BIOETHICS AND MEDICAL ISSUES IN LITERATURE

**Recent Contributions in
Exploring Social Issues through Literature**

Literature and the Environment
George Hart and Scott Slovic, editors

Youth Gangs in Literature
Claudia Durst Johnson

BIOETHICS AND MEDICAL ISSUES IN LITERATURE

Mahala Yates Stripling

Exploring Social Issues through Literature
Claudia Durst Johnson and Lynn Malloy, Series Editors

GREENWOOD PRESS
Westport, Connecticut • London

Library of Congress Cataloging-in-Publication Data

Stripling, Mahala Yates.
    Bioethics and medical issues in literature / Mahala Yates Stripling.
        p. ; cm. — (Exploring social issues through literature, ISSN 1551–0263)
    Includes bibliographical references and index.
    ISBN 0–313–32040–3
        1. Medicine in literature.   2. Fiction—19th century—History and
criticism.   3. Fiction—20th century—History and criticism.   4. Bioethics.
    [DNLM: 1. Medicine in Literature.   2. Bioethical Issues.   WZ 330
S918b 2005]   I. Title.   II. Series.
    PN56.M38S76   2005
    809'.933561—dc22   2005001493

British Library Cataloguing-in-Publication Data is available.

Library of Congress Catalog Card Number: 2005001493
ISBN: 0-313-32040-3
ISSN: 1551-0263

First published in 2005

Greenwood Press, 88 Post Road West, Westport, CT 06881
An imprint of Greenwood Publishing Group, Inc.
www.greenwood.com

Printed in the United States of America

∞

The paper used in this book complies with the
Permanent Paper Standard issued by the National
Information Standards Organization (Z39.48–1984).

10 9 8 7 6 5 4 3 2 1

NOV 1 5 2005

In loving memory of Irene Yates and Anna Bland Stripling, the grandmothers who taught many great lessons to my daughters, Whitney Harding and Lauren Stripling

The sole advantage to possessing great works of literature lies in what they can help us to become. . . . It is only they, in so far as they are appropriate food and not poison for us, that can add to the present value and dignity of our minds.

—George Santayana, *Three Philosophical Poets*

Contents

Series Foreword

Exploring Social Issues through Literature was developed as a resource to help teachers and librarians keep pace with secondary school curriculum developments in the language arts such as integrated studies and teaching literature across the curriculum. Each volume in the open-ended series confronts an important social issue that has both historical ramifications and contemporary relevance to high school students. The initial topics developed for the series reflect the 'hot button' issues most requested by educators. Themes—such as environmental issues, bioethics, and racism—encompass a considerable body of literature. The books in this series provide readers with an introduction to the topic and examine the differing perspectives offered by authors and writers from a variety of time periods and literary backgrounds.

This resource was developed to address students' needs and appeal to their interests. The literary works selected range from standard canonical works to contemporary and multicultural adult fiction that would be familiar to teens and to young adult fiction readers. Many titles are found on curriculum reading lists; other considerations in selection include pertinence, interest level, subject and language appropriateness, and the availability and accessibility of the text to the nonspecialist. The authors of these volumes, all experts in their fields, also sought to include a wide spectrum of works offering as many differing perspectives on the issue as possible.

Each volume begins with an introductory essay tracing the historical and literary developments related to the identified social issue. The chapters provide brief biographical information on the writer and present critical analysis of one or more works of literature. While the focus of the chapters is generally full-length fiction, it is not limited to that and may also include plays, poetry, short stories, or non-fiction—such as essays or memoirs. In most chapters works are arranged chronologically to reflect the historical trends and developments. In other cases works are grouped according to thematic subtopics. The analysis includes discussions of the work's structural, thematic, and stylistic components and insights on the historical context that relates the work to the broader issue. Chapters conclude with bibliographic information on works cited and a list of suggested readings that may be helpful for further research or additional assignments. Please see author's Preface for this book's extended uses.

Educators looking for new ways to present social issues will find this resource valuable for presenting thematic reading units or historical perspectives on modern problems of conflict. Students of literature as well as general readers will find many ideas and much inspiration in this series.

Preface

Bioethics and Medical Issues in Literature has multiple uses. First, it is part of the Exploring Social Issues through Literature series developed to meet the needs of secondary school students and their teachers who will delve into social issues identified in a range of accessible literature. When used in the language arts curriculum, the book intersects social studies issues and literature. Furthermore, educators in the arts and humanities and sciences can benefit from examining social issues in the intersection of literature and science. Along with the clear interdisciplinary benefit for students, the material fosters communication skills by building vocabulary because literary, scientific, and medical terms are clearly defined, giving easy access to the nonspecialist. The provocative topics also inspire writing while offering the opportunity to study both the technical and human side of medicine. Through investigating medical topics situated in literature, the book informs, develops thinking skills, and challenges students who may feel encouraged to pursue higher education in science, medicine, and the humanities. Second, high school librarians will find this book a valuable reference for units in English, language arts and literature, history, cultural studies, science, and social sciences.

Third, students from high school through pre-med and other college students will find that topics in this book engage them in ethical debate, informed decision making, and career exploration. In addition, the topics teach important interdisciplinary lessons such as respect for diversity and the art of medicine. In fact, the depth of material presented here makes this book ideally suited for any one in or entering a health care profession because the stories included serve as ethical guides. They also address the socio-cultural as well as the psychological and physical dimensions of medical practice, showing how humanistic attitudes combine with scientific facts to represent different aspects of healing. For these reasons, it is not surprising that literature and medicine courses are flourishing at all levels from high school and college to medical school and throughout post-graduate training, as educators see the need of enhancing a science or medical education with the humanities. *Bioethics and Medical Issues in Literature* develops the desired critical and empathic thinking skills with its references all the way back to ancient medicine and selections that span a two hundred year period since the birth of modern medicine in the early nineteenth century to the present. Therefore, and last, public and academic librarians can recommend this book to the general reader to be read alone or to serve as a companion to the referenced literature written by insightful authors who blend literary and medical ideals into interesting and lively reading. It offers an amazing journey.

Besides drawing facts from the major disciplines of science and medicine to develop medical issues, this book considers ethical and humanist issues by frequently citing two other significant bodies of knowledge, bioethics, a discipline founded in the late 1960s, and literature and medicine, an interdisciplinary field of study established in the mid-1970s. It develops topics such as the Human Genome Project, stem cell research, Frankenscience, cloning, gene therapy, eugenics, utopias, organ transplantation, contagious and chronic diseases, doctor-assisted suicide, and public health issues such as sexually transmitted diseases and bioterrorism. The obesity epidemic, mental illness (diagnosis and therapies), cultural rituals, clinical studies, longevity and aging, compassion in end-of-life care, dying, and death are also addressed. Our rapidly changing technology has introduced many ethical controversies, making the medical field—both its education and practice—increasingly complex. Therefore, this book spotlights concerns such as the importance of communication in the doctor-patient relationship and the pertinence of issues relating to how we should now define death. It identifies the resources we will need to draw on in our brave new world of stem cell research to solve problems. Contemporary bioethicists even ask, What does it mean to be human? What science cannot explain, literature explores.

Some of the works chosen, like Shelley's *Frankenstein* and Huxley's

Brave New World, are familiar, regularly assigned classics because their important themes relate to contemporary issues. Medical topics are situated in these stories with references to hard science texts, with the common thread being we have much to learn from the past. Most of the titles have been translated to the big screen, showing how they have captured our imagination. The ten classical and contemporary works of fiction—seven novels, two plays, and a short story—selected for their relevance to twenty-first-century medical news stories ripped right from the headlines are contained in chapters with these thematic titles: "Technology's Creature," "A Brave New World," "Contagions/ Isolations," "Illness and Culture," and "End of Life—Disease and Death." The "Historical Context" section for each work contains a short author biography and defines the medical issues and humanities topics, giving an overview of their development in time. An in-depth evaluation of the issues set within the literature follows in the "Literary Analysis" section.

Each of the two sections in five chapters can be read alone. In addition, their arrangement is chronological so that each successive work builds on concepts that precede it. For example, Shelley's *Frankenstein,* although written 200 years ago, sheds light on Cook's *Coma* and late-twentieth-century organ transplantation by emphasizing scientific hubris and the need to monitor research. Camus's *The Plague* reflects on Walker's *Possessing the Secret of Joy* by showing how the media can be both charlatan and savior when alerting the public to medical dangers. Updike's *Rabbit at Rest* and Edson's *Wit* look, respectively, at heart disease and cancer, diseases that continue to plague humankind. Hawthorne's "Rappaccini's Daughter" and Feldshuh's *Miss Evers' Boys* reveal the dire consequences of medical discoveries both unconscionably applied and withheld. Huxley's canonical work *Brave New World* and Kesey's popular *Cuckoo's Nest* demonstrate that many mysteries of the human psyche are still left to solve. These are just a few of the ways to compare and to contrast the various issues in each section, which also contains a plot synopsis. The book includes a helpful historical overview, "Chronology of Events in Literature, Medicine, and Science," and at the end quick-reference definitions appear in "Glossary of Terms: Literary, Medical, and Scientific." In addition, with the belief that every text should offer an opportunity to build vocabulary skills, whether it be for personal use or for academic testing, potentially unfamiliar words are glossed at the end as well. Four appendixes list additional resources and references, such as recommended movies, Internet sites, books and articles, and specific ideas for teaching.

At the end of each section students respond to the topics posed for oral and written discussion, as further contemplation builds the all-important critical thinking skills. For instance, noting that we live in a global community, students might argue the different sides of the main issue in Walker's *Possessing the Secret of Joy:* Should a First World country interfere with the culturally entrenched morality of a Third World African female ritual? Or, as featured in Camus's *The Plague,* they can scrutinize the ongoing role the media play both to educate and to sensationalize contemporary medical issues such as HIV and the Ebola virus, creating both informed and fearful citizens. By exploring sensitive distinctions, students develop a national social and international cultural perspective. These provocative issues lead to animated class discussions that create camaraderie among students with diverse backgrounds, interests, and career goals. By responding in writing to the questions, students usually delve deeper into their emotions. There is broad student interest in this book's central interdisciplinary concept that as science forges ahead, we will need the humanities to put the human face on medicine. By actively encountering bioethics and medical issues situated in stories, students make the significant connection that literature reflects the social issues incumbent in our world culture. Then they can apply this knowledge, combined with their own meaningful experiences and a mindful life, to form values and to make reasoned deliberations on ethical issues in our increasingly complex and interesting world.

At last, the intent of this book is to add to the growing body of literature that identifies and addresses these mounting twenty-first-century concerns by grounding students in an interdisciplinary program. Literature reveals the human condition, which after all is the subject of scientific endeavors, and this book declaratively answers the question, What is the role of the humanities in bioethics? Besides, adding humanities and social studies to science makes for lively discussions. As I respond thusly to these issues, I note that from Harvard University on down education reform is embracing a "skills across the curriculum" approach, arguing that all students are as capable of learning science as they are of mastering subjects in the humanities and social sciences. Educating our citizenry to make informed decisions with a dual facility is imperative as we face ongoing bioethical and medical challenges in our brave new world. "The unexamined life is not worth living," said Socrates, and the contents of *Bioethics and Medical Issues in Literature* should spur teachers and students on to conduct further research, resulting in critical thinking about the many new issues presented in the twenty-first century. It will be my pleasure to guide you toward that goal.

There are many people to thank who helped me over the three-year researching and writing period to complete *Bioethics and Medical Issues in Literature*. Although an author's life is necessarily one of aloneness, I have not been intellectually isolated. Besides keeping company with the great thinkers whose ideas have contributed to this book, I have relied on numerous people and resources to authenticate my views. I want to thank my editors, Claudia Durst Johnson and Lynn Malloy, for their knowledge and support in helping me conceptualize the book and bring it to fruition. I appreciate Harris Methodist Fort Worth Hospital Director of Ethics David Isch for giving me an overview of hospital procedures, policies, and ethics. In educating myself about the role of institutional review boards in overseeing clinical research, I have benefited from communicating with The University of Texas Southwestern Medical Center Institutional Review Board Administrator Pat Fisher. Also from Southwestern, medical student and Doris Duke Fellow Louise P. King, J.D., described her medical school routine and experiences. Neuroradiologist Dr. Michael O. Harding was helpful in general medical discussions. I am further indebted to The University of North Texas Health Science Center Medical Humanities Director Sue Lurie, Ph.D., for comments on specific text and for helpful insights on related curriculum issues. A special thanks goes to the unsung heroes of literary achievement, the Fort Worth Public Library interlibrary loan researchers who in a timely fashion got for me an eclectic assortment of scores of books and articles from all over the country. I appreciate Linda Lucas's diligence and keen eye while reading my manuscript and commenting on its ability to reveal important social issues in pertinent literature. I am grateful to Beverly Robertson, R.N., for her insights on the human condition—the wonderful bodies we possess—especially our hearts and minds. In addition, as I worked on *Bioethics and Medical Issues in Literature* I tapped into the vast knowledge accruing from 10 years of research and interviews with medical luminaries who contributed to my forthcoming biography on Yale surgeon-writer Richard Selzer. He bears the responsibility for inspiring my medical humanities pursuits. Finally, I owe a very special debt of gratitude to my husband, James L. Stripling, for his continuing support, love and encouragement, and meticulous editing. I could not have written this book without him.

Chronology of Events in Literature, Medicine, and Science

These Western medicine selections relate to the works included here. This is not a comprehensive timeline, but for context some unrelated historical events are shown.

B.C.

c. 4500   Sumerian and Egyptian cultures begin

c. 3000   Writing invented

c. 450   Hippocrates, the Father of Medicine, wrote *Corpus Hippocrates*, a systematic and scientific approach to medicine; his definition of a doctor's position and role in society is incorporated into his Hippocratic Oath, central to medicine today

A.D.

129   Birth of Galen Pergamum, Greek physician called the Father of Sports Medicine, who refined and organized the humoral system of medical knowledge and gave a good account of the skeleton and the muscles that move it

476–1000   Fall of the Western Roman Empire; the Dark Ages begin when classical learning and literacy decline

c. 750–1485—The Middle Ages

1037   Death of Ibn Sina (Avicenna), author of the *Canon of Medicine*

1137   St. Bartholomew's Hospital founded in London

1270   Invention of spectacles in Venice

1336–1453   Hundred Years' War

1340   End of the Plague of Justinian, which followed trade routes to France and Italy, killing 70,000

1347–52   The Black Death (the Bubonic Plague) hits England the hardest in 1348–49, killing 40 percent of the population; in western Europe one-third of the population (20 million people) dies

1440–50   Printing invented, spreading medical knowledge

c. 1455   Gutenberg's Bible printed at Mainz

1485–1660—The Renaissance

1492   Discovery of America (by Columbus)

1494   Syphilis appears in Europe

1493–1541   Paracelsus, German alchemist and physician called the Father of Pharmaceuticals, introduces remedies derived from chemicals; he stressed that nature heals, and he described syphilis, applying a mercury remedy; he discovered silicosis results from inhaling mine dust and first realized goiter is related to the presence of minerals and lead in drinking water

1505   Royal College of Surgeons established in Edinburgh

1510–90   The great surgeon Ambroise Paré writes about his work

1519–22   Magellan circumnavigates the world, a voyage plagued by scurvy

1532   London bills of mortality become our present-day death certificates

1543   Nicolaus Copernicus writes of a sun-centered planetary system; Andreas Vesalius publishes his great work on human anatomy, *De Humani Corporis Fabrica*

1605   Champlain defines scurvy during an autopsy

1610   Galileo is the first person to apply the telescope to the study of the skies and makes a series of astronomical discoveries

1628   William Harvey publishes on the circulation of blood, *De Motu Cordis*

1665   The Great Plague of London kills 17,400 people; fire ended the outbreak

1677   Cinchona bark (from which quinine is obtained) is listed in the London Pharmacopoeia as a fever treatment

1683   Anton van Leeuwenhoek, with a microscope, identifies and sketches bacteria

Eighteenth Century—The Age of Enlightenment in Europe (Reason and Individualism)

1714	Gabriel Fahrenheit constructs the mercury thermometer
1717	Giovanni Lancisi suggests mosquitoes transmit malaria
1747	James Lind discovers citrus fruits cure scurvy
1753	Linnaeus, Swedish botanist, physician, and taxonomist, publishes *Species plantarum*, an attempt to classify all known plants; later he classifies Africans as a subspecies of humans, helping to establish prejudice; his peers were jealous of his academic fame
1756	Benjamin Franklin helps found the oldest American hospital in Philadelphia, Pennsylvania
1759	Caspar Wolff shows specialized organs develop out of unspecialized tissue
1766	Albrecht von Haller proves nervous stimulation controls muscular action
1770s	**The Industrial Revolution** begins in Europe
1770	William Hunter establishes a school of anatomy in London
1773	The first mental institution, a holding facility, is established in Virginia
1774	Joseph Priestly discovers oxygen; Franz Mesmer uses medical hypnosis
1776	**The American Revolution** (the Declaration of Independence, July 4)
	Smallpox kills 130,000 North Americans; the Colonies use variolation (inserting smallpox into the skin, causing an inoculation to produce immunity)
1780	Benjamin Franklin invents bifocal lenses
1785	William Withering introduces digitalis (from foxglove) to cure dropsy
1789	**The French Revolution** (storming of the Bastille, July 14)
1794–96	Erasmus Darwin writes *Zoonomia, or The Laws of Organic Life*; Philadelphian Dr. Benjamin Rush, the Father of American Psychiatry, performs revolutionary, but cruel, treatments to cure insanity
1796	Edward Jenner's smallpox vaccination is based on evidence that dairy maids exposed to cowpox never catch it
1798	Thomas Malthus's *An Essay on the Principle of Population* is a cornerstone to Darwin's views on the theory of natural selection

1800   Marie-François Xavier Bichat's *A Treatise on Membranes* provides an understanding of tissues as basic building blocks and prime pathological sites; Humphry Davy announces the anesthetic properties of nitrous oxide, changing surgical procedures forever

Nineteenth Century—The Age of Modern Medicine

1811   Massachusetts General Hospital is founded in Boston

1815   Waterloo (Napoleonic Wars)

1816   René Laënnec invents the stethoscope, beginning the age of modern medicine

1818   Mary Shelley publishes *Frankenstein or, The Modern Prometheus*

1820s   Homeopathy gains popularity in Canada and the United States when in the late eighteenth century German physician and chemist Samuel Hanemann, frustrated with conventional invasive medical techniques, developed the system from experiments on natural sources (plants, minerals, metals, etc.), rediscovering the principle of "like can cure like"

1832   Hodgkin describes cancer of the lymph nodes

1834   Chloroform is discovered and used as a painkiller

1843   Dr. Oliver Wendell Holmes writes *The Contagiousness of Puerperal Fever*

1844   Horace Wells uses nitrous oxide to pull his own tooth painlessly; Hawthorne publishes "Rappaccini's Daughter"

1846   Boston dentist William T. G. Morton uses ether during surgery, ending indescribable pain and overwhelming dread associated with surgery; Eduard Seguin describes Down syndrome

1847   Ignaz Philip Semmelweis, the Father of Infection Control, links unwashed hands to puerperal fever in the Vienna Lying-in Hospital

1860   Florence Nightingale establishes St. Thomas Hospital nurses' training program

1858   Rudolf Virchow in *Cellularpathologie* demonstrates every cell is the product of another cell, concluding that diseases result from disturbances in cellular structures

1859   Publication of Charles Darwin's *On the Origin of Species by Means of Natural Selection*

1863   T. H. Huxley, Aldous Huxley's grandfather and "Darwin's Bulldog," publishes *Evidence as to Man's Place in Nature*, extending Darwin's *On the Origin of Species* to human evolution

1867	Joseph Lister introduces antiseptic surgery
1869	Friedrich Miesher discovers nucleic acid
1874	Louis Pasteur boils instruments in water to sterilize them
1876	Robert Koch identifies anthrax bacillus
1881	Louis Pasteur creates a vaccine for anthrax bacillus
1895	Wilhelm Roentgen discovers X-rays; H. G. Wells, the Father of Modern Science Fiction, publishes *The Time Machine*, a dystopia with a divided humanity
1896	Antoine Becquerel discovers radiation
1897	Ronald Ross locates the malaria parasite in the *Anopheles* mosquito
1900	Sigmund Freud publishes *The Interpretation of Dreams*

Twentieth Century—The Age of Global War

1904	Ivan Pavlov wins the Nobel Prize in physiology for research on digestion (the Pavlovian stimulus-response)
1905	German bacteriologist Robert Koch wins the Nobel Prize for tuberculosis research, presenting an airtight case that a single bacterium causes the condition
1906	First corneal transplant by Austrian ophthalmologist Dr. Edward Zim
1909	Oslo study begins on autopsied white males to report the natural history of untreated syphilis
1912	The *Titanic* sinks on its maiden voyage
1914	**World War I** (precipitated by the assassination of Archduke Franz Ferdinand)
1917	The Russian Revolution (Czar Nicholas II, last of the Romanov dynasty, abdicates)
1918	Spanish influenza kills at least 30 million people; first blood transfusion
1920s	Jean Piaget begins work on describing the stages of cognitive development; Earl Dickson invents the Band-Aid
1928	Alexander Fleming discovers penicillin in a mold; Harvey Cushing first uses penicillin and sulfa antibiotics
1930	Cholera epidemics
1932	In *Brave New World* Aldous Huxley predicts a controlled world in which art, science, and religion are banned
1933	Horrendous concentration camp medical experiments take place when Nazis seize control of the German government

1935   The Mayo Clinic establishes the first blood bank

1936   Dr. Walter Freeman performs the first lobotomy in the United States

1938   B. F. Skinner publishes *The Behavior of Organisms* (operant conditioning)

1939–45   World War II

1943   Waksman discovers the antibiotic streptomycin

1945   The birth of bioethics, facilitated by World War II when science and technology were both beneficial and threatening; first randomized clinical trials of streptomycin for treatment of tuberculosis; returning U.S. soldiers assessed for neuropsychological disorders

1946   French philosopher Albert Camus publishes *La Peste (The Plague)*

1947   The Nuremberg Code signed

1949   Establishment of the U.S. Navy Tissue Bank; the National Institute of Mental Health is created, recognizing the need to diagnose and to treat the mentally ill

1952   Jonas Salk develops the first polio vaccine; Briggs and King clone tadpoles from cells

1953   James Watson and Francis Crick describe the double helix structure of DNA; Rosaline Franklin's earlier work inspired them, causing controversy over who deserved the Nobel Prize

1957   Albert Sabin develops a live polio vaccine; Thorazine, the "prescription straitjacket," is put into widespread use, beginning the psychopharmaceutical revolution in mental health care in which drugs treat and ameliorate depressive or compulsive disorders without hospitalization

1960   The birth control pill is approved for general use

1962   Murray and Hume perform the first successful cadaveric kidney transplant; Ken Kesey's *One Flew Over the Cuckoo's Nest* takes another look at electroshock therapy; in October the United States confronts the Soviet Union about Cuban missiles, and many frightened Americans take to bomb shelters; school children are taught to "duck and cover"

1963   Dr. Thomas Starzl performs the first liver transplant; a vaccine for measles is introduced; Martin Luther King, Jr.'s, "I Have a Dream" speech mobilizes supporters of civil rights

1964   Civil Rights Act of 1964 is signed into law by President Johnson

1966   *Star Trek* TV series, created by Gene Roddenberry, debuts (science fiction)

1967   South Africa's Dr. Christian Bernard performs the first heart transplant; the recipient has normal heart function for 19 months

late 1960s Birth of the field of bioethics (See Dr. Albert R. Jonsen's *The Birth of Bioethics*. NY: Oxford University Press, 1998.)

1968   Brain death criteria are established; the Uniform Anatomical Gift Act allows the gift of organs

1969   Lunar module *Eagle* lands on the moon, July 20; astronauts Neil Armstrong and Buzz Aldrin walk on the lunar surface, fulfilling President John F. Kennedy's 1961 commitment

1970   The American Lung Association begins its "Kick the Habit" antismoking campaign; President Nixon signs legislation banning cigarette advertising on radio and television; the antibiotic vancomycin, regarded as the so-called silver bullet against *Staphylococcus aureus,* is introduced; the FDA approves lithium for manic depressives; an anthrax vaccine is first used

1972   The Uniform Anatomical Gift Act's Uniform Organ Donor Card is a legal document in all 50 states, making it possible for anyone 18 and older to donate organs upon death; front-page national news blows the whistle on the U.S. government-sponsored Tuskegee Syphilis Study

1974   Phelps, Hoffman, and Pogossian invent the first PET scanner

1975   The birth of the field of literature and medicine (See *Healing Arts in Dialogue: Medicine and Literature*. Ed. Joanne Trautmann. Carbondale: Southern Illinois University Press, 1981.)

1976   President Ford orders mass vaccination against swine flu; an earthquake in Tangshan, China, kills 255,000 people

1977   Robin Cook's *Coma* predicts a world in which organ harvesting has run amok

1978   Louise Brown, first test-tube baby, is born (Edwards and Steptoe developed the technique)

1979   The World Health Organization certifies smallpox as eradicated, a great accomplishment in a world devastated by the disease for 3,000 years

1981   The Commission for Study of Ethical Problems in Medicine and Biomedical Research expands the criteria establishing brain death

1982   Barney Clark receives the first permanent artificial heart at the University of Utah

1983   FDA-approved cyclosporine becomes the most successful anti-rejection medication

1984   Baby Fae receives a baboon heart at Loma Linda University Medical Center and lives 21 days; the National Organ Transplant Act establishes a nationwide computer registry, the United Network for Organ Sharing, authorizes financial support for organ procurement organizations, and outlaws the purchase or sale of organs

1985   Rock Hudson, popular Hollywood leading man, dies of AIDS at the age of 59, forcing a reevaluation of stereotypes and making AIDS a household word

1987   Prozac is introduced as a treatment for depression

1990   Dr. Joseph Murray, who performed the first kidney transplant, is awarded the Nobel Prize for medicine; Dr. E. Donnall Thomas, who pioneered bone marrow transplants in 1956 as a cure for leukemia, is awarded the Nobel Prize for medicine; David Feldshuh's *Miss Evers' Boys* dramatizes the Tuskegee Syphilis Study; John Updike writes the last in his trilogy, *Rabbit at Rest*

1991   A cyclone strikes Bangladesh killing 138,000 people

1992   Alice Walker's *Possessing the Secret of Joy* exposes a horrendous tribal ritual

1996   Dolly the sheep is cloned using somatic cell nuclear transfer; subsequently, many states make human cloning illegal; in June President Clinton, with National Bioethics Advisory Commission recommendations, signs a five-year moratorium on federal funds for human cloning research

1999   The National Institutes of Health establishes the Human Genome Project; Margaret Edson writes *Wit*

2000   Celera Genomics announces it has mapped 99 percent of the genome; the publicly financed Human Genome Project announces it has mapped 97 percent of the genome, of which 85 percent has been placed in order; each method differs, but biomedical discoveries soon follow; Carlsson, Greengard, and Kandel win the Nobel Prize for their discoveries of nervous system signaling

Twenty-First Century—The Age of Cloning

2001   Neo-Enlightenment and Biotechnical Revolution—worldwide stem cell research and cloning; the University of Oregon clones the transgenic monkey with jellyfish gene DNA that glows a fluorescent green; September 11—terrorists hijack four commercial jet airliners (two hit the twin towers of the World Trade Center in New York City, killing thousands; one hits the Pentagon near Washington, D.C., killing 196 people; and the fourth plows into a field near Pittsburgh, killing all aboard); a month later a dozen people are infected through the mail with anthrax and several die

2002   The President's Council on Bioethics cannot reach a consensus on the ethics of human stem cell use; scientists grow tissue from cloned cells and transplant them into other animals; an international academic and commercial research consortium begins work on a three-year, $100 million project to build a next-generation human genome haplotype map (HapMap), available for free on the Internet; the Advisory Committee on Human Research Protections revises its charter to define unborn human embryos as "human subjects" with protection rights (but not afforded the same current protections for fetuses, children, and adults); the Centers for Disease Control and Prevention recommend doctors and nurses wash their hands between patients with fast-drying alcohol gels to avoid giving patients life-threatening infections; the FDA approves a 20-minute HIV test

2003   The U.S. House of Representatives votes to criminalize any effort to create cloned human cells, even for medical research; researchers create a genetic blueprint for the SARS (severe acute respiratory syndrome) virus, which causes a mysterious flu-like illness that sometimes leads to fatal lung congestion; scientists complete the map of the human genetic code, improving diagnostic testing, treatment, and prevention; scientists link depression and gene-controlling brain serotonin levels by showing depression has roots in genetics and personal history (new drugs may help); on March 19, President Bush, fearing continuing homeland terrorism, takes proactive action and sends United States troops into Iraq, stating a democratic, peaceful, and nuclear-free region is desirable and that it would be "reckless to accept the status quo" in the Middle East. (By the end of 2004, 1,329 American troops had been killed and 9,981 wounded.)

2004   NASA rover touches down on Mars and signals Earth; South Korean scientists clone a human embryo for therapeutic research; the FDA reminds 70 universities of regulations on creating transgenic animals; Cohen and Boyer share the Albany Medical Center Prize in Medicine and Biomedical Research for developing recombinant DNA technology (gene cloning) and basic research for genetic engineering to develop drugs such as human insulin to treat diabetes, growth hormones for under-developed children, and interferon for cancer patients; Ronald Reagan, 40th president of the United States, dies on June 5 from complications of Alzheimer's disease, bringing attention to stem cell research; Chinese scientist Dr. Huang Hongyun succeeds in treating spinal cord patients with cultured and trans-planted fetal nerve cells; 58 U.S. senators sign a letter asking President George W. Bush to expand federal funding for human embryonic stem cell research; H. Lee Sweeney, in the *Scientific American* article "Gene Doping" (July), says the 2004 Olympic Games may be the last without genetically enhanced athletes, and he asks what will we humanly lose by doing this; on De-cember 26 a massive Indian Ocean earthquake, a force measur-ing a magnitude of 9.0 or equal to 2 million nuclear bombs the size of the one that destroyed Hiroshima, causes tsunamis or tidal waves to pummel the shorelines of Southeast Asia and Af-rica. It was called one of the worst natural disasters in modern history, killing more than 180,000 and leaving the 5 million homeless looking for food, shelter, and water. Lacking sanitation and health care, the survivors are now susceptible to diseases such as diarrhea, cholera, typhoid, hepatitis, and dysentery. Globalization and modern technology bring the scope of the natural disaster directly into our daily lives, and countries around the world pledge billions of dollars in disaster relief. Some New Year's Eve parties are replaced with memorials.

2005   As the New Year turns, Americans are resolving to safeguard and to improve their health on a personal level, and, at the same time, they are extending their resolutions toward building a healthier global community

Introduction

Bioethics and Medical Issues in Literature, in the Exploring Social Issues through Literature series, defines specific bioethical and medical issues, gives an overview of their development, and analyzes them in literature. In addition, it relates current perspectives on these issues and cites specific ongoing concerns. The 10 works of fiction analyzed in this book for their relevance to contemporary social issues succeed because their authors placed characters in situations beyond the realm of what was known. That is, what science had not yet broached, their writings explored. The selections spanning 200 years from Mary Shelley's romantic British novel *Frankenstein, or, The Modern Prometheus,* in the Industrial Revolution, to Margaret Edson's Modern American play *Wit,* in today's Biotechnical Revolution, show that as much as things seem to change, the same fears expressed long ago persist. In particular, the question concerning the advancement of science taking precedence over individual human rights looms large. The authors have used creative license in their fiction to explore this important social issue as well as others that continue to form and test us. As the chain of events since the age of modern medicine shows, we have much to learn from the past, which literature encapsulates.

In five thematic chapters, bioethics and medical issues revealing the human character and condition are set into the 10 fictional works as follows. In chapter 1, "Technology's Creature," the two works, Mary Shelley's *Frankenstein* and Nathaniel Hawthorne's "Rappaccini's

Daughter," have been warning us for a long time about scientific hubris and unmonitored research. In *Frankenstein* a stealthy young scientist invents life and unleashes a monster; in "Rappaccini's Daughter" an unconscionable father turns his innocent daughter into an experiment. While Shelley's nineteenth-century lifetime highlights other specific issues, such as women's rights and health-care concerns as documented in incidents of puerperal fever, currently *Frankenstein* is being invoked as a cautionary tale. Like Victor Frankenstein, are stem cell scientists playing God in trying to create and to alter life, with the outcome unknown? Or, are these fears unfounded, outweighed by the potential benefit to mankind? Hawthorne's work further elaborates on the scientific mind—in particular, rivalry and abuse of the Hippocratic tenet, "First, to do no harm," two concerns applicable in today's race to achieve.

As the United States entered the brave new world of stem cell research and cloning, in 2002 President George W. Bush appointed an 18-member Council on Bioethics. It is made up of medical doctors, lawyers, philosophers, theologians, biomedical and social scientists, policy experts, and medical ethicists to advise him on ethical issues arising from biomedical and technological advances in science. The council's reports also influence the U.S. Congress, future legislation, and government funding. Called "the conscience of the country," the council has deliberated on many issues, but on April 1, 2004, it released its long-anticipated recommendations on stem cell research. The council reached consensus in recommending a ban on cloning-to-produce-children and a four-year moratorium on cloning-for-biomedical-research. It would not outlaw human embryonic stem cell research altogether, saying it needs time to review current practices. In federally funded research the council calls for more self-regulation and a ban on "outlying experimental practices." Trying to reach a compromise, President Bush approved of therapeutic stem cell research on existing embryos up to 14 days maturity discarded from in vitro fertilization clinics, which are in short supply and contamination may limit their use. He also reaffirmed his moratorium, following the lead of the council, on spending federal funds to create new embryos for reproductive human cloning research or that which might result in the development of a full-term baby.

The report is troubling to many antiabortion groups, tying into the fundamental debate on determining when life begins. Conversely, the report is heralded by those who are looking for cures. Researchers grow from stem cells replacement muscle and nerve tissues that could be used in a damaged heart or as remedies in specific diseases like cystic fibrosis. The council, furthermore, has asked for a temporary moratorium on research into creating hybrid embryos using human egg and animal sperm and vice versa and gestating human embryos in animal bodies. It ponders the ethics of buying, selling, or patenting human embryos, which is of viable commercial interest. Concerns linger about the kind of creatures technology can create, and the council wishes to discourage rogue researchers intent on cloning embryos grown specifically for harvesting human parts or into a full-term human baby.

The President's Council on Bioethics will continue to debate these and other issues, including, Is research cloning in humans morally justifiable in principle? Maintaining human dignity—asking what does it mean to be human—is a chief concern. Nonetheless, two weeks before the council's report, what was once theoretical was taken into the realm of reality on February 11, 2004, when South Korean scientists announced they had cloned human embryos. Using the same somatic cell nuclear transfer technology applied to the 1996 cloning of Dolly the sheep in Scotland, they produced human embryos solely for the purpose of harvesting the all-important therapeutic stem cells. Clearly the genie has left the bottle—the age of cloning has begun—with this achievement demonstrating that science cannot be stopped. Nonetheless, it raises the specter of Frankenscience, a scientific creation that has the potential to destroy its creator. The clear and present danger is that technological achievement is running well ahead of public policy, reinvigorating political, religious, and ethical debates. While some U.S. states proceed without government funds and approval, and other countries are on a swift march into scientific discoveries, the 2005 U.S. federal budget—reflecting drains from wartime, national health-care costs, and worldwide disease and disaster relief—continues to limit funds for scientific research and education. In summary, a few issues chapter 1 highlights are: problems with the stealth of scientific research; the fear of technology, especially the unknown outcome of scientists playing God and of developing technology's creature; and the inherent problem in seeking perfection and in attempts to develop a utopia (Who decides?).

It is not a great leap into chapter 2, "A Brave New World," to discuss Huxley's description of dispassionate eugenics in *Brave New World* and Cook's imagined commercial avarice in the human transplant industry in *Coma*. The former predates the horrors documented in the 1940s U.S. sterilization movement and subsequently in the Nazi war experiments. The latter predicts the continuing shortage of human transplant organs and problems with assignment, imagining a horrific solution. In both novels individuality is sacrificed for the greater good. In *Brave New World*—in order to restore order after anthrax attacks—the government controls and conditions its people, who lack free will. It shows the inevitable harm from genetically determining a society and psychologically conforming it with pharmaceuticals from birth through the end of life. The 1932 novel sheds light on our twenty-first century brave new world of genetic engineering and cloning, underscoring the technical ability to create and to manipulate human life that runs well ahead of public policy. Science has the ability to alter human DNA, for better or worse. Now, along with the reality of these new and exciting biotechnologies that prevent and cure disease may come ethical problems. In a Huxleyan manner, will high-tech eugenics promote caste-like discrimination and undermine equality?

Similarly, Cook's gruesome theme of harvesting organs from unwilling donors, as depicted in his medical thriller *Coma*, is not only possible but even probable, he says. He spotlights research advanced in secret and the dangerous mixture of drug-addicted doctors and dehumanized patients leading to medical mistakes. The legal procurement and fair dissemination of human organs in the transplant industry, as well as the definition of brain death, are central issues in *Coma*. The thriving international black market brokering the organs of the poor to save the lives of the rich is addressed in Michael Finkel's article "Complications." Chapter 2 also discusses the many myths and inadequate procedures that inhibit the transplant process and the informed consent guidelines governing it. Every year 85,000 anxious Americans wait for lifesaving organs, and 6,000 die before they arrive. The National Organ Transplant Act bans the purchase or sale of human organs because, understandably, only the rich would benefit. Some states offer living donor tax deductions to offset expenses; other states are proposing laws to reimburse the expenses of living donors and of the families of deceased donors. In recent times xenotransplantation, the use of animal tissues and organs in humans, is a commonplace alternative, but rejection and cross-species infection are factors. The technology is here for growing body parts, such as kidneys and corneas, for transplantation. But will they be available to everyone in need? In this brave new world, biotechnology promises to reshape nature as we know it. And, indeed, recombinant gene therapies can even alter human DNA. Anthropologists ponder how benefits accruing from reproductive innovations will compare to natural selection? The widespread fear of the unknown, as magnified in Michael Crichton's 1990 depiction of chaos theory in *Jurassic Park,* should accelerate public debate.

In chapter 3, "Contagions/Isolations," Albert Camus's *The Plague* reveals a plague-stricken community's dynamics, especially after a self-sacrificing doctor isolated from the rest of the world, must deal with medical issues. In the unrelenting nature of plague his medical ethics are challenged, provoking philosophical discussions about man's morality in an atmosphere of every-man-for-himself. It also defines true heroism, a term assigned freely today. *The Plague* highlights political, social, economic, and religious issues that arise from a medical emergency, offering an ideal segue into the next section, David Feldshuh's *Miss Evers' Boys,* which describes a baseline syphilis study initiated before effective treatments were available. Richard A. Schweder in "Tuskegee Re-Examined" holds a contemporary view that hindsight moralizing will not heal wounds and recalls that paternalism—the withholding of information from patients—was a standard of care for blacks and whites in the 1930s. The Public Health Service medical professionals should not be characterized as racist evildoers, he says, especially because the 1950s standard of care including penicillin had not proved effective in a late-term syphilitic's quality of life or morbidity. The idea of the prejudicial application of medical treatments is extended into the reality of Nazi war experiments and into our international age of AIDS. Both the Nazi war crimes resulting in the Nuremberg Code and the Tuskegee Syphilis Study influencing the Belmont Report shed light on human subject research protocols, including informed consent, evolving into the creation of institutional review boards (IRBs). With the new age ushering in dazzling possibilities such as pharmaceuticals and gene therapies that alter who the person is, IRB watchdogs must continually ask whether research contributes to the general good more than it devalues individual human life.

The focus of chapter 3 is to show that plague—all infectious disease—which antedates humans, continues to determine the course of history and is never gone for good. The solid evidence of this appears in daily headlines warning of recent global outbreaks of polio, influenza, tuberculosis, the newly discovered SARS, and the yet to be known. Only now are the worldwide ramifications of AIDS—first identified in the 1970s—being felt. Medications commonly administered in the United States are not cost-effective in other countries, creating an upsurge in orphans, an abhorrence stressed during World AIDS

Day. Otherwise, critics say the media's focusing attention on sporadic incidents of mad cow disease takes the emphasis off of the biggest food-borne risks from salmonella, *E. coli,* and other bacteria killing thousands every year. While it behooves everyone to be informed health-care consumers, the downside to media overexposure is seen in the current population of "worried well" neurotics who self-diagnose, always expectant of the next emerging disease. Fearful overreaction to sensationalized reportage and commercial drug advertising taxes doctors and other therapeutic resources. *The Plague,* in which the media falsely report and withhold information as well as advertise false cures, and *Miss Evers' Boys,* in which a 1972 whistleblower ended the study, both raise questions about the increasingly symbiotic relationship between the media and twenty-first century medicine. The American public looks to medical news reports on television and in newspapers. It devours medical thriller novels and absorbs often sensationalized plotlines in fictionalized television shows. In addition, the Centers for Disease Control and Prevention (CDC) in Atlanta and other governmental agencies rely on their collaboration with the media to report legitimate stories as well as to advance agendas.

In summary, the key to controlling infectious disease outbreaks is early detection, establishment of vaccine protocols, and public education. Hygiene and quarantine may be the first line of defense in containing infectious diseases. Moreover, understanding how they originate and generate, as in insect-animal-human transference, is crucial. No matter what firewalls are put up, however, the truth espoused in chapter 3 is that infectious disease, recorded since the earliest historical accounts, has proved indomitable. Epidemiologists continually try to keep up with the next generation of diseases. They maintain a hypervigilance on known pathogens coming out of hiding somewhere in the world after lying dormant for decades and on those recombining into superbugs.

The main theme in chapter 4, "Illness and Culture," is that illness is often culture-specific and that diagnostic methods and treatment options change over the years. America's path has been long and arduous since the early days when the mentally ill and retarded roamed the streets. There are now many different approaches to diagnosing and treating the mentally ill, such as using brain scans and DNA analysis as well as using psychotherapy and drugs. Ironically, many who should seek help (schizophrenics, for instance) find themselves homeless and untreated since the National Institute of Mental Health, created in 1946, activated human rights laws including privacy and autonomy.

The two works in this chapter, Ken Kesey's *One Flew Over the Cuckoo's Nest* and Alice Walker's *Possessing the Secret of Joy*, continue to influence twenty-first-century medical issues and ethics by describing the cultural origins of mental illness. In 1962 Kesey horrified readers with his graphic depictions of electroshock treatments and lobotomy, causing the mental health industry to rethink its approaches. These so-called barbaric methods are back into use for treating depression when drugs and psychotherapy are ineffective.

Nonetheless, the new age of pharmaceuticals provides a variety of magic bullet cures. Some drugs, however, along with effectively treating symptoms, may change the recipient's personality. For instance, a new therapeutic forgetting drug is in clinical trials. It has the potential to eliminate disabling emotions such as fear and guilt in soldiers or rape victims. Opponents argue that blocking post-traumatic stress disorders (PTSDs) reduces capacity for empathy, reshaping who that person is as in soma administered in Huxley's *Brave New World*. Proponents believe the drug, by eliminating a person's crippling emotions, restores quality of life (Henig, "The Quest to Forget"). Should the Federal Drug Administration (FDA) approve the drug after more extensive study, bioethicists will have to determine whether the drug's benefits outweigh the side effects and risks, especially in the 70 percent of PTSD patients who eventually recover anyway. In the nineteenth century Ralph Waldo Emerson expressed his belief that there is innate value in all experience, whether positive or negative, because it defines who we are and how we interact in the world.

In *Possessing the Secret of Joy* Walker illustrates how our views on normalcy depend on the culture and time in which we live. Actions deemed criminally insane and unethical in one area of the world are culturally entrenched in another. The World Health Organization estimates that 100 million women worldwide have undergone female genital mutilation (FGM), a difficult issue to explore. The African culture Walker depicts has socially constructed a practice with detrimental mental and physical health consequences, linking health, education, and human rights. *Possessing the Secret of Joy* describes women subjugated to fundamentalist beliefs and denied equal protection under the law, even though the Universal Declaration of Human Rights states human rights are inalienable: "No one shall be subjected to torture or to cruel, inhuman, or degrading treatment or punishment" (United Nations General Assembly Resolution, 1948). Changing ritualistic behavior takes several generations, however, a fact understood by an Italian surgeon who offered to "safely" perform the rite, preventing the germ-laden hut-butchering of girls. He caused an international outrage. Showing that education is the key, 200 FGM practitioners attended the 2004 International Women's Day in Kenya, announced they had abandoned the practice, and vowed to fight it. Although the 2002 Children's Act outlaws the practice, in northeastern Kenya 98 percent of the girls between ages five and nine undergo radical FGM. Local magistrates levy light punishment, if any, for violations. Kesey and Walker illustrate the long-term detrimental consequences of socially constructed practices. The historical perspectives in chapter 4 build worldwide awareness on the value of education.

At last, the intent of chapter 5, "End of Life—Disease and Death," is to demonstrate, in the words of Thomas Mann, that "all interest in disease and death is only another expression of interest in life" (*The Magic Mountain,* 495). Two radically different protagonists give views of heart disease and ovarian cancer, respectively, in John Updike's *Rabbit at Rest* and Margaret Edson's *Wit.* In the former, Rabbit Angstrom, who is filled with male angst, does not engender sympathy; however, in the latter, Dr. Vivian Bearing, who is subjected to technology and the inhumanity of research protocols, experiences a nurse's kindness. Other topics developed in *Rabbit at Rest* include the obesity epidemic and the popularity of gastric bypass operations, the Me Generation and family values, and cocaine addiction and therapy. Immense strides have been made against heart disease, including gene therapy, transplants, and even cloned replacement parts. New early screening techniques are changing prognoses. Less efficient, it seems, are efforts to educate the general public about preventive measures, including maintaining an ideal weight and blood pressure, and lessening stress. Gastric bypass operations, while often effective, include risks from wound infections to death. In 2004 the U.S. Surgeon General declared obesity an epidemic, and second only to smoking as the leading cause of preventable death. At the same time, in the United States 13 million children go to bed hungry most nights.

In the engaging play *Wit,* Edson looks at cancer, research, and ethics. Once considered the silent killer because of its often late detection, ovarian cancer, the subject of *Wit,* now has more clearly defined symptoms making earlier detection and treatment possible. In fact, many other types of cancer, once a death sentence, often may be cured if detected early. Or, rather than using toxic drugs, cancer may be left uncured and treated like a chronic illness with surgery and a new generation of drugs. In 2003 the National Cancer Institute reported cancer killed 556,000 people in the United States; in 2004 8.9

million people were living with it. The drive to find a cure fuels scientific research. Breakthroughs include shutting off the blood supply to tumors, cancer vaccines, and new-age cocktails or combination drugs. With heightened screening and gene diagnosis, new drugs even tackle precancerous phases. *Wit* also addresses psychic and physical pain. With greater understanding of their similarities and differences come new therapies. For instance, brain imaging techniques reveal a cross talk between the two, leading to new approaches, including anxiety medications.

In an analysis of *Wit,* the duties and responsibilities of medical professionals are scrutinized as they interact with Dr. Bearing during the last phase of her life as a research volunteer. Human research ethics evolved from twentieth-century concerns over yellow fever treatments, having deep ethical roots in Hippocrates' tenet "First, to do no harm." The system for protecting human research participants improved following the World War II Nazi experiments on Jews, set out in an international guide called the Nuremberg Code of Ethics. Later, the effects of the experimental drug thalidomide administered to pregnant women, which caused severe birth defects, led to a better formulation of informed consent in clinical trials. A primary concern of the research community, which also polices itself, is to maintain the human dignity of research volunteers. Good science and good ethics should go hand in hand. Outrage at the Tuskegee Syphilis Study prompted the National Research Act of 1974, which in turn established local-level IRBs and the National Commission for the Study of Human Research. The important moral and social responsibility integral to human research is summarized in the Belmont Report, which sets out the basic principles for research ethics: respect for persons, beneficence, and justice. In addition, *Wit* highlights intangible qualities such as kindness and hope as they relate to patient care and quality of life.

The 10 works in *Bioethics and Medical Issues in Literature,* ranging in scope from a classical novel to a contemporary play, teach lessons in a wide range of medical and social issues. They cast a light on rapidly advancing technology, the need for public education, and the urgency of health-care reform. Science education now includes not only education in science and technology but also in social responsibility, often taught with literature. As new science and dazzling technology continue to contribute to Western medicine, literature reminds us of the human condition. Uncovering the pathophysiology of disease and solving the puzzle of its progression go hand in hand with acquiring the moral ability to apply this knowledge to sick and suffering humans.

Twenty-first-century medicine promises many great things in nano-technology, imaging techniques that reduce the need for invasive surgery, and gene analysis and therapy. Again, humans are the basis of these enterprises. At last, the primary lesson taught throughout this book that should feel highlighted from the first page to the last is the need to balance advancing science and technology with individual human rights as well as responsibilities.

BIBLIOGRAPHY

Finkel, Michael. "Complications." *The New York Times Magazine*, 27 May 2001, 26–59.

Henig, Robin Marantz. "The Quest to Forget." *The New York Times Magazine*, 4 April 2004, 32–37.

Kass, Leon R. "Why We Should Ban Human Cloning: Preventing a Brave New World." *The New Republic*, 17 May 2001, http://www.tnr.com/052101/kass052101.html.

Mann, Thomas. *The Magic Mountain*. Translated by H. T. Lowe-Porter. New York: Knopf, 1946.

Monastersky, Rich. "South Korean Researchers Harvest First Stem Cells from Cloned Human Embryo." *The Chronicle of Higher Education*, 12 February 2004, http://chronicle.com/prm/daily/2004/02/2004021201n.htm.

President's Council on Bioethics. *Monitoring Stem Cell Research*. Washington, D.C.: President's Council on Bioethics, 2004, http://www.bioethics.gov/reports/stemcell/index.html.

Schweder, Richard A. "Tuskegee Re-Examined." *Spiked-Science*, 8 January 2004, http://www.spiked-online.com.

1

Technology's Creature: An Analysis of Mary Shelley's *Frankenstein* and Nathaniel Hawthorne's "Rappaccini's Daughter"

INTRODUCTION

Mary Shelley wrote her famous monster story as a reaction against medical treatments that did more harm than good. She also tapped into the fear that rapidly advancing nineteenth-century technologies were turning her agrarian society into an urban technocracy. In fact, to bring her monster to life Shelley used the technologies of her time such as Luigi Galvani's discovery of the electrostatic spark. To imbue her monster with the need to survive, she also incorporated the revolutionary social thoughts of Erasmus Darwin. Shelley's Victor Frankenstein, a modern Prometheus, sutured dead parts into life, but his original beneficence turned into scientific hubris. Instead of helping mankind, he opened a Pandora's box filled with ethical and spiritual concerns that society now weighs against the advancement of new scientific discoveries. Another key issue developed in *Frankenstein* is how "the fiend's" horrific appearance and lack of nurturing led to human prejudice against him, causing the creature to turn on his creator. The idea that the technology we create may in the end destroy us is termed Frankenscience, which today relates to fears of bioterrorism, xenotransplantation, and cloning.

Hawthorne's "Rappaccini's Daughter," like Shelley's *Frankenstein,* comes from the romantic gothic tradition of literature. Both stories evoke a time when science seemed to promise perfection but in which people grew wary when things went terribly wrong. In particular, "Rappaccini's Daughter" characterizes two polarized schools of thought, the traditionalists and the empirics. Scientific rivalry drives the plot. The empiric Dr. Rappaccini has thrust his own innocent daughter into a life of isolation as an experiment, and at issue is understanding the type of detached intellect that allows a father to imbue his own innocent daughter with poisons. Rappaccini rationalizes that his daughter's becoming "invincible" is reason enough, but his archrival Baglioni jealously obstructs Rappaccini's contribution to science. Dr. Rappaccini demonstrates that even a father's love can be contaminated by scientific avarice, and his fatal flaw is exalting the mind at the expense of the heart, also known as head versus heart. At issue is the importance of striking a balance between human needs and scientific progress. The story implicitly plays out the theme in modern medicine of the value of sacrificing the one for the many.

Steady advances in technology since the nineteenth century make the application of Mary Shelley's *Frankenstein* and Nathaniel Hawthorne's "Rappaccini's Daughter" pertinent to the changing nature of bioethical and medical issues. Both stories encapsulate the romantic vision of distrusting science and are based on the Faustian theme that man's unchecked search for knowledge and for godlike perfection threaten humanity. Frankenstein's fiend and Rappaccini's daughter are technology's creatures, and their stories continue to fuel scientific debate about what is acceptable technology and who decides.

MARY SHELLEY'S *FRANKENSTEIN OR, THE MODERN PROMETHEUS* (1818)

Did I request thee, Maker, from my clay
To mould me man? Did I solicit thee
From darkness to promote me?

—John Milton, *Paradise Lost*
Frankenstein's title page epigraph

HISTORICAL CONTEXT

In 1816 during the romantic English literature era, the 19-year-old Mary Godwin (1797–1851) wrote *Frankenstein or, The Modern Pro-*

metheus. It is a famous gothic novel with graveyards and corpses, but the specters of natural and scientific power replace the traditional ghosts. As a precursor of the science fiction novel, *Frankenstein*'s monster symbolizes modern technology. It is both a cautionary and a prophetic tale that has led to a whole horror genre.

Mary Godwin Shelley was the only child of famous literary parents. Her mother Mary Wollstonecraft wrote the 1792 feminist manifesto *A Vindication of the Rights of Women* that openly criticized the practice of male physicians displacing midwives, who by law could not use surgical instruments such as forceps. Shelley's father was the philosopher and novelist William Godwin. When Mary was born, her mother's midwife could not remove the disintegrating placenta, so a renowned obstetrician from a lying-in hospital was called. As was acceptable medical practice, with unwashed hands he groped in her womb for hours. Mrs. Wollstonecraft-Godwin became ill and probably died of puerperal fever, also known as childbed fever or puerperal sepsis. In *The Contagiousness of Puerperal Fever* (1843) Dr. Oliver Wendell Holmes first identified it as a placental site infection that in serious cases passed from the uterine wall into the bloodstream, resulting in fever and death. Usually the wise chose to stay at home tended by midwives because the poor and unwed, who had their babies in English hospitals, had a mortality rate of more than 20 percent. In 1847 Dr. Ignaz Semmelweis, a Hungarian doctor teaching in the Maternity Department of the Vienna Lying-in Hospital, made an observation leading to a broader understanding of puerperal fever. His close friend died from a cut finger contaminated with cadaveric material during an autopsy. The symptoms resembled puerperal fever. Observing medical students going from dissecting cadavers right into the delivery room, Semmelweis made an important leap in linking unwashed hands to puerperal fever. Because the prevailing belief was that puerperal fever resulted from a bad quality to the air (miasma), he conducted clinical studies. When he instituted a policy for doctors to soak their hands and medical instruments in chlorinated lime after an autopsy and before examining patients, mortality rates dropped to 2 percent. Unfortunately, Semmelweis's medical colleagues did not accept his findings until long after his death, and it took 20 years before Joseph Lister established his technique for killing germs.

As a child made motherless through the inadequacies of nineteenth-century medicine, Mary went on to voice her deep-seated fears in *Frankenstein.* Her suspicions, along with the influence of a literary circle of friends including the first-generation romantic poets William

Wordsworth and Samuel Taylor Coleridge, melded into a theme of what happens when technology runs amok. Another important influence in Mary's life was the second-generation romantic poet, Percy Bysshe Shelley (1792–1822), who initially befriended her father and was influenced by his *Political Justice*. While at Oxford Percy embraced the doctrines of the Enlightenment (a movement stressing individual happiness), and he wrote and circulated a pamphlet titled "The Necessity of Atheism" (1810) that maintained a thinking person must deny God's existence because there was no proof of it. As a result, he was expelled from Oxford. Percy, a married man with children, ran off with Mary when she was 16. They became social outcasts except for a small circle of friends including the second-generation English romantic poet Lord Byron. Mary and Percy had two children within 14 months. The first, born in 1815, died after 12 days. Nine months later she gave birth to William. When William was three, Shelley writes in her journal, he became deathly ill after a doctor gave him excessive purgatives for worms. He later died from malaria. Births and sudden deaths were commonplace, and nineteenth-century medicine provided few remedies. For example, besides using toxic doses of the mercury-derived calomel to purge worms, nineteenth-century English doctors used other crude "cures" such as massive bleeding and prescriptive laudanum (opium and alcohol). Medical practices differed little from those of the eighteenth century and earlier, when doctors saw the body as a machine that became diseased when the nerves and blood were overstimulated. The medical cure for overstimulation was using so-called heroic measures to restore the natural balance, such as bleeding, blistering, purging, and vomiting. A patient presented any manner of complaints, and this is usually how it went:

> *Bleeding:* 1) venesection—each visit collect a pint of blood from an opened vein; 2) scarification—with a spring-loaded instrument make small bleeding cuts; or 3) cupping—place a warm glass over a cut to fill it with blood as the pressure drops. Next,
> *Blistering:* Place hot plasters on skin to raise blisters; drain blisters.
> *Purging:* Drink small doses of calomel (derived from mercuric chloride, now known to be toxic) as a laxative; or drink in large doses to purge the system. Or, try vomiting: administering tartar emetic.

By today's standards, medical doctors did more harm than good using these crude methods, and it is not surprising that Mary's growing awareness of nineteenth-century medicine's inadequacies is reflected in *Frankenstein*'s cautionary theme. In fact, only three effective remedies were in use at the time: an inoculation for smallpox; quinine for fever; and ipecacuanha for dysentery (Stone, 80).

Mary and Percy Shelley eventually had four children, only one of whom survived childhood. Most children died of neglect, including being too tightly swaddled for hours; smothered in their parents' bed; and starved due to poverty or to wet nurse indifference. The child mortality rate led to an average adult life expectancy of only 43 (Stone, 81). At the time she wrote *Frankenstein* Mary was in the midst of several other tragedies: both her half-sister and Percy's wife committed suicide. Trying to find some relief, Mary and Percy traveled with their infant son to Lake Geneva in Switzerland, where their neighbor was Lord Byron. Mary explains in her 1831 introduction to *Frankenstein* that one night they were all reading ghost stories from *Phantasma-goria*, a French translation of German gothic tales, because stormy weather had forced them indoors. Then Byron challenged his four guests, Percy and Mary, Claire Clairmont (Mary's stepsister), and Dr. John Polidori, to write one themselves. That night, Mary had a nightmare about the "effect of any human endeavor to mock the stupendous Creator of the world," and she started to write the novel *Frankenstein*.

Mary Shelley wrote *Frankenstein* during a period of dramatic change partly caused by the many shifting polarities of revolution. The failure of the French Revolution (1789) revealed a crisis in humanism, and in the early nineteenth century England was in turmoil as the Napoleonic Wars consumed its economy, leading to civil unrest. In *Frankenstein* Shelley, in fact, describes people escaping dire situations by fleeing their homeland, which highlights the new times brought on by the Enlightenment, an eighteenth-century philosophical movement. Mary Shelley wrote in her journal that she believed in the enlightenment of her fellow creatures but did not condone violence. Percy Shelley obviously influenced Mary in this direction because at the time he was reading the Enlightenment philosophy of two French philosophers, Denis Diderot (*Pensées philosophiques*, defending human passion) and Jean Jacques Rousseau ("Discourses on the Sciences and the Arts," rejecting the notion that scientific progress increases human happiness). The increasingly literate population read these works, and ideas spread throughout Europe that rejected traditional social, religious, and political beliefs. Now the emphasis was on the human ability to think rationally. As individual happiness increased, religious fervor declined. People stopped postponing gratification in this world for the promises of the next. A few Enlightenment, or Age of Reason, ideas that influenced Shelley's thinking as she wrote *Frankenstein* were:

- Women should be educated with men and freely choose their spouses, although parents have the right to delay marriage; women should have marital love and express their emotions; and women should lead sexually fulfilling lives (an affective family).
- Parents should bond with their children, and men must stop brutalizing their children, servants, and wives. (An acceptable pastime for drunken husbands was wife beating.)
- Men and women should reject puritanical beliefs that human misery resulted from original sin; rather, a bad environment and laws led to the human condition of misery expressed through alcoholism, gambling, filthiness, and promiscuity (secular humanism). (Stone, 239–46)

Frankenstein's monster, in particular, embodies the Enlightenment view that his horrendous behavior is the product of his social environment rather than his innate capacity for evil. Commonly referred to as the nature versus nurture debate, it asks the complex question, What part of us is genetic and what part is a code of conduct imprinted by society? Are we a blank tablet (*tabula rasa*) at birth or genetically predisposed with habits? Will a twenty-first century human clone have free will or be bound by evolutionary constraints? In Shelley's novel the monster is "born" without much fanfare, unlike the riveting scene in the movies. More significantly, though, Mary Shelley thoroughly explains how Victor Frankenstein (the father) abandons his monster (the child) to a life without any friends and relations. The nameless monster reflects on this:

> No father had watched my infant days, no mother had blessed me with smiles and caresses; or if they had, all my past life was now a blot, a blind vacancy in which I distinguished nothing. From my earliest remembrances I had been as I then was in height and proportion. I had never yet seen a being resembling me or who claimed any intercourse with me. What was I? (*Frankenstein*, 115–6)

The intelligent and sensitive monster, with no links to the past, feels he has no hope for the future. As a fatherless and motherless "child," he yearns for a human connection, for personal history and family identity. When he learns to speak and to read he becomes fully aware of his "accursed origins" and hungers for someone like himself. In reviewing *Frankenstein* Percy Shelley endorsed its Enlightenment view that society, not an innate propensity to evil, shaped the monster's morality. The monster's criminal actions thus were as "the children . . . of Necessity and Human nature," and Shelley felt the universal moral of the book is:

> Treat a person ill and he will become wicked. Requite affection with scorn; let one being be selected for whatever cause as the refuse of his kind—divide him, a social being, from society, and you impose upon him the irresistible obligations: malevolence and selfishness. (Shelley, "On the Moral Significance of *Frankenstein*," *Complete Works* 6:265)

According to Percy Shelley, then, because society failed to nurture the monster, his being scorned and isolated led to his misdeeds. Even Frankenstein's final words underscore the view that his experiment might not have failed if the creature had appeared more loveable.

Another factor incorporated into *Frankenstein*'s modern theme was the turmoil of the Industrial Revolution (1780–1830). Workers worried that sophisticated new technology, such as looms in the hosiery and lace industries, would replace them, and profound social changes occurred as the culture changed from an agrarian to an urban society. People feared that in the long run this new technology would harm its creators and exploit nature. Mary Shelley's basic plot reflects these new fears about technology, which were reported in the popular press as the Luddite movement. Her novel also embodies elements of new scientific discoveries such as Galvanism. In the 1790s Italian physician Luigi Galvani jolted frog muscles with an electrostatic spark, demonstrating the electrical nature of nerve impulses. In Shelley's day, people regarded this new science with wonderment. However, when *Frankenstein* was published Galvanism implied the release, through electricity, of mysterious life forces. Shelley ingeniously combined the new sciences of chemistry and electricity with the older Renaissance tradition of the alchemists' search for the elixir of life to conjure up the possibility of reanimating dead bodies. She imaginatively envisioned how, shocked with electrical impulses, her corpse might spring to life.

She also gave him the drive to survive, influenced by physician-naturalist Erasmus Darwin's *Zoonomia, or, The Laws of Organic Life* (1794). Darwin's was one of the first formal theories on evolution (how one species evolves into another, how male competition and sexual selection causes changes in species, and how in this contest among males the strongest and most active animal propagates and thus improves the species). Sixty years later his grandson Charles Darwin elaborated on these ideas in his theory of natural selection and survival of the fittest.

Besides scientific discoveries, medical advances suggesting a human mastery over the physical universe begged the question, Were we trying to play God? In 1796 Edward Jenner gave the first smallpox vaccination prepared from lesions of people infected with cowpox (a milder form of the disease). In 1800 Marie-François Xavier Bichat published *A Treatise on Membranes*, providing a new understanding of anatomy pathology. Incredibly, without a microscope Bichat examined 600 bodies and identified 21 kinds of tissue, leading to a better understanding of disease and death. He lived until only age 31, but he published two more works that contributed to nineteenth-century medicine: *Physiological Researches on Life and Death* (1800) and *General Anatomy* (1802). Chemist Humphry Davy in 1800 transformed medical practice by showing the anesthetic properties of nitrous oxide, thus lessening the overwhelming dread of the indescribable pain associated with surgery. All these discoveries pointed toward a powerful but frightening new medical age that included the reanimation of dead tissue that Galvanism suggested. Would the end of disease and death, formerly in God's province, be far behind?

At the time she wrote *Frankenstein or, The Modern Prometheus*, Mary Shelley was reading and influenced by two other works in particular. She got her theme and subtitle, *The Modern Prometheus*, from Ovid's *Metamorphoses* (circa A.D. 8), a series of tales in Latin verse. One of Ovid's tales is about Prometheus, a Titan whose name means "Forethought." There are several versions of Prometheus's tale. But Shelley drew from the one in which Prometheus created humans from mud and clay, then stole fire from the gods on Mount Olympus and gave it to the humans in defiance of Zeus, king of the Greek gods, who wanted to keep them ignorant and in darkness. Zeus warned Prometheus that humans were happy in their innocence, and every gift to them brought a penalty. Zeus further warned Prometheus that the human state of awe for the gods should not be tampered with, otherwise pride would soon poison people. But Prometheus did not listen, desiring to give meaning to human life and to free people from servitude. He saw how they lived. He knew that with fire they could now be warm, cook meat, and come out from the cave. That is, in giving fire (knowledge) to humans, Prometheus had brought civilization and power to humanity, but the gift angered the gods, especially Zeus. When Zeus looked down on Earth and noticed everything changed, he was enraged. Seeking revenge, he started to hurl his largest thunderbolt at Earth. Then he changed his mind and directed his anger at Prometheus. For defying him, Zeus chained Prometheus to Mount Caucasus where each day a vulture (or eagle) ate away at his liver, which regenerated each night.

After many centuries, the strongman Hercules freed Prometheus from his torture. But Zeus's revenge had not cooled. He still wanted to punish humans for accepting fire. So Zeus ordered a girl molded out of clay in the likeness of the beautiful Aphrodite. She was given in marriage to Prometheus's brother, Epimetheus. The gods gave the girl gifts such as song, curiosity, and a pearl necklace. Her name became Pandora, the "all-gifted." But Hermes had given her a golden box, warning her never to open it. When she could withstand her curiosity no longer, however, she did. Lizards with burning red eyes swarmed out of it. They became human ills: famine, insanity, pain and sorrow, old age, disease, and death. In the end, though, Pandora rescued humanity by shutting foreboding into her box. Otherwise, people would have no hope. In summary, Prometheus gave humans fire (knowledge); Pandora brought evil into the world, but not without hope (Evslin, 57–64). Likewise, Victor Frankenstein, the modern Prometheus, defies God's will in thinking he can create a man, and his actions unleash evil into the world.

To shape her theme, Shelley also used John Milton's epic poem *Paradise Lost* (1667), a retelling of the story of Adam and Eve. To set the tone of the story, *Frankenstein*'s opening quotation, or epigraph, comes from *Paradise Lost*: "Did I request thee, Maker, from my clay to mould me man? Did I solicit thee, from darkness to promote me?" Victor Frankenstein in his scientific hubris defies the natural order and plays God, first creating and then abandoning his Adam, who is not molded from clay but sutured together from graveyard corpses and slaughterhouse parts and then sparked to life. Unlike Milton's Adam, Frankenstein's monster is a horrific yellow-eyed being who is spurned by society. Although the desolate monster becomes increasingly hostile, he shows his humanity in desiring a mate (Eve) like himself. In the end, Victor Frankenstein feels internal conflict from his misapplied knowledge (or technology), and both he and his loved ones—as well as his creature—suffer for it.

LITERARY ANALYSIS

The focus of this analysis is to reveal pertinent bioethical and medical issues in *Frankenstein,* supported by the discussion of hard science. In the third millennium Mary Shelley's *Frankenstein* taps into a spectrum of specific issues and is a cautionary tale that asks: What happens when technology runs amok? *Technology* is defined in the *Oxford American Dictionary* as "the scientific study of mechanical arts and applied science." In applying his technical knowledge, Victor Frankenstein's first intentions were benevolent: to "banish disease from the human frame and render man invulnerable to any but a violent death" (*Frankenstein,* 40). But later, scientific hubris adds to the mix, and now he must create a superhuman species with "happy and excellent natures"—but they will owe their existence to him and will "bless" him (*Frankenstein,* 52). He is the scientist playing God. His creation, although superhuman in size and speed, is repulsive in appearance, becomes isolated, and is continually rejected by society.

The novel was written 200 years ago. In the tradition of romantic literature, the theme is often revealed through a series of letters, which is called the epistolary novel technique. Today's sophisticated reader needs to suspend disbelief while certain aspects of the plot unfold. For example, although the monster is "born" full grown, at birth his emotional and intellectual age is that of an infant. Nonetheless, given an adult brain, he teaches himself to talk by overhearing the De Lacey family. He learns to read when he finds a copy of Milton's *Paradise Lost.* Putting Milton's epic poem in his hands, as such, helps develop Shelley's theme, that her monster is God's creature, an Adam looking for love and acceptance from a mate. Shelley's early-nineteenth-century narrative seems awkward at times, and inconsistencies in description pop up. More fundamentally, though, readers must forget certain characterizations, plotlines, and images created by James Whale's classic 1931 film starring Boris Karloff, which spawned generations of pop culture. First, Mary Shelley's Victor Frankenstein is a 17-year-old science student, not the more mature Dr. Henry Frankenstein of the movies. Popular culture also has planted in our heads that Frankenstein is the monster's name, when in fact the monster is a nameless being referred to as "the fiend" or "the creature."

What is of utmost importance in *Frankenstein,* however, is that

Mary Shelley gives us the viewpoints of both creator and creature. She aligns the relative humanities of Victor Frankenstein and his "fiend" so that readers can decide for themselves on the humanness of each. Yale Literature Professor Harold Bloom states in the afterword to *Frankenstein*:

> The greatest paradox and most astonishing achievement of Mary Shelley's novel is that the monster is *more human* than his creator. This nameless being, as much a Modern Adam as his creator is a modern Prometheus, is more lovable than his creator and more hateful, more to be pitied and more to be feared, and above all able to give the attentive reader that shock of added consciousness in which aesthetic recognition compels a heightened realization of the self. (*Frankenstein*, 215)

That is, when readers immerse themselves in the story, their connection with, or sense of empathy for, the monster should heighten. Empathy is having an awareness of another's feelings and thoughts; it is what creates man's sense of humanity to man. The ability to have empathy and to show compassion is a key issue discussed today in medical and scientific circles. Victor Frankenstein, the maniacal yet detached scientist, keeps a safe emotional distance between himself and the monster. He abandons him immediately with no interest in observing or understanding the monster's feelings and thoughts. It would take empathy for Frankenstein to bond psychologically with his creation and to understand and to nurture him. Near the end of Shelley's chapter 10, the monster in his need for companionship and understanding confronts his creator, but his rational attempt to connect is thwarted. In frustration he threatens his creator. Right up until the time Frankenstein takes his last breath on Walton's ship, his tragic flaw does not arise from his Promethean ambition to create life, but rather in his mistreatment of, or lack of empathy for, the fiend he "fathered."

Other social issues emerge from *Frankenstein*, including how science and religion are misunderstood and misused; how human prejudice toward repulsive appearance leads to desolation and striking out; and even, in feminist terms, how the male scientist is seen metaphorically as raping natural resources perceived as feminine (*see* appendix D). Nonetheless, the most relevant bioethical theme centers on the Prometheus syndrome of creating technology without thinking ahead of the consequences. *Frankenscience,* a term coined by the popular press, warns us about the inherent dangers of technology going awry and the potential for chaos in mainstream science.

Frankenscience

The creature warns Victor Frankenstein: "Remember that I have power . . . I can make you so wretched that the light of day will be hateful to you. You are my creator, but I am your master" (*Frankenstein*, 160). Have we released a monster—called Frankenscience—that has the power to destroy our civilization? Victor Frankenstein wanted to eradicate disease and death, but then his scientific curiosity turned into an obsession to create life and to become famous. At the end, he even warned his rescuer, Captain Walton, who is on a quest of his own, to learn from him about the dangers of acquired knowledge. While the benefits of technology, such as lifesaving vaccines, are clear, is it prudent to be constantly vigilant about the downside of technology? In recent times, examples of Frankenscience include splitting the atom, which led to nuclear bombs, and using computers, which some say may dehumanize our society and have great potential to harm us (Y2K millennium bug, computer viruses, and hacking damage, also known as cyberterrorism). Following are more examples of Frankenscience, or the possibility of technology running amok.

Xenotransplantation

From *xenos,* the Greek word for "stranger" or "guest," a xenograft is an organ or tissue transplant from one species to another. With new biomedical technology, patients condemned to early death might live longer with baboon hearts, pig livers, or other animal organs. Oftentimes the health risks of these xenotransplantations are unknown, and animal viruses pass to humans. Mary Shelley's book adds to the debate warning of the dangers of usurping the natural order. In 1984, for example, the infant known as Baby Fae received a baboon heart transplant. She lived only 20 days with it. After a two-year effort for FDA permission, in 1996 AIDS patient Jeff Getty received baboon bone marrow, intended to boost his immune system. This is called the facilitator cell approach. Animal parts successfully transplanted into people may end serious maladies such as diabetes, but often the long-term consequences of cross-species transplantation are unknown.

Cloning (creating a genetic duplicate)

In 1996 Scottish researchers cloned Dolly the sheep at the Roslin Institute. There was widespread excitement in the scientific community, but also there was considerable speculation about the downside of this technology. Were we aware of the risks? What kind of restraint would we put on this type of scientific power? Because of intense publicity on the issue in all broadcast media, President Bill Clinton issued a moratorium on human cloning pending a National Bioethics Advisory Commission investigation. While Victor Frankenstein completed his research in secret, scientists today have more governmental oversight of their plans and procedures, especially if federal money is used. As a nation, we also have to decide how much we value individuality and diversity in our population.

Another cloning project begun after Dolly's successful cloning captured the imagination of the country. Texas A&M University received several million dollars from an anonymous couple who wished to clone their beloved dog Missy, a 13.5-year-old border collie-husky mix. Aided by new biotechnology, scientists attempted to make the right factors come together. Unfortunately, Missy died in 2002 at age 15 before the cloning succeeded, but her DNA remains in a gene bank. The project spawned commercial cloning projects, with investors looking at licensing rights that could run in the millions of dollars, even though Missy's owners just wanted to reproduce the dog they loved. They expected Missy #2 would resemble the first Missy but may not have acted like her. Successful cloning projects might answer several questions. Do genes dictate behavior? If Missy #2 is raised the same as Missy #1, will she act the same? Bioethicists who study the ethical aspects of cloning are interested in this nature versus nurture experiment. The Missyplicity Project scientists were bound by a nine-point Code of Bioethics. Point 9 states: "No data, personnel, or other resources shall be knowingly shared with people or programs seeking to clone human beings." However much the Missyplicity Project intended to limit access to its technology, on May 4, 2003, the first member of the horse family, Idaho Gem, a cloned mule, added to the lengthening list of cloned animals, including cats, bulls, and a dozen others. Project Noah's Ark hopes to preserve the genes of endangered species and to re-create prehistoric DNA, such as from woolly mammoths. On February 11, 2004, South Korean scientists announced they had cloned human embryos, with the growth process terminated in the early stages for therapeutic research purposes. The genie has left the bottle, making the age of cloning a reality. With the postmodern Frankensteinian ability to create life, public policy and laws must now address the social issues incumbent in reshaping our world.

Bioterrorism

One of these major issues is bioterrorism because terrorists have the ability to use recent advances in technology to disseminate disease, to cause illness, and to inflict mass death. In 1984 the first documented case of bioterrorism occurred in The Dalles, Oregon, a quiet town along the banks of the Columbia River. Followers of the Indian guru Bhagwan Shree Rajneesh spiked salad bars with salmonella at 10 restaurants and sickened about 750 people. Fear was widespread in the area as many residents thought cult members would try to spread the AIDS virus and to contaminate the water supply. Scared people would not go out alone, becoming prisoners in their own homes. The cult's motivation was to keep voters from the polls so that their candidates would win county elections. This incident received little national attention because it was perpetrated by a local fanatical fringe cult. Cult members fled to Europe; their leader died in India in 1990. The story is told in Portland State University Professor Gary Perlstein's *Perspectives on Terrorism* (1991).

Inciting further fears of bioterrorism, the World Health Organization warned in 2001 that it is technically possible to disseminate lethal quantities of smallpox or anthrax to kill millions of people. Local governments are slowly receiving advice from the Centers for Disease Control and Prevention (CDC) in Atlanta on how to combat germ warfare, which at times has led to grounding crop-dusting planes. A small number of people in a large city could be infected with smallpox, spreading it to many more before it is detected. U.N. treaties ban biological and chemical weapons stockpiled during the Cold War, but on and after September 11, 2001, bioterrorist threats became real. Terrorists proved their technical capability by hijacking four commercial jet airliners; two hit the twin towers of the World Trade Center in New York City, killing thousands; one hit the Pentagon near Washington, D.C., killing 196 people; and the fourth plowed into a field near Pittsburgh, killing all aboard. A month later, a dozen people in five areas of the country were infected with anthrax through the mail, including in Nevada, at a tabloid newspaper in Florida, at the Senate Office Building in Washington, D.C., and at television networks NBC and ABC in New York City. Several people died; many others became ill but were successfully treated with antibiotics. The CDC routinely issues other warnings for smallpox, food poisoning, and deadly viruses like Ebola. But the United States had not experienced a homeland attack since the Japanese bombed Pearl Harbor on December 7, 1941. With the terrorists identified as religious fundamentalists from several countries, American men, women, and children began talking about the meaning of good and evil and how to rebuild a moral world shattered by horrific events.

While the term Frankenscience takes on a pejorative meaning, the Visible Human Project sponsored by the National Library of Medicine is one recent example of how advanced technology had a favorable outcome. In 1993 the donated body of an executed murderer was sliced into thousands of razor-thin sections. They were photographed and digitized and can be freely viewed on the Web to teach anatomy and surgical techniques. The researchers had the condemned man's informed consent, but it took years of public debate before a social consensus was reached approving this human dissection and viewing it as something other than horrific Frankenscience.

In a related matter, when science is conducted secretly without the oversight of the collective conscience and public laws, there can be tragic consequences. During World War II, for instance, Nazi medical experiments on Jews in concentration camps, without their informed consent, led to horrendous suffering, disease, and death. While it is not popularly discussed, however, the results of these experiments included the first documentation that smoking caused emphysema. Nonetheless, the tobacco industry has been criticized for keeping silent about the addictiveness of nicotine and the inherent physical dangers of smoking. The price in human suffering and medical costs has been high. In the case of the Human Genome Project, which promises breakthroughs in genetic research leading to medical cures, the National Institutes of Health has opened its databases. The potent knowledge embodied in the international decoding of human DNA could be abused if kept secret. In Shelley's *Frankenstein* Victor Frankenstein also keeps silent about his grisly project and does not warn society about his monster's escape (even though he is aware of his brother's murder), making him complicit, or a participant in, the monster's crime. *Frankenstein* is a prescient warning of the stealth of science in developing gene therapy, cloning, and cyborgs.

Alone in his laboratory Victor Frankenstein created a monster who was unleashed onto humanity. Today's society, too, weighs the benefits of medical discoveries against ethical and spiritual concerns. But how do we impose a limit on the human quest for knowledge and how that knowledge is applied? In 1818 Mary Shelley could not have imagined how strongly *Frankenstein* would relate to early-twenty-first-century headlines declaring scientific breakthroughs. For two centuries Mary Shelley's ghost story has permeated our culture, spawning science fiction and horror films such as Ridley Scott's *Blade Runner.* Its themes have given shape to plays, films, and the television series *Star Trek;* and it was even a Marvel comic book series in the 1970s. Bobby "Boris" Pickett, sounding like Boris Karloff, and the Crypt Kickers made the song "The Monster Mash" a 1962 hit. Given all of *Frankenstein*'s influence on pop culture, in the end this classic tale continues to throw a cautionary light upon the rampant advances in technology and how humans use them to penetrate the secrets of nature. In chapter 2, "A Brave New World," ideas gleaned from *Frankenstein* will be extended into further discussions of eugenics, transplantation, and cloning.

SYNOPSIS OF THE NOVEL

Much of the plot of *Frankenstein* unfolds through letters a young Artic explorer writes to his sister in England. Captain Walton, who is searching for a northwest passage to the New World, tells her about coming upon the mortally ill Victor Frankenstein adrift on an iceberg. The nearly frozen man is searching for the monster he created and talks about his obsession to learn the secret of life. He tells Captain Walton about his family in Geneva, Switzerland: his parents; Elizabeth Lavenza, an orphan adopted when he was five, whom Victor calls his cousin; and two younger brothers, Ernest and William. His closest childhood friend is Henry Clerval, the well-read, gentle son of a merchant. In youth Victor marveled at the natural world and desired to divine its secrets from studying natural philosophy ("the genius that regulated his fate"). He read the works of Cornelius Agrippa, Paracelsus, and Albertus Magnus. Seeing lightening strike an old oak, its stream of fire interested him in the laws of electricity. In learning about the natural sciences, Victor dreamed of eradicating human disease.

At 17 Victor left home to study chemistry and anatomy at the University of Ingoldstadt. From Professor Waldman he learned about the new discoveries of blood circulation and of the nature of air. Clearly, Victor thought, modern science has power over the natural world. Then, suddenly, Elizabeth was struck with scarlet fever. Victor's mother nursed her through it but soon died herself. On her deathbed, she joined the hands of Elizabeth and Victor who became betrothed. Back at the university Victor's interests turned with renewed vigor toward examining the processes of life and death. Might he, in time, bring life to lifeless matter? He spent nights in burial vaults and charnel houses, filling his laboratory with dissected human and animal parts, all of which disgusted him. But he knew that from them he would create a perfect man and that this new species would "bless" him for it. With a singleness of purpose Frankenstein devoted himself to his task for more than two years, absenting himself from family and friends until his work was complete.

On a dreary November night the exhausted Victor Frankenstein sparked life into his sutured corpse, and the superiorly designed eight-foot creature opened its dull yellow eyes, breathed hard, and flailed its limbs. While proportional, the features Frankenstein had selected for his creation were not beautiful: yellow, taut skin scarcely covered muscles and arteries; lustrous black, flowing hair and pearly white teeth were in horrid contrast to its watery eyes set into dun-white sockets; and straight black lips traversed a shriveled complexion. Frankenstein's beautiful dream vanished at the sight of his horrible creation, and he ran to his bedchamber where his fretful sleep filled with prescient dreams of Elizabeth morphing into his mother's wormy corpse. All at once the monster startled him from his sleep, and Victor escaped to the lower courtyard. He remained there for the night, listening for the "demoniacal corpse."

Suddenly Clerval, who arrived to attend the university, surprised Victor with a visit. They returned to the laboratory only to discover the monster had fled. In maniacal relief, Victor fell down into a fit, exhausted. Clerval nursed him for several months, disbelieving his ranting as the product of a wild imagination. When Victor stabilized, Clerval gave him a letter from Elizabeth with news and entreating him to write. Feeling some normalcy again, Victor abandoned his former work, holding his terrible secret inside. Back at the university he introduced Clerval to his professors, but hearing their praise of his work, Victor writhed at their words. He turned away from scientific endeavors toward Clerval's studies of language and literature. Then one day Victor received a letter from his father with the cruel news that his brother William had been murdered. Victor went home to Geneva to visit the spot where William died, and a figure not of human shape passed him. It was the creature. Victor did not tell the authorities and cause immediate pursuit because they would only consider it the ranting of a lunatic. His silence exacted a terrible price.

Elizabeth, William's caretaker, anguished in self-reproach over his death. Few felt relief when the servant girl Justine was accused of the crime on circumstantial evidence—the picture William wore around his neck was found in her pocket. Eyewitnesses, caught up in mob hysteria, testified falsely. When the Roman Catholic Justine confessed to the crime to obtain absolution, Victor knew himself to be "the true murderer" but did not speak up. Thus, William and Justine became the first hapless victims of Frankenstein's "unhallowed arts." Feelings of remorse and guilt preyed upon Victor's health, and he and his family retreated to their house at Belrive. A sense of impending doom followed them, and while hiking in the Alps one day Victor saw the monster who entreated him to remember that he was his creation, now irrevocably excluded from humanity because appearances made him a fiend. He described an existence in hiding, except for time spent near a cottage in Germany where the De Lacey family lived. They consisted of an old blind peasant and his daughter, his son, and his son's lover. Compared to the monster's forlorn state, they were blissful, having found asylum from horrendous events in Paris. He observed them clandestinely and gained speech and an understanding of love. Feeling benevolent, he cut firewood for them. Then walking in the forest one day, he found a book, John Milton's *Paradise Lost,* and he slowly learned to read. Born intelligent and sensitive, the monster's emotions were profoundly stirred by reading the book as he compared his situation to Adam's. But God had not made him into a perfect creature; rather, he was hideous, abandoned, and alone. Feeling more like the fallen angel Satan, the creature envied the family's happiness. Finding the courage to meet them, he saw only how frightening he was, and he fled.

On his travels he saved a child's life, but contacts with other fearful humans added to his growing despair and sense of isolation. By the time he ran into Frankenstein in the Alps, he was despondent and depressed. He demanded Frankenstein make another hideous creature like himself—but of another sex. "We shall be monsters, cut off from all the world," but closer therefore, he argued. Happiness may not always be theirs, but having each other would keep them misery-free and harmless to others. "Let me see that I excite the sympathy of some existing thing; do not deny me my request," he implored his creator. Because normal society would not embrace him, his mate must also be deformed and horrible. The creature Frankenstein abandoned as ugly and unnatural now sought his creator, yearning for love and acceptance. At first Frankenstein considered the implications of adding to this new species, but then he consented. He traveled to Scotland with Clerval, leaving him to withdraw to a lonely Orkney Island to undertake his dreadful task. But then Frankenstein thought of the curse he might bring on future generations by producing "a race of devils" and destroyed the work he had begun. With no mate forthcoming, the monster, who had followed Frankenstein to Scotland, vowed to kill all whom Frankenstein loved.

The monster found and killed Clerval in Ireland—Frankenstein was accused but acquitted of the crime. Later, back in Switzerland, Elizabeth was murdered on her bridal bed. Frankenstein swore he would destroy the monster and pursued him to the Arctic where Captain Walton encountered him. Broken from months of vengeful pursuit, Frankenstein entreated the captain, who like himself was on a quest, to avoid scientific ambition. Hallucinating about his dead loved ones, Frankenstein died. As Captain Walton prepared for home, the monster entered the ship's window. Standing over Frankenstein's coffin, he described his unspeakable torments while he longed only for happiness. Expressing remorse for his misdeeds, the monster jumped onto a nearby iceberg and was lost in the darkness. The tragic tale of Victor Frankenstein ended.

TOPICS FOR ORAL AND WRITTEN DISCUSSION

1. How did the Enlightenment's views on individual happiness, the Industrial Revolution, and barbaric medical procedures influence Shelley's thinking as she was writing *Frankenstein*?
2. What scientific discoveries and social views did Shelley incorporate into her novel?
3. How does Shelley's use of Milton's *Paradise Lost* relate to *Frankenstein*'s theme?
4. Describe the Prometheus syndrome as it derives from Ovid's *Metamorphoses*. Is Victor Frankenstein's obsession to create life a sin against God or nature?
5. Thinking about the complex relationship between Frankenstein and his creature, how do we decide what is human and what is nonhuman?
6. How can society balance the benefits of new medical discoveries and technologies against the ethical or spiritual questions they may pose?
7. Define Frankenscience and give several examples.
8. What are Victor Frankenstein's and Justine's respective misunderstandings and misuses of science and religion, and how do they contribute to their deaths?
9. Society rejects Frankenstein's intelligent, kind, and articulate creature because of his scary appearance. If the aliens described in science fiction exist, what lessons learned from Shelley might influence our reaction to them?
10. Relate Frankenstein's ability to create life to the ethics of human cloning.

BIBLIOGRAPHY

Evslin, Bernard, et al. *The Greek Gods.* New York: Scholastic Books, 1966.

McElheny, Victor K. *Watson and DNA: Making a Scientific Revolution.* Cambridge, Mass.: Perseus Books, 2003.

Milton, John. *Paradise Lost.* In *Complete Poems and Major Prose,* ed. Merritt Y. Hughes, 173–454. New York: Macmillan, 1957. A Garden of Eden tale of good and evil.

Perlstein, Gary, and Harold Vetter. *Perspectives on Terrorism.* Belmont, Calif.: Wadsworth Publishing Co., 1991.

Risse, G. B. "Semmelweis, Ignaz." *Dictionary of Scientific Biography,* ed. C. C. Gilespie. New York: Scribner's, 1970–80.

Shelley, Mary. *Frankenstein or, The Modern Prometheus.* New York: New American Library, 1965. (3rd rev. and corr. ed., 1931, contains the author's introduction and a preface and afterword by Harold Bloom.)

———. *Mary Shelley's Journal.* Edited by Frederick L. Jones. Norman: University of Oklahoma Press, 1947.

Shelley, Percy Bysshe. "On the Moral Significance of Frankenstein." In *The Complete Works of Percy Bysshe Shelley,* ed. Roger Ingpen and Walter E. Peck. 10 vols. New York: Scribner's 1926–30. *See also* "Prometheus Unbound," vol. 6, 263–5.

Stone, Lawrence. *The Family, Sex and Marriage in England (1500–1800).* New York: Harper, 1977.

Wollstonecraft, Mary. *A Vindication of the Rights of Woman.* New York: Norton, 1975.

SUGGESTED FURTHER READING

Bear, Greg. *Darwin's Radio.* New York: Ballantine, 2000. A cautionary tale describing a human species that only survives by mutating beyond what is acceptably human.

Bulgakov, Mikhail. *Heart of a Dog.* Translated by Mirra Ginsburg. New York: Grove Press, 1968. Creature turns creator's life into a nightmare.

Clarke, Arthur C. *Childhood's End.* New York: Harcourt, 1953. After many years, humans find out what kindly aliens who land on Earth look like.

Ehrenreich, Barbara, and Deirdre English. *Witches, Midwives, and Nurses: A History of Women Healers.* New York: Feminist Press, 1973.

Keyes, Daniel. "Flowers for Algernon." In *Science Fiction Hall of Fame, Volume One,* ed. Robert Silverberg, 605–35. New York: Avon, 1970. A brain operation triples Charlie's intelligence.

Miller, Henry I. and Gregory Conko. *The Frankenfood Myth: How Protest and Politics Threaten the Biotech Revolution.* Greenwood Press, 2004.

Selzer, Richard. "Poe's Light-house." In *The Doctor Stories,* 147–71. New

York: Picador, 1998. A gothic, suspense-filled short story with a medical twist.

Seymour, Miranda. *Mary Shelley*. New York: Grove, 2001. A comprehensive biography.

Stapledon, Olaf. *Sirius*. 1944. Reprint, New York: Penguin Books, 1973. A lonely dog has the mind of a man.

Stevenson, Robert Louis. *The Strange Case of Dr. Jekyll and Mr. Hyde*. In *The Complete Short Stories,* ed. Ian Bell. London: Holt, 1994. Split personality.

NATHANIEL HAWTHORNE'S "RAPPACCINI'S DAUGHTER" (1844)

Rappaccini! Rappaccini!
And *this* is the upshot of your experiment?

—Signor Pietro Baglioni in "Rappaccini's Daughter"

HISTORICAL CONTEXT

As Shelley did in *Frankenstein,* Hawthorne drew from his background to create a supernatural tale in "Rappaccini's Daughter." Born in 1804 in Salem, Massachusetts, Hawthorne descended from Puritan immigrants. One ancestor was a judge during the Salem Witch Trials of 1692, which influenced Hawthorne's thinking on the nature of good versus evil as well as on the differences between science and religion. The witches on trial seen hallucinating and convulsing were believed to have supernatural powers given to them by the devil. The Puritan community felt at risk believing Satan could capture their souls. Religion explained natural phenomena because seventeenth-century science could not. Late twentieth-century forensic science has reevaluated the Salem witches' bizarre behavior, comparing it with similar events like St. Vitus' dance and St. Anthony's fire, and has theorized that a rye grain fungus eaten in bread caused the LSD-like behavior (Caporael, "Ergotism: The Satan Loosed in Salem?").

When Nathaniel was just four, his sea captain father died of yellow fever, leaving behind his wife and three children. All of Nathaniel's aunts and uncles helped raise him, and he attended Bowdoin College, where he befriended the poet Longfellow. He returned home to write but was not immediately successful, so he worked in the Custom House. Then he lived briefly at Brook Farm, an experimental utopian community based on transcendentalist philosophy. Finding it too difficult to write, he left in a huff. As a nonconformist, Hawthorne's commune experience might explain why his garden setting for "Rappaccini's Daughter" reflected more of Dante's inferno than romantic idealism. Later Hawthorne married Sophia Peabody. They moved to Concord, Massachusetts, where they raised several children.

Sophia's upbringing directly influenced Hawthorne's themes. Her father, Dr. Nathaniel Peabody, grew the purple wildflower *Solanum dulcamara* in his Salem garden, using it for tooth pain relief. From her early childhood Sophia kept records on the garden. Her father, despite his homeopathic tendencies, made her the object of some experiments, as Dr. Rappaccini did with Beatrice. He dosed her with paregoric (opium), laudanum, and mercury, and Hawthorne, to his horror, later found it necessary to cure his wife of these addictions. Another incident central to Hawthorne's theme was the bitter medical rivalry between two famous regional doctors, Dr. Oliver Wendell Holmes and Dr. Robert Wesselhoeft. In 1842 at the prestigious Boston Society for the Diffusion of Useful Knowledge, Holmes accused Wesselhoeft of quackery and ran him out of town, denouncing his delusional use of homeopathy (a water cure) and calling him an empiric with fantastic theories. In addition, Wesselhoeft's brother, William, used experimental hypnosis on the young Sophia Peabody, which Hawthorne viewed as a violation. Hawthorne re-creates the Drs. Wesselhoeft and Peabody in the empiric Dr. Rappaccini, reconstructing the bitter Holmes-Wesselhoeft rivalry into the driving force of "Rappaccini's Daughter" (St. John).

Other well-known Hawthorne works, *The Scarlet Letter, The House of the Seven Gables,* and *The Blithedale Romance,* also visit the theme of how good fends off evil. They reflect America's age of romanticism, a literary movement drawn from European literature to invent the gothic terror genre, a gloomy, dense, and dark style that aroused in readers a sense of the supernatural. Nathaniel Hawthorne and his contemporaries Edgar Allan Poe and Herman Melville used Puritan legends to create mysterious and evil characters. Two other romantic authors who influenced Hawthorne were Henry David Thoreau *(Walden),* who used the scientific method to observe and record natural phenomena, and Ralph Waldo Emerson *(Nature),* who believed God created nature and held dominion over everything, including science. Thoreau and Emerson rejected harsh Puritan beliefs to found transcendentalism, which like nineteenth-century Enlightenment caused a cultural awakening. In their flourishing utopian communal societies they cast off the idea that Satan caused illness and disease to punish man. Instead, they held the belief that man was innately good and that using his intuition, alone, he could arrive at a deeper truth than experience offered. Transcendental views helped to spread democracy and social reform, such as the abolition of slavery and the fight for women's rights. When compulsory school attendance was enacted into law, a more literate population spread progressive ideas that set the cornerstone for medical reform. As in Europe, the United States was changing into an industrial and urban society. In fact, in 1829 the term *technology* was coined to describe new inventions: the cotton gin, the sewing machine, and the telegraph.

It is important to note that "Rappaccini's Daughter" is set in Renaissance Padua, Italy, where at Padua University, a thriving medical center, a sixteenth-century scientific controversy brewed. Up until that time old medical traditions were practiced based on the Roman-era views of Galen of Pergamum (A.D. 130–201); he is called the Father of Sports Medicine. Galen was primarily a gladiatorial surgeon who synthesized all that was then known of medical practice. His framework for explaining the body and its diseases included numerous anatomical and physiological discoveries about heart-muscle action, kidney secretion, respiration, and nervous-system function. Primarily, he believed in the balance of four body humors: blood, phlegm, and yellow and black bile. Debates ensued when Paracelsus (1493–1541), a Swiss alchemist and physician considered the Father of Pharmaceuticals, broke with the long-held traditions of Galen to revolutionize medical practice.

Paracelsus observed plants and minerals like sulfur, iron, and copper sulfate, and he conducted experiments with their active ingredients. He taught that the activities of the human body are chemical, with health depending on the proper chemical composition of the organs and fluid, what are now called pharmaceuticals. Paracelsus encouraged research into the nature of poisonous substances, proving that if they were given in small doses they could often cure the disease they caused. It was the principle of "like can cure like," relating to present-day inoculations. "Rappaccini's Daughter" introduces the Paracelsian idea of an antidote based on the principle that what makes a person ill may also be the cure. Unfortunately, in the plot's denouement, or outcome, when Rappaccini's daughter grabs the antidote from Giovanni's hand and swallows it, she dies in a Romeo and Juliet twist of fate. However, rather than two families being at odds over their star-crossed lovers, Hawthorne reenacts the bitter rivalry between the Galenic whole-body approach and Paracelsian pharmaceutical advances, or, the traditionalists and the empirics. The idea of "like can cure like" is also a forerunner to today's homeopathy, which stresses looking at the symptoms of each individual patient for clues to a cure rather than at classical definitions of disease. In homeopathic medicine, practitioners identify cellular abnormalities that hinder the body's ability to remove toxins, and they introduce pharmaceuticals to augment the body's natural healing process.

Another term used to identify a Paracelsian approach is holistic. Paracelsus believed that a physician should be an alchemist, astrologer, and theologian in order to tend the body, soul, and spirit. He also gave us the best definition of syphilis up to that time, and, although now known to be toxic, invented a mercury treatment for its cure. Hawthorne, who understood the Galen-Paracelsus debate, characterized Dr. Rappaccini as a Paracelsian who observes nature and experiments. In fact, Baglioni tells Giovanni that Rappaccini is a "vile empiric" who does not respect "the good old rules of the medical profession." On the other hand, Baglioni, as Rappaccini's counterpart, is more of a Galenist, a traditional academic. Carol Marie Bensick offers another interesting interpretation of "Rappaccini's Daughter" in *La Nouvelle Beatrice: Renaissance and Romance in "Rappaccini's Daughter."* Reconstructing the historical Padua setting to be the site of syphilis research and drawing on the Galen-Paracelsus controversy, she diagnoses the main characters with syphilis. She says descriptions in the story of fever and strange bursts of energy support her supposition. In her view, Beatrice inherited syphilis at birth through her father (thereby developing an immunity to it), and Giovanni is simply an unknowing carrier. Bensick adds that Baglioni's vial carrying the antidote was made by Benvenuto Cellini, a known syphilitic, and she points out that in the sixteenth century the common term for syphilis was poison.

Medical topics arising from Hawthorne's story include cures for syphilis and theories of inoculation, the premise being that today's lethal toxin may contain tomorrow's lifesaving drug. Primarily, however, Hawthorne pits the conservatives who endorse the tried and true ways against the innovators who endeavor to advance new and sometimes more radical treatments. While scientific discoveries range from the basic to the lofty, such as looking into prehistoric dinosaurs, studying DNA and stem cells, and exploring the stars, the nature of scientific rivalry is always two-fold. On a multinational level scientists compete to advance scientific discoveries, and on a personal level they may want to expose a rival. It can all take place on a battlefield, as exemplified in "Rappaccini's Daughter."

LITERARY ANALYSIS

Scientific rivalry drives Hawthorne's famous supernatural tale of poison and intrigue. It reconstructs an Italian Renaissance setting at Padua University when two camps were at war: the traditional Galenists and experimental Paracelsians. Paracelsus was an empiric, the Faust of Renaissance medicine, whose new science of medical chemistry transcended tradition. He opposed the orthodox Galen, who until that time was regarded as an indisputable source. Andreas Vesalius, professor of anatomy at Padua University, a famous center for medical training, was another central figure of Renaissance medicine supporting Paracelsian reform. In 1543 his famous anatomical text, *The Fabric of the Human Body,* was published, based on stolen criminal bodies because the church did not allow dissection. For the first time, he proved Galen's observations wrong, which had been based largely on animal observations. Vesalius also helped establish surgery as a separate medical profession.

Paracelsus's and Vesalius's remarkable convergence of ideas with Renaissance humanism was the beginning of the great transformation from archaic medicine to modern technology. Their medical breakthroughs, along with William Harvey's discoveries on blood circulation, contradicted the old ways, which led to suspicions and bitter rivalries. Likewise, in "Rappaccini's Daughter" the traditionalist Baglioni opposes the experimentalist Rappaccini, a Faustian character in search of knowledge or perfection. In a scientific research scenario replayed many times over the years, archrival Baglioni uses his apprentice Giovanni as a pawn against Rappaccini. And, at a time when views of sexuality caused doctors to examine women with their clothes on, Beatrice's sexuality motivates all three men: Rappaccini must control her, Giovanni must dominate her, and Baglioni fears her.

Demonstrating how great literature can be viewed many different ways, "Rappaccini's Daughter" is variously included in anthologies of 1) the best nineteenth-century science fiction; 2) great American love stories; 3) famous poison stories; and 4) Garden of Eden stories. The story always evokes a strongly polarized and viscerally emotional male-female response in animated discussions on the nature of Beatrice's and Giovanni's romantic love. In literary analysis, however, Hawthorne's Garden of Eden allegory pits good against evil using literary allusion and devices such as symbolism and ambiguity. In addition, he plays out the romantic themes of nineteenth-century science seeking perfection and, when things go terribly wrong, the scientist's unpardonable sin for not asking for forgiveness. Dr. Rappaccini, ultimately the hubristic scientist playing God, shows his tragic flaw in using his own daughter in a life-threatening experiment. He has exalted the mind at the expense of the heart, expressed symbolically in the head (intellect) versus the heart (emotion). A hotly discussed issue today is the need to balance clinical medicine with human rights. When Rappaccini thrusts his innocent daughter into a life of isolation, he rationalizes that she will become invincible and thank him. Through no fault of her own, she turns deadly. But she is ignorant of her poisonous nature because her only companions have been her father and her "sister," a poisonous purple bush that mocks her beauty and is symbolically rooted in evil. In fact, the duality of nature, also seen in the garden's broken fountain, is expressed throughout "Rappaccini's Daughter" as a major theme. Ultimately, Dr. Rappaccini's unconscionable plan extends into "infecting" Giovanni, an intended bridegroom who is excited by a beautiful young woman and puzzled by her eccentric father.

Hawthorne repeatedly shows Beatrice's and Giovanni's inner feelings, and how they fall in love. Giovanni's is an idealized romantic love—until he realizes he has taken on her poison. In the end Rappaccini's detached intellect allows him to value science over humanity, reprehensibly sacrificing his own daughter to add to his "heap of knowledge." Indeed, the theme of sacrificing the one for the many is often played out in modern medicine. Dr. Rappaccini's "fatal love of science" envelops Beatrice and Giovanni into an inescapable situation; only death will liberate them. Rappaccini's destiny remains ambiguous. Baglioni's conservative view is that Rappaccini's flaw is not having a "sounder view of the healing art." And a universal science fiction theme including a "vile empiric" scientist whose scientific method is exalted over human life, is the main focus of this analysis. For all of the reasons highlighted in the themes, including scientific hubris, stealth of research, and scientific rivalry gone awry, today's human research subject guidelines are strictly monitored. The story's major theme in the context of a scientific rivalry is the importance of striking a balance between human needs and scientific progress, a concern many medical professionals and bioethicists face today. In the end, "Rappaccini's Daughter," like Shelley's *Frankenstein*, reminds us of what happens when unsupervised scientific experiments go terribly wrong, especially when scientific rivalry intervenes. The theme extends into medical research today where we all have to decide what is acceptable.

SYNOPSIS OF THE SHORT STORY

"Rappaccini's Daughter" opens with Hawthorne mocking himself as its allegory-loving author, M. de l'Aubepine (French for "Hawthorne"). Then he gets right into the sixteenth-century story of Giovanni Guasconti, an impressionable, self-absorbed young man leaving home for the first time to attend medical school at the University of Padua. Giovanni's room overlooks a garden where the eccentric Dr. Rappaccini, a genius but an outcast from the medical establishment, cultivates plants for medicinal purposes. One day Giovanni is excited to see the doctor's beautiful daughter, Beatrice, enter the garden; at the same time he is puzzled when Rappaccini carefully inspects a purple shrub without touching it, while Beatrice embraces it.

Giovanni's mentor, Signor Pietro Baglioni, tells him more about the mysterious Dr. Rappaccini and his daughter, but his view is tainted by years of professional jealousy, saying that Dr. Rappaccini cultivated poisons for their medicinal virtues without hesitating to sacrifice what was dear to him. Secretly, the less brilliant former colleague Baglioni fears that Rappaccini is grooming Beatrice to unseat him from his professorship and that he may be taking over his promising young protégée.

Besides having Baglioni's skewed point of view—unreliable and libelous—we draw conclusions about Beatrice and Rappaccini out of Giovanni's own paranoia and lust. In fact, most of what he and the reader think they know of this father-daughter duo comes from these two sources. In the key garden scene in which Giovanni "sees" proof of Beatrice's poison—a lizard drops dead after a few drops from the purple flower fall upon it—he has just come from Baglioni. Giovanni is drunk, according to his own admission, and almost everything he suspects is undermined by the author. At last, as Giovanni is finally drawn into her garden, the reader is drawn in through Giovanni's viewpoint, fed again by paranoia and lust. The ever-scheming Baglioni has warned Giovanni that Rappaccini is a "vile empiric" who plans to use him in one of his experiments, and he gives him a silver vial containing a poison antidote. In a test Giovanni plans to hand some flowers to Beatrice, but, inspecting them in his room, they wilt in his hands. In a scene in which he turns on her, Giovanni rushes into the garden to meet Beatrice. He offers the vial to her, declaring they must first drink to purify themselves. In actions showing her to be innocent and of a loving heart—not poisonous—she grabs the vial from his hands and drinks the antidote. What she says rings true: "Was there not more poison from the first, in thy nature than in mine?" She is poisonous only in that she is sexual; he is "poisoned" by her because she sexually excites him. That is what he resents and fears. In the final analysis, isn't Giovanni's poison lovelessness and a lustful nature; isn't Beatrice's poison more literally sexual—ultimately related to our humanness and mortality?

Rappaccini then enters the garden and tells Beatrice that Giovanni was to be her bridegroom. While Beatrice felt her father had inflicted a lifetime of horrible pain on her, he believed he had given her a great gift: she was invincible to any power and could defeat any enemy. Declaring that love would be preferable to fear, she died. The antidote, which Giovanni avoided taking first, was a poison to her. In the last line of the story, our suspicion of Baglioni's professional jealousy and his view of Rappaccini as an evil experimenter are confirmed when, after seeing Beatrice die as a result of his antidote, he diabolically gloats "in a tone of triumph mixed with horror": "Rappaccini! Rappaccini! And *this* is the upshot of your experiment?"

TOPICS FOR ORAL AND WRITTEN DISCUSSION

1. What Italian Renaissance advances improved the scientific method in studying medicine?
2. Relate the sixteenth-century Galen-Paracelsus debate to Baglioni's and Rappaccini's scientific rivalry. Who does Hawthorne cast as the villain?
3. Define and relate the homeopathic principle, "like can cure like," to the story. Discuss the theory of inoculations, specifying recent innovations in cancer and AIDS vaccines.
4. Define and apply to the story "vile empiric," detached intellect, and head versus heart.
5. How did Paracelsus's and Vesalius's works transform medicine from archaic to modern?
6. How has late-twentieth-century forensic science explained the bizarre behavior of the Salem witches in the seventeenth century?
7. Was Rappaccini's experiment a rational and/or unconscionable action?
8. Relate the story to the romantic view of scientific hubris and being wary of seeking perfection; then attribute characteristics of good and evil to the four main characters.
9. Apply the main theme in "Rappaccini's Daughter"—striking a balance

between human needs and scientific progress—to 2004 arguments put
forth by the President's Council on Bioethics recommending a ban on
human reproductive cloning.
10. Who should decide what is acceptable research?

BIBLIOGRAPHY

Bensick, Carol Marie. *La Nouvelle Beatrice: Renaissance and Romance in
"Rappaccini's Daughter."* New Brunswick, N.J.: Rutgers University
Press, 1985.

Caporael, Linnda R. "Ergotism: The Satan Loosed in Salem?" *Science* v. 192
(2 April 1976); or http://web.utk.edu/~kstclair/221/ergotism.html.
Also, PBS film incorporating her work: "Secrets of the Dead: Witches
Curse." http://www.pbs.org/wnet/secrets/case_salem/resources.html.

Genesis 2–3. The Holy Bible. Authorized (King James) Version. The Garden
of Eden story.

Harvey, William. *An Anatomical Study of the Motion of the Heart and of the
Blood in Animals.* 1628. http://www.fordham.edu/halsall/mod/1628
harvey-blood.html.

Hawthorne, Nathaniel. "Rappaccini's Daughter." In *The Complete Novels
and Selected Tales of Nathaniel Hawthorne,* ed. Norman Holmes Pear-
son, 1043–65. New York: Random House, 1937. http://bartelby.com/
310/1/3000.html.

Roslin Institute, Edinburgh. http://www.roslin.ac.uk/public/cloning.html.
Biotechnology and Biological Sciences Research.

St. John, Thomas. "Dr. Wesselhoeft in Rappaccini's Daughter." In *Nathaniel
Hawthorne; Studies in The House of the Seven Gables,* 1993. http://
www.geocities.com/seekingthephoenix/h/hawthorne1.htm (accessed May
12, 2002).

Transcendentalists. http://www.transcendentalists.com/index.htm (accessed
May 12, 2002).

SUGGESTED FURTHER READING

Carlson, Laurie Winn. *A Fever in Salem.* Chicago, Ill.: Ivan R. Dee, Inc.,
1999. A mosquito- or bird-borne encephalitis outbreak caused symptoms leading to witch trial inquisitions.

Doyle, Arthur Conan. "The Curse of Eve." The Literature Network. http://
www.online-literature.com/doyle/red_lamp/6/.

Doyle, Sir Arthur Conan. "The Adventure of the Copper Beeches." In *The
Complete Sherlock Holmes.* 316–32. Preface: Christopher Morley. Garden City, New York: Doubleday, 1930. Holmes to Watson on the scientific method in "The Adventure of the Copper Beeches": "You have
perhaps erred in attempting to put colour and life into each of your

statements, instead of confining yourself to the task of placing upon record that severe reasoning from cause to effect which is really the only notable feature about the thing."

Harrison, W. C. *Dr. William Harvey and the Discovery of Circulation.* New York: MacMillian Company, 1967.

Hawthorne, Nathaniel. "The Birthmark." The Literature Network. http://www.online-literature.com/hawthorne/125. A doctor renders his bride perfect.

Fisher, Helen. *Why We Love: The Nature and Chemistry of Romantic Love.* New York: Henry Holt and Company, 2004.

Poe, Edgar Allan. "The Facts in the Case of M. Valdemar," "The Fall of the House of Usher," "The Black Cat," and "The Tell-Tale Heart." In *Complete Tales and Poems.* New York: Barnes & Noble, 1992. Anti-utopian themes like Hawthorne's.

Selzer, Richard. "Imelda." In *The Doctor Stories,* 83–97. New York: Picador, 1998. A story recounting a doctor's obsession and personal growth.

Turner, Arlin. *Nathaniel Hawthorne: A Biography.* Oxford: Oxford University Press, 1980.

White, Michael. *Acid Tongues and Tranquil Dreamers: Eight Scientific Rivalries That Changed the World.* New York: Perennial, 2002.

2

A Brave New World: An Analysis of Aldous Huxley's *Brave New World* and Robin Cook's *Coma*

INTRODUCTION

Aldous Huxley wrote *Brave New World* to show how individuality is sacrificed when the government controls and conditions its people with science and technology. It casts a cautionary light on the inherent dangers from genetically determining a society where pharmaceuticals and psychological conditioning try to keep everyone healthy, happy, and conformed until it is their time to die. The novel is timely as we enter a brave new world of genetic engineering and cloning, highlighting the issue that our technical ability to create and to manipulate human life runs well ahead of public policy. While other countries boldly advance biotechnology promising perfected, disease-free humans, in 2001 President George W. Bush said he was deeply troubled and remarked, "We have arrived at that brave new world that seemed so distant in 1932 when Aldous Huxley wrote about human beings created in test tubes in what he called a hatchery." Indeed, many elements of Huxley's science fiction dystopia have come true: anthrax threatening economic stability; drugs controlling thoughts and feelings; artificially fertilizing and growing babies in surrogates; and lifelong conditioning by government and commercial concerns. But the significant advance in the late twentieth century of mapping and sequencing the genetic pattern for most organisms, called the Human Genome Project, means that we can now alter human life by going for a cure rather than for a quick fix. Rapidly advancing biotechnologies give rise to hope and fear, putting legal, religious, and scientific communities at odds over our sometimes un-checked faith in technology. Advocates favor government funding for National Institutes of Health projects that will fuel discovery and create medical miracles; opponents argue that the technology in-volved in genetically altering life is moving far ahead of a necessary ethical and regulatory framework.

Similarly, Robin Cook says his medical thriller themes in *Coma* are not only possible but even probable. They are definitely not science fiction, he adds. He puts the organ transplant industry under a mi-croscope, giving a Hippocratic "first, to do no harm" warning to doctors. Cook's horrific plot of turning healthy patients into profit-able donors develops within the power struggle of the lower and upper worlds of the hospital hierarchy. He shows the problem of drugged doctors and the dehumanization of patients and how weak-ening the doctor-patient relationship contributes to medical mis-takes. Research advanced in secret is also a problem. The key issues are the safe procurement and the fair dissemination of human organs and the definition of brain death, which continues to undergo medi-cal, religious, and cultural interpretations. At present, organ harvest-ing gives back life and adds to its quality; its protocol is fairly well established. However, Cook says there is a problem when the black market in human organs sells a rare commodity to the highest bidder. In addition, with genetic engineering advances 25 years after *Coma* was published, some fear scientists are bending the rules of nature and heredity by cloning transgenic or cross-species transplant organs. But, stem-cell-derived organs or those cloned from our own tissue promise transplant without rejection. The science is here, already be-ing applied from other mammals to humans.

In this twenty-first-century brave new world of scientific and tech-nological advances into the secrets of life, we will all need to under-stand the new scientific knowledge and decide how far we want to take it. Aldous Huxley's *Brave New World* and Robin Cook's *Coma* highlight important bioethical and medical issues that stimulate discussion.

ALDOUS HUXLEY'S
BRAVE NEW WORLD (1932)

> The theme of *Brave New World* is not the advancement of science as such; it is the advancement of science as it affects human individuals.
>
> —Aldous Huxley (1946 foreword)

HISTORICAL CONTEXT

The prolific author Aldous Huxley (1894–1963) wrote essays, novels, short stories, poetry, and screenplays. While *Brave New World* is his best-known novel, others such as *Point Counter Point* (1928) were successful as well. As is the case with every author, Huxley's background shaped his work. He was born in Surrey, England, on July 26, 1894, the third of four children. His father, Dr. Leonard Huxley, was an author, and his mother, Julia Arnold Huxley, was a girls' school founder. Tragedy befell the household when his mother died of cancer. Later the 16-year-old Aldous attended Eton but left a year later with the serious eye disease *keratitis punctata*. He was blind for more than a year, which prevented him from finishing rigorous science training and ended his dream of becoming a medical doctor like his famous grandfather T. H. Huxley. Instead, he received a degree in English literature from Oxford. He married his first wife, Maria, in college, and they had a son. After Maria died in 1955, he married another writer, Laura Archera Huxley. Huxley's literary ancestors include a novelist aunt and great-uncle Matthew Arnold who wrote the famous poem "Dover Beach." Aldous's brother Julian was a respected biologist. An element clearly present in Huxley's novels is the indomitable human spirit, an ideal that tested the family when one of Aldous's brothers committed suicide. Huxley moved to the United States in 1937, and in 1959 the American Academy of Arts and Letters gave him the Award of Merit for the Novel. He died of cancer on November 22, 1963.

Brave New World, written in the post–World War I period of industrialization and the rise of fascism, derived from Huxley's fascination with science, medicine, and technology as well as from his concern for problems arising from their unchecked advances. Huxley drew

from several past influences and projected them into an imagined totalitarian World State. First, he drew on the work of his outspoken
grandfather, T. H. Huxley (1825–95), a biologist, educator, and medical doctor, who was called Darwin's Bulldog because his work *Evidence
as to Man's Place in Nature* (1863) dared to embrace Charles Darwin's
unpopular theory of natural selection. T. H. Huxley inspired his grandson to courageously assert within the theme of *Brave New World* that
our individual freedoms must be carefully guarded, even if the stance
we take is unpopular. A second influence on Aldous Huxley was
geneticist-psychologist Francis Galton (1822–1911), the father of eugenics and Darwin's cousin, who believed science could increase human happiness through improving breeding patterns. He favored
genetic determination over environmental influences (i.e., nature over
nurture). Galton's influence is clear in Aldous Huxley's genetically
determined caste system. The third to influence Huxley was political
economist Thomas Malthus (1766–1834), whose work fueled Darwin's theory and influenced Huxley's economy-driven, population-
controlled brave new world by describing how plants and animals
naturally produce more offspring than can possibly survive. Malthus
blamed nineteenth-century England's decline on too few resources for
the increasing population and on an irresponsible lower class. He believed that only curtailing reproduction would prevent a global famine,
a natural phenomenon he thought God created to keep man from
being lazy. Lastly, Aldous Huxley's concept of lifelong neo-Pavlovian
conditioning in *Brave New World* stems from behavior scientist Ivan
Pavlov's 1880s work in human behavior. Russian chemist and physi-
ologist Pavlov studied the digestive system, drawing a link between
salivation and the stomach's action in his stimulus-response theory. He
rang a bell at the same time he offered food to dogs; then, even when
no food was present, the bell's ring caused the dogs to salivate. He
called his result a conditioned reflex.

Drawing from his forbearers T. H. Huxley, Francis Galton, Thomas
Malthus, and Ivan Pavlov, Huxley created ways in his future world to
artificially reproduce humans and to condition them to be content with
their predetermined lots. Writing *Brave New World* was his way to
address a fear that the world was becoming spiritually bankrupt and
settling into an abhorrent conformity. A similar theme is reflected in
1984, the work of his contemporary George Orwell. Huxley's novel
describes an economy-driven population in which physical and psychological control is essential. How we choose to advance humanity
through breeding techniques is the novel's main concern, casting a
cautionary eye on eugenics, the term Francis Galton coined in 1883.

While Galton's pioneering scientific study of twins helped advance knowledge of inborn and learned characteristics, in 1953 James Watson and Francis Crick gave deeper access to life's secrets. They fueled contemporary genetic engineering by deciphering the structure of DNA and by identifying the basic inherited molecular characteristics of life. This event and the plant and animal biotechnical advances since that time are fully described in Bernice Schacter's *Issues and Dilemmas of Biotechnology* (1999). Since *Brave New World*'s 1932 publication, cautionary lessons have been evoked by moralists who fear each significant leap in understanding the biotechnology of creating life. For instance, although the general population took little notice in 1952 when Robert Briggs and Thomas King cloned tadpoles from cells, much later in 1978 there was considerable concern as the first test-tube human baby was born through in vitro fertilization, or combining eggs with sperm in a dish, then implanting the fertilized eggs into a human womb. In 1990 the U.S. Human Genome Project extended Watson's and Crick's work, setting a 15-year goal to fully map and sequence human DNA. Encrypting DNA's 100,000 gene pairs is to discover "the language in which God created life," President Bill Clinton asserted.

Brave New World was evoked again in 1996 when Dr. Ian Wilmut of the Roslin Institute in Scotland cloned Dolly the sheep through somatic cell nuclear transfer (SCNT). The public and press, scientists and clerics raised the dreaded specter of Frankenscience. As an embryologist, Dr. Wilmut said his primary objective was therapeutic (to help mankind); subsequently, he produced a human protein in Dolly's milk, creating transgenic or cross-species organisms from cloned genes. In 2005, the British government granted Wilmut a license to clone human embryonic skin cells for therapeutic use in research on motor-neuron diseases like Lou Gehrig's disease. In December 2000, Texas A&M University advanced the science and presented its transgenic bull, 86 Squared, cloned from donor cells frozen 15 years before and naturally resistant to tuberculosis, salmonellosis, and brucellosis, making the species more fertile and better milk producers. Although 90 percent of the attempts have failed, researchers see great potential for saving endangered species. With a somewhat eerie result, in October 2001, the University of Oregon cloned the monkey ANDi (ANDi stands for "inserted DNA" spelled backward). Differing from Dolly and 86 Squared, ANDi's DNA contained a jellyfish gene inserted into the egg. Genes, segments of DNA, contain the "recipes" for making biological molecules, usually protein. When ANDi is stimulated, he glows a fluorescent green. The therapeutic goal is to create transgenic research monkeys containing genes for human diseases such as Alzheimer's, AIDS, or breast cancer. Because monkeys are close genetic cousins to humans, there is concern the same method soon will be applied to humans. Signaling the continued meteoric advance in biotechnology, in 2002 the University of Missouri cloned piglets modified to yield transgenic transplants to humans. Although better breeding techniques have been used in cattle for decades, many scientists fear the unforeseen consequences of the leap to transgenic cloning. With the science already in place for cloning mammals, these techniques can be applied readily to humans. Lay, religious, legal, and science communities are urgently posing specific questions about what some consider the horrific cloning of human beings:

- Is it morally justifiable to clone a dead child to fulfill his or her lost destiny?
- Couples using in vitro fertilization can choose the desired sex from their collection of eight-cell embryos and then discard the rest. Is this preimplantation genetic diagnosis sex selection sex discrimination when sperm-sorting effects the same result? During the embryo selection method horrendous diseases are genetically screened, but how does it affect humanity when other characteristics such as eye color and intelligence are isolated?
- Parents have procreated a child to provide tissues, organs, and bone marrow for another child. Is there anything wrong with cloning a donor child for a perfect match?
- If you cloned yourself, who would that be?

Incredible advances in genetic engineering help infertile couples and eliminate inherited disorders such as Tay-Sach's disease, sickle-cell anemia, and Down syndrome. The ability to clone, or to duplicate, humans, almost as described in *Brave New World,* is here. With biotechnological advances begun when Watson and Crick identified the molecular code of DNA and continued with the Human Genome Project, ethical challenges follow. Some twenty-first-century bioethicists are asking the question, how soon we will forget World War II and the Nazi's eugenics-driven genocide?

The Embryonic Stem Cell Controversy (Therapeutic versus Reproductive Use)

While *Brave New World* was published in 1932, the themes in Huxley's novel clearly take us into the debate over human cloning, with the technical ability to create and genetically manipulate human life running well ahead of public policy. Stem cells are found in human embryos, umbilical cords, and placentas and, when divided, can become any kind of body cell. When terminated at the five-day stage, the in vitro fertilization process yields embryonic stem cell lines that can grow into 200 cell types, potentially repairing or even replacing damaged body parts. Proponents argue the value of therapeutic cloning, including finding missing clotting factors in hemophilia, benefiting cystic fibrosis, and creating new antirejection factors, far outweighs the fact that the so-called activated cells are terminated. Opponents of therapeutic cloning fear the precedent set for experimenting on life, born or unborn, and believe no way exists to bar reproductive cloning once therapeutic cloning is legal and government-funded. The National Academy of Sciences opposes reproductive cloning. Other private and governmental bodies concur, asserting that once we have designer children and clones, the brave new world will have arrived.

In 2002, after President Bush announced he favored using existing stem cells lines for therapeutic research but banned federal money for creating new stem cell lines, the U.S. Congress debated the issue, and Bush appointed a national Council on Bioethics to deliberate on research ethics and to make policy recommendations. In July the council, which seems representative of the nation as a whole, was sharply divided on creating new stem cell lines for therapeutic research, but in the end, calling cloned cells "nascent human life," favored a four-year moratorium on attempts to create cloned cells for medical research. They needed time for studying moral and scientific issues and to make policy recommendations. The council was at odds with President Bush, who favored a permanent ban. The dissenting members saw this as failing to be patient advocates and feared a delay would block development of important medical therapies. At the same time, the U.S. Senate stalemated on the issue. Nonetheless, the privately funded cloning of cells for reproduction and therapeutic research is very much underway. Since the council's debate, scientists have announced promising work on adult stem cells that prove more versatile than formerly believed. The University of Minnesota Medical School used a specific bone marrow cell in mice to grow in the laboratory into a variety of cell types, including blood, bone, fat, brain, and liver cells. With more positive research on humans—which is years away—these findings might soften the ethical debate over creating and disposing of embryonic stem cells. Nonetheless, noting that existing stem cell lines are limited, in poor condition, or useless for research, in September 2002,

California passed its own legislation to fund state-wide embryonic stem cell research, attracting world-wide talent to what has been termed the skin cell gold rush.

The New Debate (Groopman versus Kass)

The bioethical debate on how far we should take cloning is focused in the essays of Leon R. Kass, bioethicist and chairman of the President's Council on Bioethics, and Jerome Groopman, Harvard professor and science correspondent for *The New Yorker*. In the 1960s Kass opposed the now common practice of in vitro fertilization, saying it would erode family values, stigmatize the children, and create a baby market. Follow-up studies proved otherwise. He now opposes creating new embryos for reproductive research but approves using existing stem cell lines in therapeutic research. In his highly publicized "wisdom of repugnance" test, he states that if it feels wrong, it must be wrong. In his May 21, 2001, essay in *The New Republic*, "Why We Should Ban Human Cloning Now: Preventing a Brave New World," Kass argues that there is a danger in creating a utopia that tries to conquer disease and even death through psychopharmacology, artificial organs, and computer chips. He is concerned about what new scientific technology will do to our humanity. Huxley's World State eliminated disease, aggression, and grief, and in the process of creating prosperity and stability, it achieved a conformity that tried to homogenize humanity. Art, science, and religion were banned; immediate gratification was compulsory. Prozac may not be soma, and somatic cell nuclear transference cloning may not be the Bokanovsky Process, but, looking at our society now, Huxley saw it coming, Kass says. We were rescued from Nazi and Soviet tyranny, but if we remain uncritical, biotechnical hubris and profit motive will undermine "genuine contributions to human welfare." Although there is a considerable difference in intent, human reproductive cloning is just a small step away from unrestricted therapeutic cloning, he avers.

Jerome Groopman, responding to Kass's views, wrote in his January 28, 2002, *New Yorker* essay that President Bush had asked the Council on Bioethics to be "the conscience of our country," and Kass, as its chairman, had considerable influence on the future of American life science. Groopman criticized Kass for asking the council to read Hawthorne and Huxley to illustrate the consequences of scientific hubris and the dangerous quest for perfection, instead of using hard facts. But the facts are, Groopman states, that in the two types of cloning a cell's nucleus is inserted into an unfertilized egg that takes on that cell's genetic characteristics. In reproductive cloning the manipulated egg grows into a baby genetically duplicating the donor; while in therapeutic cloning, the manipulated egg grows into a microscopic clump that provides stem cells, at which point the process is terminated. Cloning stem cells for research promises cures for millions of people suffering from spinal-cord paralysis, Alzheimer's, Parkinson's, and juvenile diabetes. Kass fears that cloning will raise the specter of Nazi war experiments by creating "genetically identical humans suitable for research" or by fostering a desire to replicate beauty, talent, and genius. Groopman worries that Kass will encourage the council to write a guideline based on his "wisdom of repugnance." The "it must be wrong if it feels wrong" argument, according to Groopman, "is impervious to reason and severely constrained by time and place." Historically, the church once deemed autopsy, important for diagnosis, as repugnant and sacrilegious. To further Groopman's argument, in 1976 the city of Cambridge, Massachusetts, home to Harvard Medical School, tried to make "repugnant" recombinant DNA research illegal. Now its NIH-regulated biotechnology treats heart disease, cancer, and rheumatoid arthritis. Groopman, in a summary response to Kass, states that he wants our national bioethical guidelines to be "based on fact, not on literature or aesthetics—one that distinguishes real science from science fiction."

Biotechnology continues to promise dazzling changes in modern society. But some fear its power to lead the human race down a slippery slope, making it vitally important for everyone—not just scientists and the clergy—to understand and to deliberate on the Groopman-Kass debate.

LITERARY ANALYSIS

This literary analysis concentrates on how *Brave New World* continues to cast a cautionary light on twenty-first-century bioethical questions on genetic engineering, especially with technology far outpacing regulation. Concerns are, how far should we go to fix what is wrong with us, and should this even include cloning a new and better species that is smarter, more beautiful, and more talented? In Huxley's World State, a technocratic government and its scientific elite make decisions for the good of the entire population, sacrificing individuality. Its motto is Community, Identity, Stability. In the previous era, anthrax bombs had threatened the war-torn economy during the Nine Years'

War. The government's response to anthrax threats, which relates to our own twenty-first-century fears of bioterrorism in the United States, was to create a one-world state and to fortify the economy by controlling the population. In order to maintain a stable community, individual identity was forsaken. The most interesting aspect of the plot is that, rather than exercising military control, biotechnologies took over. Humans were mass-produced, then physically and psychologically conditioned into a specific class, each with its own destiny. Although less time is spent on character analysis here than on bioethical issues, the five classes or castes—Alphas, Betas, Gammas, Deltas, and Epsilons—all were fixed into their predestined tasks to keep the economy running. Likewise, the American education system once tracked children into specific slots throughout their school years. And in countries like China, where the birth rate is strictly controlled, students' high school scores either afford them additional educational opportunities or place them into trade occupations for life.

Huxley's imagined ectostatic (outside of the womb) method of creating human life by placing fertilized eggs into bottles eerily comes close to the now-common practice of in vitro fertilization and the artificial womb created in 1997. Moralists fear Huxley's imagined world in which two parents are no longer required to make a baby and the word *family* is vulgar. Huxley's idea that one fertilized egg would be cloned into 96 identical lower-class Epsilons to lock in conformity highlights the hot contemporary debate in cloning. Geneticists argue that cloned humans have 100 percent identical DNA but that transfer of genetic material is not the transfer of consciousness. In fact, it would be no different from naturally conceived identical twins who maintain unique personalities. But psychologists now theorize that as much as 50 percent of a clone's psychological traits, such as shyness and fearlessness, are influenced by genes. The half-mile-long assembly line Huxley called the Bokanovsky Process modifies embryos into lifeforms to serve in specific roles. The related idea of cloning perfected humans or of creating cloned tissues that promise a myriad of therapeutic cures is receiving both loud criticism and stalwart support. Every country is evoking the Huxleyan dystopia in debates over the far-ranging bioethical issues relating to human cloning.

With some changes in terminology, the human condition in Huxley's futuristic brave new world does not sound very different from our twenty-first century. Instead of the pleasure-inducing drug soma to control thoughts and feelings, we have Prozac and Ritalin. The Internal and External Trust extracts hormones to keep people young and happy; we have hormone replacement therapy and Viagra. Instead of the neo-Pavlovian conditioning and hypnopaedia, some say our subliminal governmental and commercial messages cause conformity in what we want to have and to be. Huxley's human babies are manufactured, and a medical procedure called a pregnancy substitute gives women the psychological experience of having babies without actually having childbirth. His Podsnap's Technique artificially speeds up the ripening of embryos for extraction (we have follicle-stimulating drugs to extract ova). Instead of Malthusian belts to discourage unsterilized women from having sex and getting pregnant, we have the birth control pill, fallopian tube-tying, and male sterilization. In Huxley's World State, imperfectly cloned humans are discarded; we routinely screen for genetic faults, aborting within the limits of the law. Both manipulate reproduction. Huxley's Liners and Matriculators work in the Bottling Room, placing artificially inseminated embryos into sow-peritoneum-lined bottles for maturation, at which point they are decanted (born); we artificially inseminate ova with sperm in a glass dish (in vitro fertilization) and implant them in a surrogate human womb or artificial womb. Underscoring Huxley's one-world utopia is the Malthusian philosophy of achieving a reproduction-consumption balance in a world without disease and fear of death. Our contemporary view is more a matter of the desire for human perfection by eliminating disease and all the while consuming however much we want, while in the end creating a painless morphine-induced death.

Hence, much of what is going on in biotechnology today is reflected in Huxley's cautionary theme, and, in particular, that we must control the rapid advances in biotechnology before they control us and our individuality. His *Brave New World,* in which economic stability supersedes art, science, and religion, was written in the early 1930s before the beginning of the totalitarian Nazi state, the communist Soviet regime, and World War II. Incredibly, however, the criticism of Huxley's World State parallels that which fell on eugenics when the Nazi government sanctioned Dr. Josef Mengele's World War II medical research atrocities. In his 1976 novel *Boys From Brazil,* Ira Levin imagined how Mengele planned to clone a new generation of Hitlers. Levin used the twentieth-century technology to turn skin cells salvaged from Hitler into his clones who are then placed into preselected homes to mimic Hitler's youthful environment. That is, the cloned babies are environmentally nurtured to become a new race of Hitlers who will then take over the world, fulfilling a destiny that World War II cut short. Using today's technology, which is not too far afield from Huxley's 1930s theories, stored cells collected even from the dead could be cloned into a Mozart, an Einstein, and a Hitler.

The memory is still fresh in Germany, which in 2001 banned creating embryos for research. Germans learned a hard lesson from Nazi eugenic experiments on Jews. In their wartime genetic determinism, they tried to control who had the right to be born and live. Indescribable human experiments horrified the world, even though some of the research still benefits us today, such as connecting smoking to lung cancer. The underlying lesson, perhaps, is that science, even when regulated by its own government, can run amok. In *Jurassic Park* (1990), another fictional account about cloning, Michael Crichton envisions a world in which prehistoric dinosaurs have been cloned and brought back to live in a twentieth-century theme park where they terrorize the very scientists who created them. Even within the sterilized adult dinosaur population, the unexpected happens and life finds a way. James Gleick's *Chaos: Making a New Science* (1987), applied to *Jurassic Park,* further theorizes that in our nonlinear world random, unpredictable and chaotic events often override whatever type of order we try to impose. Both the novels of Levin and of Crichton replay the *Frankenstein* theme describing what can go terribly wrong when biotechnical scientists are left to their own devices.

In essence, *Brave New World*'s reproductive methods derive from the Malthusian idea that anything not contributing to the economy, for the greater good, should be forbidden. In Huxley's dystopian vision, the family unit is obsolete because reproductive sexual intercourse would be too genetically risky and would relinquish the government's control. Instead, eggs are harvested from women taking Hormone Stimulate Surrogate, which releases their eggs and diminishes any maternal impulse. To continue a comparison of Huxley's future world and ours today, his reproductive process equates with the willing surrogate (paid or not), her womb available to host the fertilized egg of two donor parents. The World State requires conformity. Subliminal propaganda called *hypnopaedia* inculcates early prejudices. Soma drugs, a chemical called Violent Passion Surrogate, and multisensory movies called *feelies* promote sexual promiscuity and a sense of well-being. The Controllers have decided what is best for all.

In *Brave New World* the World State seeks to perfect human life without disease and discontent, replacing individual identity. It has created conditions it believes are good for the community as a whole. Unfortunately, Huxley's imagined social engineering, taking drugs to numb a harsh existence and having few family bonds, is not foreign to today's reality. Furthermore, the Controllers use neo-Pavlovian stimulus-response to condition their people to relate death to something pleasant. Critics say today's American way of isolating and drugging dying people tends to sanitize or "to domesticate" death. In a like manner, the World State conditions its people to not fear death, and, when faced with it, they are repulsed. The contrast between Huxley's imagined future world and ours today shows what might go wrong when the government controls art, science, and religion. The World State discourages literature because it might cause discontent in people thinking about the old ways. Science not contributing directly to the overall plan is outlawed, and religion has no place in a world without disease and fear of death.

In his plotline, Huxley contrasts his main characters, the nonconformist upper-class Bernard with the highly conditioned lower-class Lenina conformed to her lot in life; and the woman Linda, raised in World State values but relegated to a Reservation life, with her savage son John, who is caught between worlds and cannot be happy where there is no hope and love. Huxley's characters set into the contrasting worlds, the World Society and the Savage Reservation, show how class discontent begins to unravel the society. Bernard and Helmholtz, independent thinkers and misfits, are joined by John, a romantic savage, to destabilize society. Passages from Shakespeare run throughout the book, signaling notions of romantic love. But achieving stability through conformity and induced states of happiness, not individual romances, are key ingredients in the brave new world. The Savage John can never be happy there because its civilization has poisoned him. He wants to join the banished Bernard and Helmholtz but is denied doing so because he is still the object of an experiment to amalgamate him into the culture. In Huxley's 1946 foreword to *Brave New World*, the author states that he erred in not giving the Savage a third choice in addition to either a primitive Reservation life or insanity in utopia. He could choose to live in sanity on the borders of the Reservation within a "society composed of freely cooperating individuals devoted to the pursuit of sanity," where the lofty question posed is, "How will this thought or action contribute to, or interfere with, the achievement, by me and the greatest possible number of other individuals, of man's Final End?"

Related to today, Huxley's brave new world of genetically engineered humans shows us what might happen when measures are taken to control and to condition us. The family unit is obsolete; chemicals keep people happy. While appearing as a utopia without disease and warfare, free will is lacking. Consumption of goods that boost the economy, promiscuous sexual interplay that keeps emotional attachments from forming, and the redefinition of religion and the banning of history and art are all elements that keep the totalitarian society intact. Huxley's novel predicts the eugenics issues we currently face, first with test-tube babies and now with human cloning. Fears center around the possibility of cloning worker and controller types as well as stagnating gene pools. In summary, Huxley's caste system includes manufactured, conditioned, and conformed human beings.

Dr. Lee Silver, a molecular biologist at Princeton University and author of *Remaking Eden: How Genetic Engineering and Cloning Will Transform the American Family,* argued in a 2002 PBS special, "Eighteen Ways to Make a Baby," that we should not fear human cloning. He suggests we look closely at genetic engineering, which has been perfected in some animals, eliminating cancer and augmenting memory. The primary purpose of human cloning, he says, would be to help infertile couples whose babies could have health advantages as well as improved personalities and better cognitive traits. In a cloned human, the process of dividing DNA in half is eliminated, so fewer chromosomal problems are expected and certain physical attributes are controlled, including the predisposition to certain diseases. Of course, environment and consciousness modify genetic endowment. In Huxley's dystopia, genetic and environmental engineering preset human personality, identity, and social structure.

Dr. Silver, nonetheless, cautions that ethical dilemmas may arise when human cloning creates a permanent gap between the affluent society boosting its children's advantages and the poor countries that cannot. And the problem with widespread genetic engineering is that it might eliminate the type of genetic diversity seen in randomly dispersed genes. The beauty in genetic diversity is that it allows any child to succeed. In addition, we must ask ourselves if manipulated genes could create a permanent divide in society between the upper and lower socioeconomic classes. When people no longer interbreed, would this divide us into two or more separate species? Many questions arise, noticeably beginning with could, would, and should. One consideration of so-called brute-force evolution—dropping manufactured traits into an organism and hoping for its genetic best—is that there may still be many failures and surprises. It is unlike Darwin's natural selection, tinkering with genes and selecting the variants over a long period of time. In the end, we must all wonder how direct biotechnological intervention in the genetic process, such as human cloning, will interfere with evolution itself and affect the human race.

Given the legal, ethical, and social backdrop of Huxley's cautionary *Brave New World*, we should ask ourselves these major questions about genetic engineering:

- Because scientists and the biotech industry have vested interests in research, will our legislatures pass effective laws to prevent genetic determinism (physical and psychological) and genetic discrimination? (Huxley's Alphas are the genetically engineered, advantaged few.)
- What would happen if our world's gene pool became controlled by the scientific elite (Huxley's Controllers)?
- The President's Council on Bioethics in 2004 approved of therapeutic research on existing stem cells but disapproved of reproductive cloning. How much does "the conscience of the country" influence the views of Congress, the scientific community, and society at large?

In our *brave new world*, which is a phrase spoken by Miranda in Shakespeare's *The Tempest*, we must all decide—not just the scientists, philosophers, lawyers, and clergy—where we want biotechnology to lead us as a human race.

SYNOPSIS OF THE NOVEL

Almost everyone seems happy in the World State's brave new world of 632 A.F. (After Ford), a "utopia" Huxley imagined in 1932 and set 600 years in the future. In the pre-Ford era anthrax bombs had created economic instability during the Nine Years' War. Now the need for security supersedes individual freedom. An autocracy of 10 Controllers manages life from an artificially manufactured birth to a painless and unemotional death. Everything is done for the welfare of the human collective. Instead of old-fashioned two-parent reproduction (viviparation), the Director of Hatcheries and Conditioning creates human life. Women receive Pregnancy Substitute to suppress maternal impulses and to produce eggs, which are then artificially fertilized and placed in bottles. The Bokanovsky Process chemically alters embryos into humans ranging from the super-intellectual Alpha Pluses to the semimoronic dwarfed Epsilons. Lower classes come from a single egg that buds into 96 identical clones, and oxygen deprivation causes the desired mental defects. Any science not suiting the Controllers' purposes is deemed "dangerous and potentially subversive." Controlled in this manner, humans have an inescapable destiny.

Besides reproductive genetic engineering, behavior conditioning controls the population. Through neo-Pavlovian conditioning infants hear loud sirens and receive electrical shocks to make them hate books and roses. They are taught that "prehistoric" pre-Ford populations suffered reading the Bible and that books taught independent thinking and history, which is "bunk." Roses have no value because they are uncommercial and may influence urban workers to love nature. In place of religion, society worships Ford, symbolized by Henry Ford's Model T replacing the Christian cross. As children grow into adulthood, repetitive subliminal messages (hypnopaedia) inculcate propaganda suggestions. All games include elaborate apparatus to increase economic consumption, and children's participation in erotic play, including multiple-sensory movies called feelies, promotes promiscuity. The word *family* is vulgar. Everyone pops the pleasure-enhancing drug soma, which has no side effects and masks discontent.

All throughout the human life span Controllers decide what is best for the common good, but from time to time things go wrong. The Alpha-Plus psychologist Bernard, a loner mocked for his Gamma-like appearance, is different. During his embryonic stage, the Controllers put too much alcohol in his blood-surrogate. Bernard and another misfit, the poet Helmholtz, become friends. Bernard attends the quasi-religious Solidarity Service where the president is the minister, the T is the cross, and everyone else leaves feeling reperfected. Unlike Lenina, the woman Bernard likes, he refuses to join in the orgy. Lenina has been conditioned with the feelings and desires of her lower class and cannot understand Bernard's nasty desire to express his individuality. They plan to vacation on a New Mexico Indian Reservation, an outpost not worth civilizing. Long ago the Director had taken a "pneumatic" Beta-Minus woman there who was lost and did not return with him. Bernard fears being banned for his nonconformity, but, bred as an intelligent Alpha, he is intoxicated with his own significance.

At the Reservation Lenina feels repugnance at the wild and uncivilized ways: children, born in wombs, nurse indecently at their mothers' breasts; the old and toothless reek of decay. Disease and death are visible. By contrast, in the civilized World State sterile internal secretions balance youthful equilibrium, and blood transfusions keep metabolism stimulated. Lenina and Bernard meet an old squaw, the Director's lost woman Linda, who bore him a son, John. Linda tried to maintain her World State civility by teaching John about the civi-

lized world's helicopters, soma, and feelies. She substituted Indian pes-
cal for soma, but her promiscuity displeased Indian wives. John, like
Bernard, feels trapped between two cultures. He reads Shakespeare,
had a father-substitute, and performed his own manhood rites, fasting
and torturing himself like Christ on the cross. Bernard empathizes with
the two savages but has an ulterior motive in taking them to his world.
He will have some leverage against the Director's banning him for his
unorthodox ways.

On return to the World State, Bernard and Lenina take Linda and
John to the Bloomsbury Centre, its 4,000 rooms buzzing with the
activity of turning embryos into whole predestined populations. Newly
decanted babies suck down pints of pasteurized external secretion, and
the napping toddlers unconsciously listen to propaganda tapes on hygiene, erotic sexuality, and sociability. To all present Bernard presented
John, the Director's son, who called him father, and Linda, his woman,
who is now embarrassingly fat and old. Caught in petrified disgust,
the astonished Director resigns on the spot. Everyone is curious about
the savage, John, but Linda repels them. She sinks into a soma-induced
trance to hide from her new reality. But Bernard revels in his new
celebrity as the Savage's friend and guardian. John and Lenina go to
a feelie, which John considers a base and ignoble experience. He has
romantic notions of love from reading *Romeo and Juliet,* and having
sex with Lenina would feel immoral. She is disappointed. Helmholtz,
who has become John's friend, finds it strange and comical that there
should be so much tension in the man-woman relationship. But, for
John, there must be a commitment, and he must feel worthy.

Besides pining for Lenina, John is grief-stricken to learn his mother
is dying, a strange emotion in a world where an individual is insignif-
icant among the masses. At the hospital the soma-drugged Linda cannot communicate, which makes John feel guilty and alone, fearful he
is losing his one human connection. The death-conditioned Bokanovsky Group comes into the room, surprised at such an extreme reaction
and horrified at seeing Linda's "flaccid and distorted senility." Their
modern medicine is able to give even a moribund sexagenarian a girlish
appearance. When his mother dies, John's grief is palpable, upsetting
the visiting group that associates death with pleasure. In his presence,
identically cloned Delta workers obediently receive their daily soma,
and John realizes in a flash he must make this slave world free again.
He throws their soma out the window, calling it "poison to soul as
well as body." A fight ensues. Bernard and Helmholtz arrive. Bernard
declares John mad while Helmholtz helps him. All three are taken to
see Controller Mond.

Mond at last bans the insubordinate Bernard and Helmholtz for causing instability. Then he explains the World State to John in a declaration of Huxley's core *Brave New World* ideology. Science, art, and religion were sacrificed for the common good. Science was first controlled during the Nine Years' War when anthrax bombs threatened the world. Now, when humans need to release residual anger and passion, chemically administered Violent Passion Surrogate stimulates the adrenals. New discoveries in pure science might be subversive and are outlawed. The high art of literature must be sacrificed for conformity. Old books like Shakespeare's tragedy *Othello* can cause people to feel self-conscious and unlearn new ways. Religion in a youthful and prosperous society, when people are safe, well, and not afraid to die, is unnecessary. "God isn't compatible with machinery and scientific medicine and universal happiness. You must make your choice," he says. They live in a utopia where security and happiness replace desire for beauty and truth. Besides, soma controls discord.

In the end, John faces a hopeless future. He isolates himself in an old lighthouse to purify himself from the contamination of civilized life. In old-world tradition, he flagellates himself, calling on God to forgive his lust for Lenina and his callousness over Linda's death. For a while he lives in peace, but then inquisitive people find his pain fascinating and invade his privacy. Giving John soma, they all engage in an orgy of pain. In futility John the Savage hangs himself. He cannot bring freedom and love to a world convincing him it is pointless to live, and he cannot return to his savage roots.

TOPICS FOR ORAL AND WRITTEN DISCUSSION

1. What scientific, behaviorist, and psychological theories influenced Huxley and how?
2. Describe Galton's eugenics and relate it to twentieth-century U.S. sterilization movements.
3. How does Huxley's totalitarian society control its people through art, science, and religion?
4. How specifically does the birth-to-death Bokanovsky Process create the class system?
5. Unlike Huxley's brave new world, our democracy gives power and responsibility to each of us to decide where we want technology to take us. If we were genetically determined through science and technology rather than born freely through natural selection, how might that change our society?
6. Argue the different sides of the Groopman-Kass debate.

7. Describe the ethical issues surrounding human cloning. Could it ever be justified?
8. How does Gleick's chaos theory describe the inherent dangers in gene manipulation? What imaginable problems might arise from restoring pre-historic DNA?
9. What specifically does Leon Kass's "wisdom of repugnance" argue for or against? Cite historical examples.
10. Relate Huxley's totalitarian state to the U.S. government's increasing control over its people since the September 11, 2001, terrorist attacks on the United States.

BIBLIOGRAPHY

Crichton, Michael. *Jurassic Park.* New York: Ballantine, 1990.

Gleick, James. *Chaos: Make a New Science.* New York: Penguin Books, 1987.

Groopman, Jerome. *The New Yorker,* January 28, 2002. http://www.new yorker.com/THE_TALK_OF_THE_TOWN_CONTENT/?020204ta _talk_groopman.

Halden, John. *The Causes of Evolution.* Princeton Science Library (1932). Princeton, N.J.: Princeton University Press, 1990.

Huxley, Aldous. *Brave New World.* New York: Harper, 1989.

Fisher, R. A. *Natural Selection, Heredity, and Eugenics.* Oxford: Oxford University Press, 1983.

Kass, Leon R. "Why We Should Ban Human Cloning Now: Preventing a Brave New World." *The New Republic,* May 21, 2001. http://www .tnr.com/052101/kass052101.html.

Levin, Ira. *The Boys from Brazil.* New York: Random, 1976.

Schacter, Bernice. *Issues and Dilemmas of Biotechnology.* New York: Greenwood, 1999.

Silver, Lee. "Eighteen Ways to Make a Baby: On Human Cloning." Interview by Sarah Holt. July 9, 2002. http://www.pbs.org/wgbh/nova/baby/ clon_silver.html.

Silver, Lee M. *Remaking Eden: How Genetic Engineering and Cloning Will Transform the American Family.* New York: Avon, 1998.

Wright, Sewall. *Evolution in Mendelian Populations* (1931). www.esp.org/ foundations/genetics/classical/holdings/w/sw-31.pdf.

SUGGESTED FURTHER READING

Atwood, Margaret. *The Handmaid's Tale.* New York: Houghton, 1985. A dystopia.

Cook, Robin. *Shock.* New York: Signet, 2001. A fertility industry exposé.

Lem, Stanislaus. *Solaris.* New York: Harcourt, 1987. Understanding what lies within us might be the key to understanding the universe around us.

McHugh, Maureen F. *Nekropolis*. New York: Morrow, 2001. The poor voluntarily sell themselves into servitude, altering their brains to love their masters.

Michison, Naomi. *Solution Three*. New York: Feminist Press, CUNY, 1995. All future couples are homosexual; reproduction is by in vitro fertilization and surrogacy.

Orwell, George. *1984*. New York: Signet, 1950.

ROBIN COOK'S *COMA* (1977)

This novel was conceived as an entertainment, but it is not science fiction. Its implications are scary because they are possible, perhaps even probable.

—Robin Cook (author's note)

HISTORICAL CONTEXT

Robin Cook, master of the medical thriller, was born in New York in 1940, received an M.D. from Columbia University, and did postgraduate work at Harvard Medical School. He is on a leave of absence from Massachusetts Eye and Ear Institute and lives in Waterville Valley, New Hampshire, with his wife and child. He was once Jacques Cousteau's Sea Lab aquanaut in the south of France. Since 1970 Cook has been writing about hot issues in the evolving medical field. His other novels include *Outbreak* (1987), *Vital Signs* (1991), and *Toxin* (1998). Cook's novel *Vector* (1999) about a bioterrorist anthrax attack on New York City foreshadowed the real-life event in 2001. Showing a knack for anticipating public debate on controversial topics, Cook's *Shock* (2001) describes the fertility industry and controversy over federal funding of stem cell research. Each novel is compelling and informing, while also exacerbating the public's fear.

The organ transplantation industry is the subject of *Coma*. Each day in 2001 63 people in the United States received an organ transplant; another 16 on the waiting list died because organs were unavailable. Driver's licenses and living wills may have an advance donor directive; however, family members often have the final word. Therefore, potential donors should tell family members of their wishes in advance. Living donors cannot donate if it is life-threatening, with uncoerced, voluntary informed consent required. Then there are brain dead donors whose cessation of brain stem function is indicated from an EEG test. Because the brain makes a person breathe, organ vitality is sustained by cardiopulmonary machines. Ethical concerns arise when harvesting from brain dead donors because brain death is a process without a distinctly pronounceable event like cardiac death. Hospice professionals, in particular, exercise ethical care in withholding food and liquid from and administering narcotics to a patient with auditory and visual responses. In a recent development, doctors who felt there was only a small window of opportunity for harvesting most transplant organs now look to a 2002 University Hospital Zurich study that shows transplant success even in harvesting older organs from cardiac death donors. This goes beyond the conventional wisdom that only a few organs such as corneas and kidneys remain viable for a time in cadavers. In heart transplantation, brain death as a criterion is distinctly different from cardiac death because only a recently beating heart can be harvested. Artificial, self-contained hearts only extend life until a donor heart can be transplanted. Bioengineering a human heart from stem cells triggered to become cardiac cells is decades and billions of dollars away. Existing stem cell lines used in research are declining, and President George W. Bush placed a moratorium on cloning to reap human parts.

While most industrialized nations legitimize brain death as a condition for organ harvesting, there are many cultural differences. In 1968, Dr. Juro Wada harvested Japan's first and only heart for transplant from a brain dead donor and was heralded as a hero and condemned as a murderer. China's primary source of transplantable organs comes from executed prisoners without their consent. Transplant proponents argue that fear and ignorance are great barriers to collecting transplant organs. Most major U.S. religions consider donation the ultimate act of charity and condone it; other views prohibiting donation include the religious belief that the body must remain intact in order to be resurrected in toto, the belief that organ harvesting from a viable body equates with abortion, and the belief that the soul still resides in the body with a beating heart.

Because transplant organs are so hard to get, there is a current debate over the donor's motivation or the commodification of tissues. The U.S. Organ Procurement and Transplantation Act makes it illegal to buy and to sell human organs. Because of the great gap between supply and demand, wealthy recipients would have inequitable access to donor organs. Right now only a donor's medical and funeral expenses are paid, so an American Medical Association ethics group suggested a small payment of $300 to $500 or tax credits to increase donation. Organ transplant organizations claim it is an urban myth that in foreign countries poor people are waylaid, drugged, and surgically relieved of their organs; nonetheless, an advertisement appears from time to time offering a kidney for sale from $1,000–$10,000. Pirated organs may be a rarity because complex donor-recipient matching, the required surgical skill, and follow-up care are essential. Other myths include the recipient acquires the donor's desires (liking certain foods, for instance), the donor is limited by age (minors need guardian consent), donation mutilates the body prohibiting open-casket funerals, and the donor's estate pays the medical costs. Potential donors may fear indicating their wishes to donate will forestall efforts to save their lives, but safeguards are in place because the donor's medical team and the transplant team are two separate entities. Besides, the organ procurement organization is not notified until brain death is determined. Kidneys and corneas are the most transplanted organs, largely because of progressive surgical skills and fewer rejection factors. Other organs and tissues transplanted are the heart and heart valves, liver, pancreas, lungs, intestines, eyes, skin, bone and bone marrow, and tendons. A national organ donation network matches donors and recipients for blood type, medical urgency, geographical location, and time on waiting list.

Because many people die waiting for a suitable organ, recent developments in transgenic cloning are making it more feasible to transplant modified animal organs into humans with fewer rejection problems and cross-species diseases (xenotransplantation). In another advance, Dr. Anthony Atala of Harvard Medical School in 2002 took a donor steer's skin cells and created functioning tissues that were transplanted into the donor steer. Three months later the implanted tissues remained healthy and were performing their respective functions. In the case of humans these same principles should apply to growing body parts using a person's own DNA, or body parts may derive from human embryonic stem cells, an issue mired in abortion politics. President George W. Bush's Council on Bioethics in 2004 only approved of therapeutic stem cell research on existing lines, limiting research potential. Public opinion is sharply divided on these issues.

LITERARY ANALYSIS

In *Coma*, Robin Cook, a trained medical doctor turned writer, describes the carefully controlled chaos of a major urban teaching hospital. He takes us all over the hospital—from the dingy basement to the lofty Grand Rounds—putting the American transplant industry under a microscope. The novel's central theme reveals the controversy surrounding our search to define *brain death* and the way transplant organs are procured and disseminated. In his author's note Cook says he intends to entertain, but *Coma* is definitely not science fiction. His belief, which contradicts the U.S. transplant industry's official stance, is that scarce organs are pirated and sold to the highest bidder every day. At the time he wrote *Coma* in 1977, he also saw as unacceptable the definition of brain death, which, as noted earlier, is contrasted with cardiac death. What medical organizations such as the American Medical Association and various transplant organizations are trying to do is to improve legislation to effect a greater number of donors by offering financial and moralistic incentives, by educating the public on the need for donor organs, and by dispelling myths and misconceptions. The significant problem remains of legally obtaining the donor's and the family's timely permission to harvest organs. The revised Uniform Anatomical Gift Act, promulgated in 1987, increased donor awareness but has not solved the problem of providing enough transplant organs.

The way Cook describes the hospital hierarchy is important to weaving *Coma*'s sinister plot. The viewpoint is mostly third-year medical student Susan Wheeler's. She has left her intensive book learning and just started her clinical surgical rotation, going on the ward with patients for the first time. She and four others are on the bottom professional rung. Doing scut work—and often learning from the more competent nurses—they do not have much credibility and power. They do not have much confidence, either, often feeling like imposters. Small accomplishments, like successfully inserting an IV needle into a vein, cause euphoria. One student faints at his first operation, not an uncommon happening. The bright and beautiful Susan Wheeler feels panicked, like the rest: "What if someone expected her to make some life-death decision to go along with her white coat and her impotent stethoscope in her pocket." The medical students' superiors are the residents (first-year residents are often called interns). Wheeler's immediate supervisor is intermediate surgical resident Mark Bellows, who is responsible for her learning and for her actions. George Chandler is the chief surgical resident, a job Mark Bellows competes for. Bellows does not want to make waves when the spirited Susan Wheeler tells him of a horrific hospital conspiracy to turn healthy patients into profitable organ donors. Her investigation shows a high incidence of prolonged coma resulting from anesthetic complications in surgery. But, one by one, as she naively approaches her superiors for help, they try to quash her efforts. The hospital's lower and upper worlds collide, as conspiratorial terror develops and her life is threatened.

As would be expected, Cook also describes the antagonism existing between medicine and disease. Surgeons, especially, are seen as the conquering warriors. Other relationships—because the book was written in 1977—have changed somewhat. For instance, Susan Wheeler describes the "paradoxical loneliness" of being the only woman on her rotation, among all-male superiors: "[S]he felt she was entering a male club; she was an outsider forced to adapt, to compromise." In the patriarchal system of men's rule and sexism toward women, a woman responding with competitive and aggressive action is labeled "a castrating bitch"; however, if taking a more passive, compliant stance, she is told she cannot compete. Susan's hard investigative data and strong intuitive feelings on the coma incidents are met with patronizing behavior toward the beautiful medical student. Now, however, with more women entering medical school than men, the system Susan entered is changing. But the hospital hierarchy Cook describes is still in effect today. He also gives enough technical medical descriptions of operations and details of diseases and autopsies to satisfy premed students. Realistic accounts of the intricacies of applying anesthesia and of the drama of performing surgeries add to the growing terror. Dated accounts of computerized medical research will make today's students appreciate what is currently available.

Interwoven into the high tension of a covert hospital conspiracy, Cook portrays the problem of drug-addicted doctors, dehumanization in the medical field, and the doctor-patient relationship. A hoard of narcotic drugs is found in an attending surgeon's hospital locker once assigned to Mark Bellows. The hospital wants the investigation kept internal and private, a conspiracy of silence. The story relates to the medical profession's continual efforts to deal with stressed-out doctors whose narcotic licenses make it too easy to self-medicate. Now programs help with recovery to return valuable medical professionals to their professions. Also as shown in *Coma*, doctors' dehumanizing patients leads to errors in their medical judgment. Often sick patients cannot easily describe symptoms to their doctors, and when their doctors cannot bridge this lack of communication, the patients suffer the consequences, which leads to medical mistakes. In 1999 the National Institute of Medicine estimated that deaths from medical mistakes exceeded 44,000 (about the same as motor vehicle accident deaths). In other words, it is "like a jet crash every day of the year" (Neergaard).

The very worse kind of medical mistakes, Dr. David Hilfiker believes, involves "a failure of will," which happens even though "a doctor knows the right thing to do but doesn't do it because he is distracted, or pressured, or exhausted" (Hilfiker, 376). Cook portrays members of the medical staff as having profit motivation and as treating each coma patient as the object it has become, "like a part of a complicated game, like the relationships between the football and the teams at play. The football was important only as an object to advance the position and advantage of one of the teams." Cook's conspiratorial and cynical doctors detach from any human connection with their coma victims, avarice and greed being chief motivators. In fact, generations of doctors were taught to have "detached concern" and not to get too close to a patient; but now having empathy is linked with communication for better doctoring. An unnatural distance also creates a level of dissatisfaction in the doctor-patient relationship and eventual physician burnout. Susan Wheeler's human connection with her two coma patients, in particular, and her attention to detail sustained her investigation all throughout *Coma*. To borrow from legendary humanist doctor Sir William Osler, with patients as texts, the best teaching during clinical rounds is done by the patients, themselves.

SYNOPSIS OF THE NOVEL

Coma is written in suspenseful daily and hourly entries over several weeks. It begins at Boston Memorial Hospital with Nancy Greenly's minor D and C procedure for excessive uterine bleeding. All seems to be going well when suddenly Greenly's heart beats erratically and she lapses into coma. The doctors are baffled. Greenly's diagnosis is cerebral hypoxia, or oxygen deprivation to the brain. She is sent to the intensive care unit where a flat EEG indicates brain death. She becomes a tube-fed, temperature-controlled machine whose fluid-electrolyte balance and ability to ward off infection are critical. Homeostasis, or a balance of her body's functions, is difficult to maintain. On her first day as a third-year medical student, the beautiful Susan Wheeler enters surgical clinical rotation on the ICU ward, and she connects with Greenly, also 23. She sees the comatose Greenly as "a casualty of medicine, a victim of technology" and wants to understand what went wrong. In her second encounter with a patient, Susan starts the IV on Sean Berman, an athletic architect in for knee surgery. They make a date, but, like Greenly, he falls into an irreversible coma. Later in the ICU Susan's superior, surgical resident Dr. Mark Bellows, draws the comatose Berman's blood for analysis while the contentious Susan Wheeler grills Chief of Anesthesia Robert Harris about the hospital's high-risk statistics. She decides to look into the problem, but the realistic, career-driven Mark Bellows bows out.

Susan's investigation begins with Nancy Greenly's physical exam, and then she pores over her chart. Trained in the scientific method, her extensive research continues in the medical school library on "anesthetic complications followed by prolonged coma." She discovers a long list of possible causative agents for coma or disrupted brain function and that her hospital had 100 times more cases like Greenly's and Berman's than the rest of the country (or 11 deaths in 25,000 surgeries). Half of the cases were never diagnosed by a medical examiner. Later Susan watches an autopsy and also learns of the hospital's high number of unexplained respiratory arrests and resuscitation failures. Susan tells Dr. Nelson, the chief of medicine, and Dr. Harris, chief of anesthesiology, about her findings and requests their help. One confiscates her research data, and the other physically threatens her. Both show her the door, close it, and immediately make a phone call. Chief of Surgery Dr. Stark seems more sympathetic to Susan, acknowledging that neurology professor Dr. Donald McLeary has signed out all the patients' charts. When Susan tells Mark Bellows about her encounters and her strong intuition of foul play, he admits problems but asks for a possible motive. He sees no conspiracy, saying he is more concerned with the cache of drugs found in his old OR locker now belonging to the missing Dr. Walters. Mark worries about Susan's delusional crusade, but their relationship takes another turn during a romantic evening date.

The next day Dr. McLeary advises Hospital Director Oren how disruptive Susan has become, and Dean of Students Dr. James Chapman switches her surgical rotation to the V.A. Hospital. On her way home from the hospital she runs in panic from someone following her. Later that evening the same man accosts her at home and threatens her family if she continues her investigation. After regrouping, Susan reviews her research and sneaks into Dr. McLeary's office to get the coma patients' charts. She tells Mark of the conspiracy she suspects involving Harris, Nelson, McLeary, and Oren. Mark informs her of finding Dr. Walters dead in his condemned house with a suicide note. Later Susan discovers all the coma incidents happened in OR8, and she finds a carbon monoxide gas line running from a hidden boiler room tank connecting to the oxygen line in OR8. Hoping to get some respite in her dorm room, she instead finds the hired hit man there, and he chases her through the vacated hospital campus. They have a grotesque confrontation in the hospital anatomy lab.

In the meantime Berman had been transferred to the private Jefferson Institute in South Boston, a state-of-the-art government-built facility for chronic-care comatose patients. It is a large rectangular building with no first-floor windows. Visitors are not encouraged, but Susan reviews the building plans on file with the city and goes disguised as a nurse for a tour. The facility has advanced computer technology that keeps 132 naked coma patients in homeostasis, eerily suspended by wires four feet above the floor in a climate-controlled atmosphere. As the tension builds, Susan goes exploring on her own in the facility to find Berman's body. She enters what is indicated on the floor plan as an OR, and suddenly the motive for creating comatose patients becomes clear: "The Jefferson Institute was a clearinghouse for black-market human organs!" She is discovered and escapes. Then she calls Dr. Stark, telling him the secret of the Jefferson Institute. All across Boston carefully typed surgical patients have had carbon monoxide added to their anesthesia. In addition, they have received shots of succinylcholine in their IVs, causing brain hypoxia, all of which was undetected in the ICU. A secret corporation has masterminded keeping the bodies alive until their organs are harvested and sold for big profits.

Susan meets Dr. Stark at his office—he has warned her not to tell anyone. After drugging her, he talks about his three-year plan to create the Jefferson Institute. The sale of its product had helped rebuild Memorial Hospital, he rationalizes. The drug-addicted Dr. Walters with a cache of narcotics in his OR locker was not a part of the organization; his suicide was faked only so the police would not investigate the hospital. Dr. Stark's transplant work, he argues, will benefit mankind, helping to learn the secrets of immunological mechanisms and to advance the transplanting of all human organs. Like Leonardo da Vinci who secretly dug up corpses for dissection, he believes the Jefferson Institute is also above the law. And sometimes secrecy is needed because the common man would not understand the immense gain to be had for the greater good. Stark schedules the drugged Susan Wheeler for an emergency appendectomy, administering the anesthesia in OR8. Bellows remembers what Susan had said about the mysterious valved line and investigates, reaching the OR just in time to save Susan and to arrest Dr. Stark.

TOPICS FOR ORAL AND WRITTEN DISCUSSION

1. When, if ever, is it justifiable to sacrifice the few, medically speaking, for the majority?
2. What cultural and religious differences influence organ donation?
3. What motivated Dr. Stark and others to create coma patients?
4. While most students on their first clinical rotation feel insecure and like imposters, what special problems does Susan Wheeler have being the only woman in a male "club"?
5. In recent years, medical mistakes have reached epidemic proportions. How do a doctor's lack of communication and empathy and Hilfiker's "failure of will" contribute to mistakes?
6. How can potential organ donors indicate, in advance, their wishes?
7. What is the difference between brain death and cardiac death in harvesting organs?
8. How will the commodification of organs change when they can be grown from cells?
9. What are the problems with xenotransplantation?
10. How do the differences in the hospital hierarchy contribute to Cook's plot?

BIBLIOGRAPHY

Center for Ethics and Human Rights. http://www.nursingworld.org/ethics/index.htm.

Cook, Robin. *Coma*. New York: Signet, 1977.

Hilfiker, David. "Mistakes." In *On Doctoring*, 371–82. New York: Simon & Schuster, 1991.

Medline Plus. http://www.nlm.nih.gov/medlineplus/organdonation.html.

Neergaard, Lauran. "Like a Jet Crash Every Day of the Year." *Times-Picayune*, 20 February 2000, A2.

Southwest Transplant Alliance. http://www.organ.org.

Transplant Network. "Timeline for Transplantation." http://www.thetransplantnetwork.com/history_of_transplantation.htm.

United States Department of Health and Human Services. "Organ Donation." http://www.organdonor.gov.

SUGGESTED FURTHER READING

Ash, Karin T. "Accident." In *Sutured Words: Contemporary Poetry about Medicine,* ed. Jon Mukand. Brookline, Mass.: Aviva P, 1987. A nursing perspective on caring for a patient in a persistent vegetative state.

Gawande, Atul. *Complications: A Surgeon's Notes on an Imperfect Science.* New York: Holt, 2002. Medical mistakes, trends, and mysteries.

Selzer, Richard. "Brain Death: A Hesitation." In *The Exact Location of the Soul*, 110–20. New York: Picador, 2001. A surgeon, who once had to remove a beating heart for transplantation, looks at brain death and wonders.

———. "Brute." In *The Doctor Stories*, 386–9. New York: Picador, 1998. A tired and frustrated doctor takes out his fatigue on a patient.

———. "Whither Thou Goest." In *The Doctor Stories*, 64–82. New York: Picador, 1998. A Christian fundamentalist donates her husband's heart and must listen to it one last time to go on with her life. Also readers' theater.

Shem, Samuel. *The House of God*. New York: Dell, 1995. A cynic looks at internship year and how residency is selected (money, lifestyle, etc.).

Williams, William Carlos. "Old Doc Rivers." In *The Doctor Stories*, 13–41. New York: New Directions, 1984. A beloved old-timey doctor self-medicates.

———. "The Use of Force." In *The Doctor Stories*, 56–60. New York: New Directions, 1984. A frustrated doctor forcibly examines a young girl with diphtheria.

Winerip, Michael. "Did You Hear about Doc Ogden?" *The New York Times Magazine*, 5 May 2002, 42–7. A beloved small-town doctor makes a fatal mistake.

Contagions/Isolations: An Analysis of Albert Camus's *The Plague* and David Feldshuh's *Miss Evers' Boys*

INTRODUCTION

Camus wrote *The Plague* as a World War II French Resistance fighter, intending "plague" to represent all imprisonments. It characterizes the despair felt in occupied France during the 1940s when Nazism sneaked up on Europe and almost destroyed it. It is a work of great literary imagination emphasizing the reemergent nature of contagions, and it sheds light on contemporary plagues such as AIDS. At issue is how the government and medical personnel in the unsuspecting town of Oran, Algeria, fail to enforce in a timely manner the city medical code by identifying the scourge, putting a vaccine into use, and isolating the town from the outside world. There are questions, as well, about media responsibilities in a medical crisis, illustrating how desperate people fall victim to quackery and superstition. Each character in the novel is exiled from the outside world and deprived of not only food but also love, teaching us lessons about how important human connection is to well-being and to happiness.

In Oran's collective destiny one self-sacrificing doctor, in particular, works within the community's changing dynamics, highlighting political, social, economic, and religious issues. In the unrelenting nature of plague his medical ethics are challenged, provoking philosophical discussions about man's morality in an atmosphere of every-man-for-himself. The label *heroism* is also scrutinized as a descriptor subject to exaggeration and abuse. In Oran's dire situation, the tactics of the spiritual leader are examined when, rather than providing comfort, he strikes fear into hearts by preaching that God afflicted them with plague as punishment. In the end, people die, and the government and priests seem ineffectual, leaving us to appreciate the value of a selfless doctor and to contemplate his warning that literature teaches us plague never disappears for good.

Just as in early views of plague, sexually transmitted diseases carry significant stigma as deserved punishment. The primary issue in *Miss Evers' Boys,* however, is how the U.S. Public Health Service conducted clinical experiments during the Tuskegee Syphilis Study (TSS) from 1932 to 1972 and how doctors, in their scientific fervor, failed to realize the black subjects were people like themselves. Racial discrimination did not end with the 1863 Emancipation Proclamation, fortified in 1865 by the Thirteenth Amendment's abolition of slavery. From the 1870s to the 1950s, the Jim Crow era extended stereotypes of African Americans and hurt them in areas including economics, politics, education, sports, and medical research. Only with the Civil Rights Act of 1964, shepherded in by President Lyndon Johnson, did racial segregation and discrimination become illegal in all of the states. But, for the 40 years of the Tuskegee Syphilis Study in a climate of segregation, the U.S. Public Health Service looked on as 399 syphilitic black men suffered and infected others. The human subjects received the standard of care in the beginning but were denied the silver bullet treatment, penicillin, until a whistleblower exposed the injustices. In 1997 President Bill Clinton formally apologized to the few survivors, calling them "a living link to a time . . . many Americans would prefer not to remember, but we dare not forget." Calling the study a betrayal by medical people who should have offered care and a cure but instead lied and denied help, he continued, "What was done cannot be undone. But we can end the silence. . . . [W]hat the United States government did was shameful, and I am sorry." The National Center for Bioethics in Research and Health Care has emblazoned these words on its Web site, after receiving a 1999 federal grant to establish a center that memorializes the TSS participants, hoping to prevent future ethical lapses in minority studies.

Other issues arise from David Feldshuh's literary medical history. What is the doctor-patient relationship in the African American experience, especially regarding autonomy, empathy, trust, and human worth? How are repercussions still felt in African American communities where the legacy of distrust makes it difficult to get subjects in research benefiting them? And what lessons have public health bioethicists learned from the Tuskegee Syphilis Study for reviewing protocol in current infectious disease medical research studies?

ALBERT CAMUS'S
THE PLAGUE (1946)

[A]s he listened to the cries of joy rising from the town, Rieux remembered that such joy is always imperiled. He knew what those jubilant crowds did not know but could have learned from books: that the plague bacillus never dies or disappears for good. . . .

—Albert Camus, *The Plague*

HISTORICAL CONTEXT

The Algerian-born French philosopher Albert Camus (1913–60) was a novelist, dramatist, and journalist. His father was killed in World War I, and his illiterate and deaf mother raised him and a brother in poverty. It was not a happy childhood. He studied philosophy at the University of Algiers, quitting for a while for health and financial reasons, and finally graduated in 1936. Camus held a variety of jobs and joined and quit the Communist Party. He was afflicted with tuberculosis and lived in poverty most of his life, motivating him to write about contagion and isolation. His criticism of French government controls of Algeria caused him to move to Paris in 1940. During World War II he became a member of the French Resistance. He wrote political essays, but his most famous work is *The Plague*. Camus viewed man's condition as absurd and meaningless, which aligned him with the existentialists; however, in *The Plague* and other absurdist works, he describes how courageous humans can be when faced with increasing alienation in an indifferent world. In 1957 Camus received the Nobel Prize for literature. He died in an automobile accident in 1960 at the age of 46.

Literary views of plague appear in Greek mythology, and, as described in the Bible's Exodus, ever since God brought 10 plagues upon the Egyptians until the pharaoh let the Israelites go, it has been seen as a deserved punishment. For the next 800 years plague, which could be bubonic plague, smallpox, or gonorrhea, descended upon unsuspecting populations, brought by trade routes and war, drastically reducing populations and bringing famine. Western Europe was relatively disease-free from 800 until the fourteenth century, and medieval civilization flourished. Then the bubonic plague (1348–50) hit Europe, killing more than 25 million people, both peasants and gentry, bringing a great recession to Europe. Sienese chronicler Agnolo di Tura wrote, "No one wept for the dead because everyone expected death himself." The bubonic plague (Greek *boubon,* meaning "groin"), a disease caused by the bacterium *Yersinia pestis*, spreads from infected rodent's fleas that bite humans, causing their lymph glands to swell. In advanced cases the skin turns black, hence the alternate name, the Black Death. The plagues had high mortality rates. Up to two-thirds of the population died in each epidemic. When the attacks lessened, so did the immunities, and populations became vulnerable again. Only a fire could contain the Great Plague of London of 1665. A nineteenth-century increase in hygiene, purer water supplies, and efficient garbage disposal decreased European plague epidemics, but in 1894—to show the global nature of contagion—plague killed 100,000 in Hong Kong. Plagues, exacerbated by famine and warfare, change the political, social, economic, and religious dynamics of a country forever.

Contrary to popular belief, the bubonic plague is not a thing of the past, although it is an extremely rare, sporadic event. About 20 cases appear in the United States each year in endemic areas of the rural West. In 1987 a Montana hunter infected by an antelope was treated with antibiotics and recovered. In 2002 two New Mexicans infected by flea-ridden wood rats were diagnosed with plague in New York City where they had traveled. Because it had not been seen in the city for more than a century, the media caused quite a stir by recalling the Black Death that had devastated medieval Europe. Plague, a naturally occurring bacteria and generally not a public health threat, is preventable, however. People—especially those with open sores—should wash their hands with soap and water and should be wary of handling, dissecting, or skinning wild animals. They should watch for fleas or ticks, keep yards clean, and properly dispose of garbage that attracts rats. Roaming household pets may bring plague inside, so a suspiciously ill animal should be immediately taken to a vet. Ironically, the second-century Greek physician Galen announced that poisonous swamp vapors spread plague, so people did not wash, believing opened pores in the skin would let it in.

Besides devastating infectious bacillus plagues, the 1918 Spanish influenza epidemic killed up to 40 million people. Through new research methods, Gina Kolata explains the medical mystery in *The Story of the Great Influenza Pandemic of 1918 and the Search for the Virus that Caused It*. Scientists at the Armed Forces Institute of Pathology in Washington, D.C., decoded the virus's molecular structure from a victim's tissue sample, theorizing it derived from a gene in a strain of pig flu virus that recombined with a gene from a human flu virus. Recombination is common in other viruses such as HIV. Flu strains commonly travel around the world on boats and in planes and are mosquito-borne to humans. Modern researchers continue to delve into the mysterious origins of flu to avoid another pandemic. In fact, in 1976 fear that the 1918 virus had reemerged caused President Gerald Ford to immunize all Americans against a swine flu that killed one solider. In 1997 a million chickens were killed in Hong Kong and disinfected to prevent the spread of a new bird virus that killed one child. Just like clockwork, every fall the Centers for Disease Control and Prevention (CDC) announce a new, molecularly reformulated vaccine to fight an emerging influenza, urging the elderly, the very young, the chronically ill, and pregnant women to get vaccinated. The severity of flu strains and their location and timing vary greatly from year to year, often making adequate supplies and treatment efficacy guesswork. Even in a mild season, 20 percent of Americans get the flu, and 20,000 people die. Advances in treatment include new antiviral medicines that must be taken within 48 hours of symptoms, and a new family of designer "plug drugs" promise halting flu viruses that invade the body.

Smallpox, another devastating viral infection, claimed more lives than the Black Death and all twentieth-century wars combined. In 1796 Edward Jenner observed that dairy maids infected with the milder cowpox never caught smallpox, and he invented the first smallpox vaccine. Vaccinations stopped in 1972 because smallpox was believed eradicated; however, after the September 11, 2001, attacks on the United States, fear of bioterrorism hit populations no longer having immunity. Reacting to these concerns, the federal government vaccinated 500,000 health-care and emergency workers against smallpox as a precaution while preparing for a mass public vaccination. An exercise called Dark Winter played out a smallpox attack scenario on the United States to gauge government response.

Like Jenner's smallpox vaccinations, Jonas Salk's polio vaccine seemed to conquer the widespread poliovirus in the United States in the 1950s and 1960s, but the World Health Organization reports that polio cases in India tripled in the first half of 2002, setting back a worldwide eradication goal to 2005. Tuberculosis, a highly communicable lung disease caused by the tubercle bacillus, is prevalent in Third World countries but is commonly reported in the United States as well. One-third of the world's population has a latent form of tuberculosis; the active form kills three million people a year. Tubercular patients and other victims of contagious bacterial infections may fail to comply with the necessary course of antibiotics, making drug-resistant germs proliferate. In 2002 the CDC renewed millions of dollars in funding to study tuberculosis, especially its drug resistance and coinfection in HIV victims. Another infection, methicillin-resistant *Staphylococcus aureus,* resulting from excessive worldwide use of antibiotics, spread throughout U.S. health-care facilities in the 1990s. This staph infection can be deadly in the ill or elderly, and finding the necessary antibiotics to keep up with resistance is a public health concern.

So-called modern plagues revitalize fears about a rapidly globalized world with everyone in close contact, and immigration, prostitution, and urban decay are contributing factors. Africa has long been targeted as the origin of disease, and, in particular, scientists have traced the global HIV-1 epidemic to a virus in Central African Republic chimps. Killing these chimps and other primates for bush meat may be spreading AIDS-like viruses. In the United States, a 1981 government health bulletin discussed a strange outbreak in Los Angeles among five gay men who had a rare pneumonia caused by *Pneumocystis carinii.* Just as in the ancient plagues, some viewed the affliction as a punishment from God. HIV, the human immunodeficiency virus that attacks the immune system leaving the body unable to fight diseases like pneumonia and cancer, progresses into AIDS, acquired immune deficiency syndrome. Since this early report AIDS has been identified across the globe in all strata of human life. Eradicating HIV, a virus spread through bodily fluids such as blood and sperm, seems unlikely, even though modern medicines prolong lives. The United Nations reported that HIV infections spiked in 2004, with 38 million people living with HIV and 9 out of 10 not getting treatment. Africa, India, China, and Russia are in crisis, reflecting Louis Pasteur's observation, "The microbe is nothing, the terrain is everything." In the wake of the AIDS epidemic, whole new generations of orphans are left behind, often left to fend for themselves. Many fear the worst is yet to come.

To show the nature of emerging infectious diseases, new varieties are identified or reclassified periodically. There is a growing demand for college students who reside in close quarters to be vaccinated for meningococcal meningitis, a highly contagious bacterial infection of

the membranes of the brain and the spinal cord that, without immediate medical treatment, brings quick death or lifelong debilitation.
Reemerging African viruses cause concern in the United States. The
Ebola virus, a filovirus, was named after a river in Zaire (now the
Democratic Republic of the Congo), where it was first identified in
1976. Severe outbreaks cause hemorrhagic fever in humans and nonhuman primates, often leading to 90-percent fatality rates. In 1989
macaques (Asian monkeys) imported into the United States from the
Philippines brought Ebola into the United States. In 1999 the West
Nile virus invaded New York City, passing through airport screening
systems. To illustrate the global nature of infection, it was first identified in Uganda in 1937, then spread to Europe, Asia, and the Middle
East. The virus is mosquito-borne from infected birds or horses to
humans, and in 2001 the CDC declared it an "emerging, infectious
disease epidemic." Victims experience flulike symptoms, which in severe cases lead to encephalitis and poliolike paralysis. Because it can be
transmitted in blood transfusions, a screening test is imperative. The
media have educated the public responsibly but also have been criticized for causing undue alarm. Nonetheless, the outbreaks pose questions about what measures should be taken to prevent the cross-species
transfer of disease. In an age of mass transportation, infectious diseases
can invade a host country at an alarming rate, especially when public
health systems let down their guard.

The ravages of incurable and chronic conditions, such as in untreated AIDS leaving desperate victims, provide a focal point for
questions surrounding the moral and ethical aspects of physician-
assisted suicide, also known as mercy killing and euthanasia. The U.S.
law on physician-assisted suicide stems from a 1997 Supreme Court
decision unanimously upholding the New York and Washington state
laws criminalizing assisted suicide and stating the Fourteenth Amendment does not provide a constitutional right to die. Most states have
laws prohibiting physician-assisted suicide and some address the issue
through common law. The ethical questions surrounding mercy killing
reached an all-time high when Oregon approved by a large majority
its 1997 Death with Dignity law. The Oregon statute legalized assisted
suicide, stating a doctor may prescribe, but not administer, a lethal
dose of medicine to a patient with fewer than six months to live. Two
doctors must confirm the patient's mental competence and uncoerced
decision. In Michigan Dr. Jack Kevorkian, "the suicide doctor," espousing compassionate care, tested the legal limits with his suicide
machine. In 1999 he was convicted in Michigan of second-degree

murder and of delivering a controlled substance without a license. Nevertheless, the right-to-die movement is worldwide. In 2001 The Netherlands legalized euthanasia, allowing doctors to end a life not worth living. Two doctors must validate the patient's terminal illness, unbearable suffering, and the wish to die. In 2002 Belgium became the second nation, stating the patient must be conscious when applying for permission, and a second physician must be consulted. Belgium's law does not distinguish between terminal illness and incurable disease. Opponents say legalizing euthanasia, like abortion, violates the unalienable right to life and its unquestioning value. The specter of Holocaust genocide—with the Nazis' dehumanizing the Jews—is raised.

The complex issues arising from doctor-assisted suicide appear in Dr. Richard Selzer's true-life diary entry, "A Question of Mercy." It is his unremittingly honest 1991 account of assisting a gay man dying from AIDS to end his life. Selzer tells how he painstakingly counseled the man and his partner on the procedure, but they botched the attempt. It is a horrific event because no doctor controlled the medical procedure. On a national level—with the urgency of an aging population—the debate continues between the right-to-life movement and the right-to-die, which sees society as being hypocritical by outlawing a procedure it knows occurs out of sight. Terminally ill people continue to take their own lives with or without medical assistance, and "A Question of Mercy" asks what is a doctor's duty to a patient, including confidentiality, and should we consider legalized physician-assisted suicide the final gift of a caring physician?

LITERARY ANALYSIS

This analysis focuses on the social, political, economic, and religious aspects of the plague's effect upon the North African coastal town of Oran, Algeria, population 400,000. Camus was a World War II French Resistance fighter when he wrote *The Plague*. Its allegorical significance begins with the epigraph, setting the tone for the plague to symbolize the scourge of Nazism and to represent occupied France during the 1940s as well as all imprisonments, past, present, or future. Through linking plague and Nazism, Camus warns the reader to learn from history and the literature that encapsulates it. In an atmosphere of unrelenting gloom, his riveting novel asks us to consider the value of human life. It describes the course of a disease at its first inkling, to isolating the city from the outside world, to finally opening the gates almost a year later under the presumption the good fight has won over the horrific disease. The narrator, who is not identified until the end, relies on data collection, eyewitness accounts, and official documents to report the medical effects of bubonic plague on Oran. It feels like we are there in the unattractive seaport whose population is so habitually intent on commerce that the town even faces away from the life-enhancing waters of the Mediterranean Sea. Existential views of finding meaning in daily accomplishments and accepting earthly existence as finite generate from Camus's work. In Oran's collective destiny where death is wide-scale, one man, Dr. Bernard Rieux, stands out for his major contributions and self-sacrifice. He works within the community's changing dynamics, showing the unrelenting nature of plague and provoking philosophical discussions about man's moral duty to preserve life. Every day the suffering he witnesses causes him to confront loneliness, and during nonstop medical rounds only minor victories bring triumph over universal despair.

Ironies abound in the novel, starting with the medical authorities' failure to face the truth, fearing they might alarm citizens. At first, the government-run newspapers give daily tallies of dying rats, but they omit human deaths. Relying on faulty statistics, Rieux is slow in identifying the scourge. There is a standoff between Rieux, who simply wants to convince the authorities to take proper medical measures to save lives, and the politicians, who are afraid of losing their positions should they err in judgment. The situation generates an atmosphere of every-man-for-himself, except for Dr. Rieux who ministers to all. The government's ineffectual response provides a study in bureaucratic reaction to infectious disease, where martial law and curfews cause panic and attempts to vaccinate are often too little, too late. Likewise, modern-day CDC officials must reach consensus before taking action, with the media, for better or for worse, influencing each situation. Although frontline Dr. Rieux urges isolation, medical association president Dr. Richard balks. Only Dr. Castel, who has seen plague in China and France, takes a stand. He invents a vaccine that is immediately in short supply and then becomes obsolete when a new pneumonic plague emerges. The authorities have the newspapers report a false optimism no one believes. In desperation, people fall victim to medical quackery, from believing a winery's slogan that consuming large quantities of wine creates immunity, to a new *Plague Chronicle*'s ads for "infallible antidotes."

The Plague is a good character study as well, showing how various people cope in forced isolation. In this human drama several people join in solidarity with Dr. Rieux to battle their common enemy. In particular, Rieux's professional ethics are apparent when he asks the Parisian journalist Raymond Rambert to write the whole truth of their situation in Oran; then, later, when Rambert, who finds himself in the wrong place at the wrong time, begs Rieux to certify him plague-free so he can return to a lover he calls his wife, Rieux cannot, for "the law was the law." All live in a state of constant fear, and their vulnerability is brought home to them when even during Gluck's opera *Orpheus* the tenor collapses on stage. The opera's theme evokes Rambert's attempt to reunite with his loved one; however, when weighing personal happiness against the greater good, he simply cannot abandon his friends and the fight. Rieux's friend, the newcomer Jean Tarrou, symbolizes the resistance fighter who organizes volunteers. Duty for Tarrou, like Rieux, is paramount, even if he is the lone survivor who remains to wash dead bodies. His moralistic code is simple: as a good person he must stay and fight the battle. For Tarrou, a threshing machine symbolizes the authorities and the plague that inflict damage upon the victim. His black-and-white morality took hold when, as a youth, he witnessed his prosecutor father cause a young criminal to die. Tarrou's swim in the sea with the young healer, Rieux, binds their friendship, until a whirlpool forces them to shore. Tarrou is the counterpart to Cottard, the symbolic collaborator, a criminal who attempted suicide, but once the authorities became preoccupied, he turned to smuggling.

In another criticism of bureaucracy, Camus portrays the municipal clerk Joseph Grand as a daily plodder so absorbed in work he does not know his neighbor. He represents the townspeople of Oran who with their noses to the grindstone let the small details of daily living overwhelm its larger significance. Grand's wife leaves because he cannot show her affection and cannot promise hope for the future, but he persists in trying to write a great novel. Finding the right word for Grand's first sentence serves as a diversion for Rieux and others, acting as the novel's leitmotif to represent the indomitable human spirit. Rieux contrasts Grand's ingrained work habits overlaid by routine volunteer activities with Rambert's more dramatic decision to stay and to fight. This causes him to reflect on the nature of morality, or acting well in a given situation. Rieux theorizes it would be simply unconscionable for the decent man not to respond, and therefore it is inappropriate to make him a hero. That is, to free themselves as prisoners of plague requires common decency, simply doing a job week by week. In a town where many survivors have become cynical, Rieux sees Grand as the closest to a hero for maintaining a business-as-usual sanity. Grand has no illusions about the dire situation. He acts well in it, exemplifying ingrained integrity, which reminds us that standards to measure goodness are imperfect and that using the label "hero" may be subject to exaggeration and abuse.

Each in his own way faces the plague's desolation, reflecting the conditions of World War II prisoner-of-war camps. Lacking freedom and at times minimal sustenance, some question God's existence. The Jesuit priest Father Paneloux's fire-and-brimstone sermon ending the Week of Prayer strikes fear into the hearts of the people. He does not hold out God's love for their salvation but rather uses Christian doctrine as a threat to bring the commerce-driven townspeople back into his fold. He first preaches from Exodus that God sent plague down on Oran to separate the wheat from the chaff, the believers from the nonbelievers, and that He was punishing them into becoming better people. A small child dying a horrible death after receiving a vaccination prompts an orthodox religious discussion. Rieux cannot understand how God would let an innocent child suffer so, but Father Paneloux says humans cannot understand "what is meant by 'grace'." The incident causes Paneloux to soften the tone of his next sermon. Suffering increases as the pneumonic vaccine-resistant plague takes hold, and so do discussions of religion. Father Paneloux, Rieux feels, is theoretical, not attuned to human suffering, and cannot possibly know the truth of their dire situation as does he who takes the bedside vigil. How can plague have a good side by helping "men to rise above themselves"? Life is sacred, period, and Rieux, even if seen as prideful, must relieve suffering and pain through whatever means available. A thinning congregation now wears prophylactic St. Roch medals and "superstition has usurped the place of religion." Priests, like government, become ineffectual as people die, and mass burials take the place of religious rites. Paneloux falls ill and dies, in the end having a fatalistic view that as a faithful priest he has no need of a doctor.

Dr. Rieux is seen as a true healer, a saint, for whom there is no rest. With a singleness of purpose he carries on, quarantining infected people. By Christmastime, the death toll is subsiding so the town plans to open its gate. Grand seems infected and burns his manuscript, then recovers to renew his efforts. Unpredictably, the valiant Tarrou contracts the plague and succumbs about the same time Rieux receives word that his wife has died. In the end, Rieux, whose exhaustion might leave him prey to crippling emotions, understands "No resource was left him but to tighten the stranglehold on his feelings and harden his heart protectively." At issue today is the horrendous challenge medical professionals face to contain their empathy for patients under a protective carapace, to borrow from Richard Selzer, and to find elsewhere the relief and love needed to maintain sanity. In Rieux's wife's absence, his mother's unconditional love must do. With the disease lessening, Cottard's fears return, and he goes insane; Rambert greets his lover at the open gates; and Grand returns to what he hopes will be a literary masterpiece. Dr. Rieux, who we learn is the narrator, focuses on finishing his plague chronicle to provide a lesson that plague can strike the strong and weak at any time.

SYNOPSIS OF THE NOVEL

Camus's *The Plague,* divided into five parts, chronicles the yearlong story of Oran, a dismal commercial seaport battling the plague. One fine April day in the 1940s Dr. Bernard Rieux, a 35-year-old physician preoccupied with sending his ailing wife to an out-of-town sanitarium, steps on a dead rat. Police magistrate M. Othon notices others. Later, Parisian journalist Raymond Rambert interviews Rieux for a story about lack of sanitation among the Arab population, but because the publication will compromise the truth, Rieux steers him to the dead rat story instead. Rieux's friend, Jean Tarrou, tells him about seeing more convulsing, dying rats. All but the doctor's mother, who comes to keep house for the doctor and his son, are unsettled by the events; she has lived through war, depression, and a husband's death. Dead rats begin appearing by the thousands, then just when a sudden drop in the numbers causes the town to feel hopeful, the concierge M. Michel has fever, thirst, delirium, and dies, the first plague victim. Rieux fails to make the diagnosis, and only his old asthmatic patient who survived the 1918 Spanish flu recognized it as the first phase of an epidemic. With increasing deaths, Rieux realizes the plague has taken their ordinary town by surprise, just as a war might. The city government issues propaganda bulletins, treating it as a problem of bad hygiene and sanitation. It takes too long to apply the municipal medical code. Dr. Castel, who had seen plague in France and China, develops a vaccine, but there is only a limited supply. Three months into the plague there are 700 deaths a week. Without quarantine, the epidemic rages out of control, and the gates of Oran are finally closed.

Rieux's medical duties never end as he connects with the isolated townspeople. For example, the bureaucrat Joseph Grand confides in him that his failed marriage resulted from working too much. He did not make his wife feel loved or offer her hope for a better future. He remains commerce-driven and loveless, obsessed with writing the perfect novel. The journalist Rambert asks Dr. Rieux to certify him plague-free so he can leave the city to join his lover. Rieux, taking an ethical, moralistic stance, cannot oblige. Sending patients into quarantine, separated from loved ones, and witnessing daily suffering and pain cause Rieux to harden his heart. A Week of Prayer culminates in Father Paneloux's fiery sermon. Citing Exodus in the Bible, he preaches that plague is a deserved scourge sent as "punishment for their sins," just as God had brought plagues down on Egypt "to strike down the enemies of God" and to "humble the proud of heart." It will separate out evildoers, or the wheat from the chaff. Salvation, he concludes, only comes to repentant sinners who embrace God's teachings. Paneloux's sermon creates widespread panic among the "condemned," especially when a new form of bacillus, pneumonic plague, causes terrible suffering and seems vaccine-resistant. Adding to the pressure, supplies dwindle, and dogs and cats are killed as possible carriers of plague. Newspapers warn of long imprisonment for breaking rules. A new paper, *The Plague Chronicle*, publishes the progress or recession of the plague but is prone to quackery, advertising "'infallible' antidotes against plague."

Some people scramble after the latest amulet, while others pour their hearts and souls into recovery efforts, causing Dr. Rieux to make observations about heroism. He cautions against "attributing over importance to praiseworthy actions," which may pander to the worse side of human nature; that is, heroes should not be coined from acts of normal human decency. To Rieux, Grand, who volunteers to record plague statistics, embodies quiet courage because he does so with the "large-heartedness that was second nature with him." Grand believes he is simply taking a stand. Rambert is another matter. Rieux finds Rambert's persistence admirable. But he has been so obsessed with the challenge of escape that he has just about forgotten his motivation: to be with the woman he loves. Most citizens of Oran are slackers, resigned to being plague victims, and by midsummer plague reaches crisis levels. Martial law and curfews help contain areas of town cordoned off, but panic strikes. Townspeople, hoping to kill plague by burning their homes, set fires that often rage out of control. In a holocaust of confinement and of deprivation, "No longer were there individual destinies; only a collective destiny, made of plague and the emotions shared by all." With mass burials, even religious death rites are abandoned. Isolated people feel the gnawing pain of separation and now face an unflagging adversary that kills off the capacity for both love and friendship.

In the fall the "town lay prostrate, at the mercy of the plague." Survivors, gripped by fear, carry on, sometimes reflecting sentimentally on what had been. At a performance of Gluck's opera *Orpheus,* the plague-stricken tenor collapses on stage. Meanwhile, the godless Rambert still plans his escape, rationalizing that he needs another human to give his life meaning. But, overwhelmed by shame, he has a change of heart, deciding the plague is everyone's fight. The battle gets particularly poignant when the new Castel vaccine is first tried on M. Othon's young son Philippe. In the final stage of the disease, Philippe's vaccination is ineffective, and, after great suffering, he dies. The incident causes great moralizing among Rieux, Castel, and Paneloux about how an all-powerful God can allow little, innocent children to suffer. Something changes in Paneloux after he sees Philippe die. It causes his second sermon to reflect on the nature of good and evil and to suggest that "the child's sufferings would be compensated for by an eternity of bliss awaiting him." In these extraordinary times, God is testing everyone, Paneloux warns, and in this fight against evil either you are saved or are damned. With "no island of escape in time of plague," echoes of fatalism ring throughout the church. For Paneloux everything is in God's hands. Later when his temperature spikes and he coughs up blood, he declares that it is illogical for a plague-stricken but faithful priest to call in a doctor. With this resolve, he dies. Then the epidemic reaches its high watermark with people scrambling to purchase waterproof clothing, believing rubberized material will safeguard against infection. With the new pneumonic form of plague spreading, fatalities increase across town. The newspapers, as ordered by the authorities, project a false optimism no one believes.

Toward the end, Tarrou has a heart-to-heart talk with Rieux about the plague within all of them. His father, a public prosecutor, was a kindly man although an adulterer. But one day Tarrou learned his father prosecuted a young criminal condemned to die. From that day on, he considered his father a murderer. He left home, becoming an advocate against the death penalty. After a long talk, Tarrou and Rieux take a symbolic swim together. As Christmas approaches, they all have become weary in the prison of plague. For Rieux, facing death and despair every day has taken its toll on him. He concludes that "a loveless world is a dead world." Then one day Rieux notes that rats have not been seen for a while, and the human death toll is subsiding. With hope restored, the authorities open the gates. The new serum is working, and it seems "the plague had been hounded down and cornered, and its sudden weakness lent new strength to the blunted weapons so far used against it." Rieux even dares to envision a reunion with his long-absent wife when Tarrou is stricken and dies, the victim of two types of plague. Rieux had been unable to help. While lamenting the loss of a friend, Rieux gets a telegram stating his wife has died of tuberculosis, which he has been powerless to cure. He has lost the human love of a friend and of his wife, but there is no time to grieve. While listening to the townspeople's cries of joy at anticipating the end of plague, he sees a dog dig at fleas. He knows the plague bacillus

> can lie dormant for years and years in furniture and linen-chests; that it bides its time in bedrooms, cellars, trunks, and bookshelves; and that perhaps the day would come when, for the bane and the enlightening of men, it would rouse up its rats again and send them forth to die in a happy city.

TOPICS FOR ORAL AND WRITTEN DISCUSSION

1. What is the allegorical significance of the absurdist novel *The Plague*?
2. Discuss Camus's views in *The Plague* of suffering, death, and religion.
3. What do Dr. Rieux's relationships with Tarrou, Grand, and Rambert reveal about his morality?
4. How are the major themes of isolation and solidarity, suffering and the value of human life, and hope and despair played out in the novel?
5. What roles do women play in the novel, especially Dr. Rieux's supportive mother and M. Othon's wife, who fights to release her husband from quarantine?
6. How does AIDS, the greatest modern disease challenge, shatter the illusion that industrialized nations are immune to epidemics? What is being done to prevent it?
7. What modern lessons should we learn from Camus's description of the increasingly complex and symbiotic relationship between the media and medicine?
8. How would you relate the self-sacrificing Dr. Rieux to today's modern practitioner?
9. Define bubonic plague and discuss its history, symptoms, and remedies.
10. In light of Dr. Rieux's views on heroism, who, in your estimation, is a true-life hero?

BIBLIOGRAPHY

Camus, Albert. *The Plague*. Trans. by Stuart Gilbert. New York: Random-Modern Library, 1948.

Kolata, Gina. *The Story of the Great Influenza Pandemic of 1918 and the Search for the Virus that Caused It*. New York: Farrar, 1999.

Selzer, Richard. "A Question of Mercy." In *The Exact Location of the Soul*, 134–46. New York: Picador, 2001.

SUGGESTED FURTHER READING

Cook, Robin. *Outbreak*. New York: Berkeley, 1988. A flu epidemic sweeps the country.

Crichton, Michael. *Andromeda Strain*. New York: Ballantine, 1969.

Defoe, Daniel. *Journal of the Plague Year*. New York: Modern Library Classics, 2001. An account of the Great Plague of London (1664–65) first published in 1722.

King, Stephen. *The Stand*. New York: Doubleday, 1991.

Maugham, Somerset W. *Of Human Bondage*. New York: Penguin, 1992. Tuberculosis.

Selzer, Richard. "A Mask on the Face of Death." In *The Best American Essays 1988*, ed. Annie Dillard. New York: Ticknor, 1988. AIDS ravages Haiti; a taboo against the truth.

DAVID FELDSHUH'S
MISS EVERS' BOYS (1990)

By too much frolickin' you can get a dangerous sore down below on your private parts and through that sore a bug can crawl inside you and you won't even know it. And then that bug goes to sleep for twenty or thirty years so it's not hurting anybody but you. Because when it wakes up, you can't walk, you can't breathe, you can't think. That's bad blood. That's what you got.

—Nurse Evers in *Miss Evers' Boys*

HISTORICAL CONTEXT

Syphilis is a chronic, contagious systemic disease caused by the microscopic bacterial spirochete *Treponema pallidum*. It cannot survive for long outside the body and enters through mucous membranes or skin, typically sexually transmitted (venereal); passed from mother to child (congenital); or spread through blood transfusions. Its four recognizable stages are primary, secondary, latent, and tertiary. Treatment should begin at first indication, usually when, in the sexually transmitted kind, a chancre or lesion appears on the genitals within four to six weeks of infection. If untreated, the secondary stage from six to 12 weeks after infection includes headache, fever, nausea, swollen lymph nodes, rashes, sore throat, and fatigue. Lesions may persist, and grayish patches with red areolae may occur on the mucous membranes of the mouth and genital region. Hair patches often fall out (alopecia areata). After three months symptoms may come and go but the whole body is now infected as bacteria invade vital organs, bone marrow, and the central nervous system. During a period of latency, from a few years to the end of life, the afflicted may appear and feel normal, except for vague discomforts or eye disorders. But one-third of untreated infections develop into the dreaded tertiary stage, often many years after first infection, bringing painful lesions or tumors. By this time, the bones are eaten away, and an infected brain and heart lead to insanity and then death. Syphilis is contagious until its latent stage. In developed countries antibiotics given for other indications may cure undiagnosed syphilis, and aggressive public health education helps contain its spread.

Christopher Columbus, who exposed the vulnerable American Indians to pathogens such as smallpox and measles, is commonly blamed for bringing syphilis back from the New World to the Old World. However, new forensic research might prove syphilis existed in Europe before 1493. What is known is that at the end of the fifteenth century a great syphilis epidemic hit Europe, with the rate of infection in French soldiers so horrendous it stopped a planned invasion of Italy. Since then, syphilis has been called the French Disease. Early treatments included mercury ointments, oral applications, and vapor baths that often did more harm than good. Often "sinful" syphilitics were isolated in leper colonies or hospitals. Later in the 1800s potassium iodide was an effective treatment, but the breakthrough came in 1905 when German microbiologists Schmudinn and Hoffman identified the bacteria. Their important discovery led in 1906 to the Wasserman test for detecting syphilis and in 1908 to Paul Ehrlich's arsenic treatment, Salvarsan (meaning "I save"). Salvarsan was a landmark "silver bullet" technique that targeted a disease without inflicting undue harm on the victim. Ironically, with the advent of Salvarsan came a strange backlash.

Elements of society believed giving a cure to the sinful intervened in God's punishment of them and promoted promiscuity. Nonetheless, only one in 100 treated patients recovered until, in 1929, British bacteriologist Alexander Fleming ushered in the antibiotic era with his accidental discovery of penicillin. Although not widely used for 15 years, it is still used today, even though bacteria continually change into penicillin-resistant strains.

In Macon County, Alabama, in 1932, the U.S. Public Health Service began the Tuskegee Syphilis Study (TSS) among 600 poor African American men, who were later excluded from new penicillin treatments. Researchers, who believed syphilis developed differently in blacks, wanted to study the population to improve health conditions in the rural South. For the next 40 years 399 subjects with late-stage syphilis and 201 disease-free subjects in a control group received free meals, general medical care, the Surgeon General's signed certificate of appreciation, and a $50 burial stipend. Even after there was widespread knowledge that penicillin could cure syphilis, only protiodide, iron, and placebos (sugar pills) were given to the study subjects. Painful spinal taps called "back shots" extracted fluid from the men's spinal cords for neurological testing, with aspirin the only analgesic. In a simultaneous assault on humanity vastly more extensive in scope, after the Nazis seized power in 1933, German doctors such as Josef Mengele, the Angel of Death, used concentration camp victims as human guinea pigs in atrocious experiments including freezing, burning, and vivisection. In an effort to accomplish "racial hygiene" to build a master race, there were forced abortions, sterilizations, and euthanasia. Camp inmates deliberately infected with bacteria or malaria had various drugs tested on them to determine effectiveness. In twin studies, if one purposefully infected twin died, the other was often killed with an injection to the heart and used in a comparative autopsy. Hitler's doctors killed millions, inflicting pain and suffering in the name of science. The Nuremberg Code, derived from the World War II criminal trials, sharply defines boundaries for moral, ethical, and legal practices in approved medical experiments.

After World War II, a second syphilis epidemic occurred in 1947, with 106,000 cases reported in the United States. Public health measures were taken to educate the public on sexually transmitted diseases (STDs), but the 1960s sexual revolution caused an increase in cases. Meanwhile, in 1972 a whistleblower, alarmed that men in the TSS were not offered penicillin, caused the study to stop. Since syphilis can pass through placentas into unborn children, many of the children had syphilis, and in 1974 the U.S. government paid an out-of-court set-tlement of $10 million. Not until 1997, however, did the government, through President Clinton, officially apologize to the surviving men and their families. Likewise, six decades after the atrocious Nazi ex-periments, leading German scientists apologized to Holocaust survi-vors for pursuing "their scientific goals beyond every moral boundary of humanity." Public health epidemiologists continue to study syphilis within populations, determining in 2001 that syphilis cases doubled to 282 in gay men in New York City, the highest in seven years. Sta-tistical studies give important data for tracking syphilis around the world and for targeting public education preventive measures, leading to lower rates of infection. Routine STD testing helps stop widespread infections.

The history of Western medical ethics goes back to 400 B.C. when Hippocrates, the Father of Medicine, promulgated guidelines for eth-ical medical conduct referred to as the Hippocratic oath, simply put, "to be useful, but, first, to do no harm." This standard, considered gentlemanly behavior at the time, holds today. Professional ethics be-came codified in the late eighteenth century when English doctor Thomas Percival published rules for morality and service. His code was adopted and modified into the American Medical Association Code of Ethics in 1846. Recent revisions emphasize public health education. Later in 1947, the Nuremberg Code derived from the trial of 23 Nazi research doctors for crimes against humanity. In an instantaneous papal response speaking to the primacy of human worth and dignity over any medicoscientific values no matter how worthy, Pope Pius XII's condemnation of the atrocities helped define the moral and social du-ties of the medical profession. The 10 principles of the Nuremberg Code, in summary, include: requiring a subject's informed, voluntary consent; showing the proposed research is necessary to benefit society and the subject's risks are not greater than the study's humanitarian importance; requiring it be based on animal studies or justifiable ra-tionale; attempting to avoid a subject's injury or mental and physical suffering; requiring a preliminary investigation of the facts to determine there is no reason to believe death or disability will occur and that the investigators be scientifically qualified; and giving the human subject the right to terminate the experiment if physical or mental conditions war-rant it. Subsequent codifications addressing crimes of science include the Declaration of Geneva (1948), which mentions maintaining dignity in the art of medicine and avoiding prejudices; and the Declaration of Helsinki (1964), which, as modified in 2000, states "the well-being of the human subject should take precedence over the interest of science and society" and that ethics committees, such as institutional review boards (IRBs), must monitor ongoing trials, especially regarding use of placebos, funding details, and conflicts of interest.

Besides IRBs, the U.S. Office of Human Research Protections is charged with overseeing human research volunteers. At present, with technologies rapidly evolving from the Human Genome Project, medical ethics (known as bioethics since 1965) must weigh the benefit to society versus the dangers to humanity. Unfortunately, unconscionable experiment protocols are not a thing of the past, continually challenging IRBs to interpret research data and to apply the ethical principles that protect human subjects. In November 2002, the Bush administration's new Advisory Committee on Human Research Protections revised its charter to define unborn human embryos as human subjects with protection rights, although they will not be afforded the same protections for fetuses, children, and adults. The Department of Health and Human Services, which administers the committee, denied abortion politics.

LITERARY ANALYSIS

David Feldshuh's *Miss Evers' Boys* derived from James H. Jones's *Bad Blood: The Tuskegee Syphilis Experiment* as well as from medical articles, 1930s Alabama field interviews, and Senate testimony. In two acts set in the Possom Hollow School House outside of the town of Tuskegee, Alabama, the play fictionally portrays how the U.S. Public Health Service (PHS) experimented on a group of black men. This analysis focuses on how the play highlights important ethical questions about human rights in scientific research. PHS venereal disease doctors set up the Tuskegee Syphilis Study (TSS) to find better ways to treat poor syphilitic southern blacks. Presuming there would be great value in studying syphilis in different races, they were eager to compare their results with the 1909 Oslo Study analyzing autopsies of white males with untreated syphilis. In an unprecedented partnership, trained black medical staff worked alongside white medical professionals who thought their subjects could not understand the research and would not consent to it without enticements. Throughout the play the black nurse liaison, Miss Eunice Evers, who was assigned to foster trust and cooperation, gives us her views on the nontherapeutic study and on her two doctors, U.S. PHS Dr. Eugene Brodus and Tuskegee Memorial Hospital head Dr. John Douglas, the only white character. The action begins in 1932 before penicillin was widely used, and it ends in 1972 after a public health whistleblower closed the study down 25 years after the Nuremberg Code influenced human rights principles. Although the 1947 Nuremberg Code requires stoppage once harmful situations are ascertained, some say a complicit PHS rationalized its good intentions. In its defense, Evers reminds us, it was a different time.

Evers, a pivotal character in Feldshuh's play, speaks intermittently to the 1972 Senate subcommittee investigators in testimony areas to give us a retrospective sense of the time period. Watching her father die from untreatable pneumonia motivated her to become a nurse, and she takes her professional oath seriously. Evers has sworn to maintain high standards by practicing faithfully, confidentially, and without administering harmful medicine. Her true dilemma comes with the second part of the oath, finding it impossible to be both loyal to her physicians' work and devoted to her patients' welfare. Incredibly, the study is set up so that Evers's duties simultaneously require her to be both a compassionate nurse who translates doctor-speak and a detached scientist who withholds lifesaving medicine, a duplicity that cannot be rectified ethically. In addition, she abridges the "boys'" ability to voluntarily consent by enticing them into the study with incentives of free meals, health care, and a $50 death benefit, affording the rare opportunity for a dignified burial. Acting contrary to the Nuremberg Code's standard informed consent rules, Evers also withholds a great deal of information to gain their trust. For example, when therapeutic mercury and arsenic treatment is stopped after six months due to lack of funds, she does not tell them the study is continuing on them as untreated syphilitics. Instead, they are promised when effective treatment comes, they will be the first in line to get it.

Drs. Brodus and Douglas have slightly different motivations for continuing the TSS. Douglas wants to differentiate racial response to syphilis, believing the humanitarian importance of the research to society outweighs the gravity of the subjects' deaths. He also wants to keep the fear level high so that more government funds will be forthcoming. Brodus initially wants to stop the study once penicillin has been proved a "silver bullet" cure, but then he compromises his integrity by going along with Douglas. Neither medical professional seems to be able to perceive the difference between his doctor and scientist duties. Instead, they both rely on the Oslo study that gave them reason to believe first disability and then death were certainties in the study group. What is most unconscionable, however, is that the

PHS medical professionals watched the men unnecessarily suffer unbelievable mental and physical pain. For this reason, as the study progressed into the 14th year, lying to her "boys" became a burden for Evers, especially when their suspicions caused them to demand "new doctorin'." In the end, Ben, the oldest, acquiesced to the study's protocol and died, proud that he had earned a government certificate and a proper burial. The superstitious Hodman went mad, drank a magic potion, and died from the poison. Caleb, the most literate, learned about penicillin and was treated in time. Evers took dancing Willie, the youngest, out of a treatment line, convinced by Douglas that penicillin in Willie's late-stage syphilis might set off an allergic reaction or kill off spirochetes, causing his heart to explode. He suffered the crippling effects of the disease. Today, with a known cure available, it would be considered a heinous bioethical injustice not to give study participants the choice to terminate.

Even with the subjects' progressive physical and mental syphilitic signs, the doctors continued the delusion to keep the study viable for comparison with Oslo's. In the end, the charade continued with the doctors' additional rationalization that if the study participants were given penicillin and died, then the thousands of untreated syphilitics in the county would feel forewarned and refuse treatment. The doctors convinced Evers that her part in the study is a chance to do something special. The study was extended beyond the period of a known cure and a proven equality in black-white response because Douglas believed extending the fear would get more government money to eradicate the disease. He rationalized sacrificing the few for the greater good and argued against invalidating 14 years of work. Taking their study "to the end point" meant to autopsy, and he ordered Evers to advise all Tuskegee doctors to refuse treatment to study participants. Ironically, once penicillin was found to successfully treat syphilis, it made the study marginally relevant. The big issue is that Evers's boys, mostly illiterate men who did not read the news, were lied to. They were told that diagnostic spinal taps were therapeutic, and that penicillin could kill them. The enticements of food and medicine negated any possibility of voluntary consent. Evers's burden is heavy especially because she watched two of her friends, the study's human guinea pigs, suffer end-stage syphilis and die. She is left guilt-ridden, reflecting on the nursing ideals that had guided her life.

By 1947, 14 years after the TSS started, in a parallel world Nazi doctors were on trial for research crimes on humans. Like Nuremberg, a legacy of distrust follows the TSS, especially the rumor that participants were intentionally infected with syphilis, promulgating notions of genocide. In a concomitant study also in direct defiance of the Nuremberg Code, at the infamous Willowbrook State School in New York from 1955 through the early 1970s newly admitted mentally retarded children were deliberately infected with hepatitis to study the course of the disease. Their parents were told it was a condition of admission and that their children would get it anyway. In this instance and in other studies of infectious diseases, live cancer, and radiation, scientific fervor took precedence over basic human rights, turning what should be autonomous human beings into scientific sacrifices. TSS folklore passed down through generations explains the distrust of white medicine, creating a health gap. By 2010 a new government initiative, Eliminating Racial and Ethnic Disparities in Health, hopes to end the practice of lower minority medical standards in six priority areas: infant mortality, cancer screening and management, cardiovascular disease, diabetes, adult and child immunization, and HIV infection, which in 1997, the National Minority AIDS Council reported, infected one in 50 black men. The catch-22 is that it is difficult to obtain more black subjects in clinical trials with such an ingrained legacy of distrust, including the notion that the statistics are a hoax.

More than 30 years later, what lessons have we learned from the TSS, a metaphor for research abuse? To begin with, it is necessary for studies to apply a careful definition of voluntary, informed consent and to have specific institutional review boards monitor research protocol to preserve the rights of human subjects. Furthermore, scientists devising study protocols must guard against believing subjects in a particularly vulnerable group are inherently inferior, and they must be wary of putting too great a significance in the biological and social difference in race. And, lastly, researchers must see their study participants as people like themselves. While it may be shocking to hear bad ethics in the TSS (as in the Nazi experiment), did not necessarily equal bad science, although the issue of trust permeates the results. The fact is that medicine still relies on the 40-year TSS as a valuable source of information on diagnosing and treating syphilis. Clearly, in teaching this medical history on the potential for immorality in research methods, a cautionary bioethical lesson should be taught along with scientific results.

SYNOPSIS OF THE PLAY

Feldshuh's seven-character, two-act play is set mainly in the sparsely furnished Possom Hollow Schoolhouse in rural Macon County near the town of Tuskegee, Alabama. A 1972 Senate subcommittee investigation is ongoing in spotlighted testimony areas. In the prologue Nurse Eunice Evers gives her professional oath of faithfulness, confidentiality, loyalty, and devotion. In act 1 (1932–Contagion), she talks about her motivation to be a nurse and how she has become a PHS nurse-liaison to four tenant farmers, Hodman, Willie, Caleb, and Ben, who are variously fidgety, superstitious, and defiant, while being tested for "bad blood." Hodman, 37, believes in magic cures like putting a knife under the bed to cut pain. Willie, 19, wants to win a gillee dancing contest and move North. The analytical Caleb, 25, is the most literate. At 57, compliant Ben writes his name with an "X" on the blackboard, but not wanting "to rile nobody," hastily erases it. Evers gains their trust and entices them into the TSS with promises of hot food and "free doctorin'." The men are afraid that blood-drawing to see if they were bitten by a "parakeet" (misunderstanding "spirochete") will cause impotence. They also suspect the government is lining them up for military induction. But Evers sells the idea of government interest in their welfare and that waiting for testing might be too late, leading to insanity and death. She gives them a ride to the gillee contest, which they enter as Miss Evers' Boys.

In scenes 2 through 5 the black Dr. Eugene Brodus, 34-year-old U.S. PHS field physician who is more of a research-oriented "medicine doctor" than a congenial "people doctor," does a trial workup on the four men, finding it necessary for Evers to interpret anemia as "low blood," potency as "hot blood," and syphilis as "bad blood." Brodus tries to connect with the men on a musical and dance level. After Evers confirms her boys tested positive for syphilis, they begin a two-year course of treatment with mercury salves and arsenic injections that is 55 percent effective—"if it didn't kill you first." They are treated for six months when government money runs out. Dr. Douglas, Tuskegee Memorial Hospital administrator, confers with Brodus and Evers, convincing them to keep the federal government's attention by studying untreated syphilis for six months, to acquire facts to differentiate the disease along racial lines, and to set new PHS priorities for allocating money and offering treatment. Their findings would be compared to an Oslo study of 300 white syphilitics, with the hope the government would stop saying, "Don't throw white money after a colored man's disease." Douglas would examine the men periodically, coordinate data, and be the liaison between Washington, D.C., and Macon County. He would be both physician and scientist, an uneasy combination. Their two-year comparison study would require X-rays, drawn blood, and spinal taps for neurological tests, then money would become available for treatment. The men must not suspect protocol change, Douglas warns. Brodus agrees, desiring recognition for Tuskegee, but Evers knows the men are only getting heat liniment treatment and will infect others. Douglas entices each man to stay in the study with $50 for a decent burial, and Evers agrees because her boys will be first in line when new treatment becomes available.

In scene 6 at the schoolhouse, Evers helps Douglas give a searingly painful spinal tap to Caleb, who does not tell the others, fearing they will be deprived of government care. Evers helps Douglas with the procedure, recalling how the only job she could get before was housework even though she was a trained nurse. Caleb trusts them to help him get healthy. Three days later, in scene 7, Evers delivers the spinal tap report to Dr. Brodus, admitting she hated lying to the boys about the taps' importance to their health and that the heat liniment was mercury salve. He rationalizes it is humane to zigzag "round the truth once in a while," and warns that a medical professional has to step back at times. Evers is offered a job in New York, which she considers because it has become difficult to carry her burden of being both a caring nurse and a detached scientist. In scene 8, one week later at the schoolhouse, the boys practice for the gillee contest that evening. Evers teaches Ben to write his name on the blackboard, and he tries to convince her they need her. While they wait for the car to arrive to take them to the contest, they talk about how a life insurance policy helped to pay another man's burial cost, but first he was taken to the hospital for an autopsy. The gillee contest is spirited.

In act 2 (1946–Progression), scene 1, penicillin has been introduced as a treatment for syphilis in all but the Tuskegee study group. Evers has been close with the men for 14 years. They seem pain free and appear healthy. But such a hidden, unpredictable disease can catch you by surprise. Besides, treatment is dangerous and no money is available. Then came the "silver bullet" penicillin that offered a cure for her men, who were to be first in line. But Willie's legs give way. The rest are concerned about him and their gillee group, demanding some "new doctorin'." Drs. Brodus and Douglas tell Evers her boys are too far gone for penicillin to help, and, in fact, it might kill them with the Herxheimer allergic reaction; or, if penicillin kills the spirochete embedded in a heart muscle, it could cause the heart to disintegrate—or to "explode."

In scenes 2 and 3 Evers finds Caleb and Willie waiting in a Birmingham center to get a penicillin hip shot, but she talks Willie out of it, telling him he is a government patient and, besides, the shot (mold) could kill him. Later Brodus and Douglas examine him, revealing a "slight slurring" of his right foot, indicating progressive syphilis, but he feels special, like he is "riding in the front of the train." Evers privately urges the doctors to tell Willie about possible treatment so he can choose the consequences, but they accuse her of unprofessional behavior and too much patient attachment. Douglas says penicillin is a small risk to Willie but there is greater danger because if he gets it and dies anyway, then all 6,000 untreated syphilitics in the county will resist treatment and spread the disease. Brodus stresses to Evers that continuing the study is a chance to do something special, pushing "past the hate, past the idea of difference." Willie comes back to the room and apologetically asks them if he needs new "doctorin'." Brodus's half-truth response is that new research science will not help every single person, but "more people are helped than hurt." Evers offers him hope, and that day the U.S. government gives each study participant a certificate of appreciation and $14, one for each year.

In scene 4, outside the schoolhouse, the superstitious Hodman tries an old May tea and moonlight cure on Willie. But Caleb knows that all over the county penicillin is the new cure. Later, Douglas convinces Brodus he will never get future funding if he wavers in this study, but Brodus says equality of penicillin's response to the disease on whites and blacks has already been proved. Douglas argues they need to foster a sense of fear in order to get more money to eradicate the disease, and sacrificing 600 men versus treating 6,000 or more is at stake. But to Evers these men are her friends and neighbors, and her doubts multiply. In scene 5, at the schoolhouse three months later, Caleb tells Evers penicillin has helped him but the moon cure has not helped Willie. Evers repeats that the government will not let her give Willie penicillin, but she must stay there to help her people. Caleb invites Evers to go with him but then leaves, saying he must use his brain and mouth. In scene 6, four months later at Memorial hospital, Ben is in a wheelchair getting breathing instructions. Evers offers him $50 for burial if he will sign an autopsy permission, but he resists, thinking he will look cut up in his open casket. She convinces him it is okay, and that he is part of something important and lasting after he passes. His government certificate is very important to him. He has been practicing for 14 years and signs his name "Ben Washington." He thanks

Evers for caring for him and for doing all she could to make him well. Besides, he loved riding in the government car. As a nurse she was following the doctors' orders, she told him, and cries remorsefully when Ben tells her he knows she will always do right by him.

In scene 7, two months later, Dr. Brodus tells Dr. Douglas penicillin would be too late, but Brodus argues it has helped others no matter what stage they are in. Douglas argues they are different as study subjects because 14 years of work cannot be invalidated and patients sacrificed with a possibly useless or lethal injection. To match the Oslo study, they need to take it to the end point by validating the facts by autopsy. He rationalizes only the best study possible will "unravel the secrets of this disease" and honor the men's sacrifices "for something greater than they'll ever understand." Ben dies a painful death but looks peaceful in his coffin, as Evers promised. But she repeats her nurse's oath before God "not to harm my patients." Dr. Douglas orders Evers to call every doctor in the Tuskegee area and tell them they are not to treat study participants with penicillin. Evers begins cracking from carrying too heavy a burden, but Dr. Brodus convinces her they each serve their race in different ways and have trade-offs. In scene 8, two days later, Evers gives penicillin to Hodman, whose eyes are being affected by the disease. Having gone insane, he drinks poison and dies. Evers wonders if the penicillin had given him the Herxheimer reaction from which he died. She gives Willie hip shots as well.

In the 1972 epilogue the Senate committee hears the evidence. A whistleblower informed newspapers the subjects were human guinea pigs watched to see what bad blood would do. Willie received a course of penicillin out of the county and partly recovered. Caleb also left, was treated, and recovered. Evers told the men the disease "had three parts: you get it, you forget it and then you regret it twenty years later when it comes back to haunts you." And that is how it was with her study participation as well. She continues reporting on the remaining subjects. Caleb uses his certificate of appreciation as evidence to sue the government that was callously watching him die. Douglas rationalizes that the study proved blacks and whites were affected the same, but Brodus counters they were not given a choice. And what about Nurse Evers who pulled Willie out of the treatment line in Birmingham? She loved her boys but, simply put, got some of them buried. In the end, Feldshuh tells us that the nursing ideals that guided Evers's life left her with "little blame" while the government and its doctors held "the big blame."

TOPICS FOR ORAL AND WRITTEN DISCUSSION

1. What did the legacy of the Jim Crow era contribute to the Tuskegee Syphilis Study and how specifically did the Civil Rights Act of 1964 change the potential for racial segregation and discrimination?
2. How did British bacteriologist Alexander Fleming's 1929 accidental discovery influence the history of syphilis?
3. Define syphilis and describe its early treatments. What do the terms "bad blood" and "back shots" mean?
4. Is Nurse Evers a traitor for using powerful incentives to entice her subjects into the trial?
5. In what way has the TSS's legacy of distrust permeated the black community and how did President Clinton take a first step to regain trust?
6. What is the U.S. Public Health Service and how do their epidemiologists educate the public?
7. What are institutional review boards (IRBs) and upon what code(s) do they base their human research protocols?
8. Describe the ethical principles that would make it illegal and unconscionable today for Public Health Service doctors to engage in subterfuge in order to entice participants into a study.
9. How do you divide Public Health Service blame in the TSS among Evers, Douglas, and Brodus?
10. What specific tenets of the Nuremberg Code did the TSS violate after 1947?

BIBLIOGRAPHY

Feldshuh, David. *Miss Evers' Boys.* New York: Theatre Communications Group, 1990.

National Center for Bioethics in Research and Health Care, Tuskegee University. http://www.tubioethics.org/.

Reverby, Susan M., ed. *Tuskegee's Truths: Rethinking the Tuskegee Syphilis Study.* Chapel Hill: University of North Carolina Press, 2000.

Syphilis. The Merck Manual of Diagnosis and Therapy. http://www.merck.com/pubs/mmanual/section13/chapter164/164d.htm.

SUGGESTED FURTHER READING

Hurston, Zora Neale. "My Most Humiliating Jim Crow Experience." In *On Doctoring,* ed. Richard Reynolds and John Stone, 121–2. New York: Simon & Schuster, 1995. Hurston's reflections on racist medical treatment.

Jones, James H. *Bad Blood: The Tuskegee Syphilis Experiment.* New York: Free Press, 1993.

King, Martin Luther, Jr. "I Have a Dream." Speech delivered on the steps of the Lincoln Memorial in Washington, D.C., on August 28, 1963. http://www.mecca.org/~crights/dream.html.

Klass, Perri. "Invasions." In *On Doctoring,* ed. Richard Reynolds and John Stone, 407–10. New York: Simon & Schuster, 1995. Sarcastic and insensitive residents' responses upon learning an elderly man has syphilis.

"Lasting Legacy: An Apology 65 Years Late." *The News Hour with Jim Lehrer,* 16 May 1997. http://www.pbs.org/newshour/bb/health/may97/tuskegee_5-16a.html.

Lederer, Susan. *Subjected to Science: Human Experimentation in America before the Second World War.* Baltimore: Johns Hopkins University Press, 1995.

Selzer, Richard. "Imagine a Woman." In *Imagine a Woman and Other Tales,* 189–229. New York: Random, 1990. AIDS and isolation.

Williams, William Carlos. "Use of Force." In *The Doctor Stories,* ed. Robert Coles. New York: New Directions, 1984. A young diphtheria patient rebels.

4

Illness and Culture: An Analysis of Ken Kesey's *One Flew Over the Cuckoo's Nest* and Alice Walker's *Possessing the Secret of Joy*

INTRODUCTION

Ken Kesey's *One Flew Over the Cuckoo's Nest* embodies the rebellious energy of the psychedelic 1960s, a prosperous time following World War II when drugs were rampant and the counterculture challenged authority. A classic description of mental illness, *Cuckoo's Nest* encapsulates Kesey's experimentation with alternative forms of perception while highlighting ethical issues. The setting is a mental institution where a power struggle exists between the staff and the patients afflicted with many types of mental illness. Paradoxically, reading this important novel feels liberating while it asks the disturbing question, who among us is completely sane? In fact, the United States has gone through a slow and arduous process to learn how to identify and to treat mental disorders. Early on the mentally ill and retarded roamed the streets, were confined by relatives, or were thrown into prisons with criminals; later, psychoanalysis led to greater understanding. Finally, in 1946 the National Institute of Mental Health was created, recognizing the need to diagnose and to help the mentally ill. With the advent of mental institutions came radical therapies such as electroshock treatment and lobotomy. Today these controversial approaches are often replaced by psychotherapy, the so-called talking cure, and by drugs such as Prozac and Halcyon. With today's brain scans and DNA analysis some mental disorders are more readily detected and treated.

Other topics *Cuckoo's Nest* develops concern sexuality and institution-alization, humor and illness, nursing and group therapy, and psychiatry and surgery.

Kesey's *Cuckoo's Nest* continues to influence twenty-first-century medical issues and ethics as does Walker's *Possessing the Secret of Joy* by describing the cultural origins of mental illness. The female genital mutilation (FGM) ritual Walker describes in a certain African culture illustrates how society constructs practices that inflict psychological trauma and have long-term physical consequences. FGM, viewed as sane in one culture, is judged unethical and criminally insane in oth-ers, linking health and human rights. Increasing immigration brings the surgical ritual, once commonplace in Puritan times, back to the United States. In addition, worldwide awareness causes petitioners seeking asylum based on sexual discrimination to flock to the United States.

Possessing the Secret of Joy also teaches morality lessons and the im-portance of the mother-child relationship all within the context of cultural relativism and Social Darwinism. The main issue, however, is of global concern, how human rights violations perpetuate women's mental and physical health problems. In the Western world the long history in which women were seen as objects springs from Aristotle's view that women were unfinished men. This thinking was at the heart of early Greek medical practices such as female circumcision, just as, ironically, was Hippocrates' "first, to do no harm" mandate. Many cultures continue to subjugate women to fundamentalist beliefs, de-nying them equal protection under the law, even though the United Nations Universal Declaration of Human Rights states that human rights are inalienable: "No one shall be subjected to torture or to cruel, inhuman or degrading treatment or punishment" (United Nations General Assembly Resolution, 1948).

Both Kesey and Walker show how illness derives from culture as well as from disease and that our views on normalcy depend on the culture and the time in which we live. While *Possessing the Secret of Joy* projects issues that for some may be difficult to explore at first, by putting a face onto the estimated 100 million women worldwide who have undergone FGM, Walker has crafted a chilling book of literary importance.

KEN KESEY'S *ONE FLEW OVER THE CUCKOO'S NEST* (1962)

The ward door opened, and the black boys wheeled in this Gurney with a chart at the bottom that said in heavy black letters, MC MURPHY, RANDLE P. POST-OPERATIVE. And below this was written in ink, LOBOTOMY.

—Ken Kesey, *One Flew Over the Cuckoo's Nest*

HISTORICAL CONTEXT

Ken Kesey (1935–2001), born in Colorado and reared in Oregon, appreciated nature and loved wrestling. He received a degree in speech and communication from the University of Oregon. Then, with a Woodrow Wilson Scholarship, he enrolled in the Stanford University Creative Writing program. While a graduate student, he participated in life-altering psychology department research involving psilocybin, mescaline, amphetamine, and LSD. For several weeks Kesey, a 24-year-old paid research volunteer, ingested these mind-expanding drugs. Later, as a Veterans Administration psychiatric ward orderly on the night shift, he observed that many of the patients, rather than being crazy, were just nonconformists in a sterile environment. While drug-induced, Kesey hallucinated about an Indian sweeping the floors, who became Chief Broom, his schizophrenic narrator in *One Flew Over the Cuckoo's Nest*. His novel was an immediate success, allowing Kesey and his wife Faye to buy a farm that became a site for an influential bohemian community experimenting with drugs, believing altered mental states could improve society. Because Kesey's parties were notorious for illegal drug use, he was soon arrested and jailed for several months. Nonetheless, with his new fame, Kesey drew the attention of Neal Cassady (hero of Jack Kerouac's *On the Road*) and others, and soon the hippie-aesthetic, antiwar group the Merry Pranksters was formed, exploding into the psychedelic era.

In 1964 the notorious Pranksters drove cross-country in a Day-Glo bus, ostensibly to see the New York World's Fair, but it became instead a creative adventure. Cassady drove the bus, and its riders dropped acid and smoked marijuana along the journey, which was filmed for posterity. The bus became a metaphor for "living your art," and the saying "You're either on the bus or you're off the bus" was Beat Generation lingo for creative tripping. The exploits of the Pranksters are the subject of Tom Wolfe's *The Electric Kool-Aid Acid Test* (1968), a book voraciously consumed by antiestablishment hippies in search of the universe within. Kesey went on to write other novels, but none achieved the success of *Cuckoo's Nest,* which subsequently influenced popular culture with its stage and film productions. Late in life, Kesey, the pied piper of the psychedelic era, took drugs only for his diabetes and hepatitis C, finding the pure adrenaline of experiencing nature enough. He died on November 10, 2001, in Pleasant Hill, Oregon, following surgery for liver cancer.

Cuckoo's Nest continues to be a prototypical depiction of mental illness by describing various mental disabilities as well as the legal and ethical issues arising from them. The novel's publication brought to the American consciousness what a slow and arduous process it has been to define and to devise treatment for mental disorders. From Colonial times, before the proper diagnosis of the mentally ill and retarded, madmen roamed free. Alternatively, shamed families cruelly locked abnormal relatives in an attic or chained them to a wall. Society's first priority was to feel safe, then to punish the evil they believed inherent in the mentally ill. The very first mental institutions were small, primitive nontherapeutic holding facilities, such as the one founded in Williamsburg, Virginia, in 1773. Until larger mental asylums were created, particularly troublesome individuals, including the poor, were incarcerated with criminals or sent to the poorhouse.

Over time many unusual theories have been espoused regarding the diagnosis and treatment of mental illness. In the late 1700s, Philadelphia's Dr. Benjamin Rush, a signer of the Declaration of Independence and the Father of American Psychiatry, challenged demonic causation and believed moral treatment that controlled the environment would cure insanity in acute patients. Thinking brain arterial disease resulting from gluttony caused mental illness, he advocated a restricted diet, extensive bleeding, emetics to encourage vomiting, and hot or cold showers to slow metabolism. He also invented the gyrator, a spinning chair or plank upon which the patient was tied, designed to increase the brain's blood supply. Rush's *Medical Inquiries and Observations upon the Diseases of the Mind* made him a revolutionary authority on madness, and he became a popular lecturer. Much later, in the mid-1800s, Christian social reformer Dorothea Dix (1802–87) raised money to establish the first state mental institution in Massachusetts after she saw the mentally ill housed with criminals in unsanitary conditions.

Her efforts brought national focus upon human rights abuses. Since that time, numerous civil rights laws help differentiate criminals from the mentally ill who are often involuntarily committed upon proof they would be a danger to themselves or others. With an increased awareness of civil liberties also came an individual's right to refuse treatment. State-specific rules apply to involuntarily committing and treating teenagers. The remedy for being confined against a person's will is to have a lawyer file a habeas corpus petition with the court asking the institution to show cause why that person should be held. Thus, insanity (lacking mental capacity) is foremost a legal term, rather than a medical one.

In the late nineteenth century the upper class with socially acceptable nervous diseases oftentimes voluntarily availed themselves of short and long-term residencies, such as in Philadelphia neurologist S. Weir Mitchell's rest cure, involving isolation, electrical massage, and a milk diet. Charlotte Perkins Gilman in "The Yellow Wallpaper" chronicles her incipient insanity and the "wise man" who withdrew her from all active stimulation by putting her to bed to rest. At the end of her treatment, she was ordered to return to domestic life and only "have but two hours' intellectual life a day" and "never to touch pen, brush, or pencil again." After three months, these conditions pressed her "near the borderline of utter mental ruin," she wrote later ("Why I Wrote 'The Yellow Wallpaper'"). Ironically, after Dr. Mitchell read her account of descending slowly into madness and the ineffective cure, he altered his future treatment for neurasthenia (meaning "tired nerves") and melancholia (depression). Another popular spa treatment to calm agitation was hydrotherapy, which was more than a nice warm bath. For instance, one practice was to wrap an agitated patient in cold (50 degree), wet sheets. A very disturbed patient could be placed in a continuous bath 18 hours a day for two to three weeks, or however long it took to change the aberrant behavior. The dangers of hydrotherapy were hypothermia, convulsions, and even drowning.

Another part of U.S. history, the 1920s eugenics movement, unfortunately influenced the 1940s Nazi practice of sterilizing the feebleminded. In Germany it led to euthanizing the congenitally inferior in order to purify the population. The movement began after the American Civil War when medical professionals, who saw few results from the Moral Movement, embraced the idea of Social Darwinism (countries fail from inherent weakness). Patients were being increasingly subdued by drugs such as chloroform, bromides, and ether, and 30 states, with the support of prominent Americans, legalized forced sterilization. In Virginia, Carrie Buck was an institutionalized 18-year-old unwed mother whose mother and child were also feebleminded. She was forcibly sterilized under Virginia's 1924 eugenics law. Her case was appealed to the Supreme Court, claiming that the plaintiff, under the Fourteenth Amendment, was denied due process and equal protection of the laws. However, Supreme Court Justice Oliver Wendell Holmes in *Buck v. Bell* (1927) upheld the state eugenics law, declaring "three generations of imbeciles are enough." With this precedent, over the next 40 years 60,000 people nationwide were sterilized for other types of unacceptable behaviors or conditions, such as alcoholism, promiscuity, criminal acts, epilepsy, and running away from home. In an attempt to make restitution, several governors have formally apologized to their states' eugenics victims.

Besides sterilization procedures performed for the greater good, in the 1930s Washington, D.C., neuropsychiatrist Dr. Walter Freeman pioneered his drastic ice-pick psychosurgery. Also known as lobotomy, it initially involved partially destroying one of the brain's frontal lobes, thus causing great disfiguration. Freeman explains in "Glimpses of Postlobotomy Personalities" how, when all else fails, the desired change in the patient's anxious and fearful personality is effected: "Without the long, painful process of developing insight in the patients, psychosurgery somehow relieves them of their sufferings and makes it possible for them to go back to their homes and to survive in the very environment in which their disorders developed" (Robinson and Freeman, 15). In his case studies, however, the postoperative realities sound grim. Patients often were described as slothful, irritable, and angry. Nonetheless, in *A History of Psychiatry* Edward Shorter points out, "The idea of operating on the brain to cure madness does not seem intrinsically unreasonable. Physicians have always intuited that a physical intervention in the brain, perhaps cutting some tract causing compulsive behavior or removing a center producing some malignant protein, might put an end to a pattern of psychosis" (Shorter, 225). The relationship between the brain and the mind is being continually studied, of course, with new methods of brain imaging such as MRI (magnetic resonance imaging), CT (computerized tomography), and PET (positron-emission tomography) proving immensely helpful in diagnosing and mapping progressive diseases. Although the adverse publicity arising from *Cuckoo's Nest* caused lobotomy to be largely replaced with antipsychotic drugs, today successful psychosurgeries like cingulotomy relieve severe compulsive neuroses and depression.

Besides psychosurgery, electroshock therapy (EST), also called electroconvulsive therapy (ECT), which is also prominently featured in *Cuckoo's Nest,* has proved a valuable psychiatric treatment for mental illness. In 1938, after an earlier scientist observed that schizophrenics seemed symptom-free following seizures, Italian scientists Cereletti and Bini devised electroshock therapy as an efficient way to manage uncontrollable patients. Today, a severely depressed patient receiving ECT, administered in a series of treatments, has an intravenous relaxant administered and a mouth guard inserted before an anesthetic renders him unconscious. The airway is protected, and electrodes are connected with conducting jelly on the temples. Electric current comparable to a 60-watt bulb shoots through the brain causing a 20-second grand-mal seizure. The patient wakes about 30 minutes later, confused and disoriented, with a headache and short-term memory loss. In essence, ECT helps disturbed patients regain the control necessary to enter into a therapeutic relationship. Short-term impaired memory follows; complications from possible fractures and dislocations caused by muscle contractions are a thing of the past. For generations Kesey's *Cuckoo's Nest* inflamed the public consciousness by depicting ECT as a means to punish misbehaving patients, easily associating it with electrocution. Over the years attempts to pass state laws banning ECT have failed. As horrific as it sounds, some neuropsychiatrists still find ECT to be an effective treatment for severely depressed and suicidal patients, especially after psychotherapy and slow-acting, cyclical drug regimens fail. Depression, more than a character weakness and feeling just down, is a brain disease often detectable on a PET scan that indicates receptor chemistry abnormality. It affects millions of Americans who often feel ashamed they cannot pull themselves up by their bootstraps. Hence, they often fail to seek help. New electromagnetic brain treatments, easily applied and without side effects, are proving effective, and recent NIH DNA studies indicate a 50 percent to 80 percent genetic component. In 2003 scientists, after working decades, documented a clear link between a gene controlling serotonin levels in the brain and depression, leading to possible new drugs. Tying genes with behavior, scientists say depression has roots in both genetics and personal history (i.e., nurture and nature).

The beginning of World War II brought more awareness to mental and emotional problems with more than a million inductees rejected for military duty as unsound. This was shocking evidence of public fragility. Returning servicemen, on the other hand, benefited both from medical advances, such as penicillin and blood banking, as well as from psychiatric screening. Subsequently, the number of psychologists proliferated and terms such as *post-traumatic stress disorder* (PTSD) were coined. PTSD, formerly referred to as battle fatigue or shell shock, is not new, but the term continues to be applied to returning soldiers with ongoing problems such as loss of concentration, sleep disturbances, nightmares, flashbacks, intrusive thoughts, and emotional stress. This spotlight on identifying prospective mental disorders brought about the National Institute for Mental Health in 1949, advocating more study on the origins of mental illness, its diagnosis, and its treatment. For the first time—in the place of hospitalization—the new drug chlorpromazine was used to relieve anxiety and control delusions. Thorazine, the prescription straitjacket, was used to treat and ameliorate depressive or compulsive disorders. With the widespread use of these drugs and others, the psychopharmaceutical revolution in mental health care began. Ironically, as the 1950s rolled in, the counterculture movement looked to their drugs, such as LSD and peyote, to escape from the conventional rationality.

The psychiatric climate in the 1960s when *Cuckoo's Nest* was published included two main schools of thought: the behaviorists and the humanists. A leading American behaviorist, B. F. Skinner (1904–90), believed we could solve major mental problems by improving our understanding of human conditioning. When he objectively observed aberrant behavior, he felt it should be ignored or punished. Good behavior, he thought, could be positively conditioned with encouragement and reward. Behaviorists tended to pigeonhole patients into categories in which they would be forever tracked. The other major view of the time came from the humanists who hesitated to label the patient but who also socially constructed mental illness. For example, Scottish psychiatrist R. D. Laing (1927–89), "the philosopher of madness," believed that a schizophrenic only acted abnormally as a mechanism to cope with a stressful situation. This view is increasingly seen as outdated as work is underway to confirm a genetic mutation as the disease's cause. Two million American schizophrenics have lost touch with reality, hallucinate, and suffer from this disabling disease. Laing vehemently opposed the dehumanizing use of ECT and lobotomy. American psychiatrist Thomas S. Szasz (born 1920) took humanism a step further by writing about "the myth of mental illness" and the ethical and moral issues physicians contend with. He advocates patient autonomy, including the right to refuse involuntary "imprisonment" and treatment. For better or worse, in recent times mental patients have greater civil rights, and more scrutiny is given to psychiatric institution admission methods, leaving the standard five-day admission to include a quick psychiatric evaluation, drug readjustment, and then release. The result is that a large population of mental patients is not benefiting from lengthy psychotherapeutic interactions with caring psychiatrists and, therefore, is left to fend for itself, often on the street.

Mental institutions in the1970s, due in part to *Cuckoo's Nest*'s adverse publicity that fostered hostility against authority, were seen as warehouses that inflicted physical and sexual abuse on patients. With the current trend toward deinstitutionalization, more patients are treated on an outpatient basis with psychotropic drugs. There are new ways to diagnose and many other types of treatment for mental illness, of course, besides psychosurgery, ECT, drugs, and confinement. In the early part of the twentieth century American psychotherapy, which tended to classify disorders by symptoms rather than causations, proliferated. It stemmed in part from the work of Austrian Sigmund Freud (1856–1939), the Father of Psychoanalysis. Psychotherapy slowly became popular and arguably successful. Some of the concepts that Freud's talk therapy popularized, as translated, included the Oedipus complex; the id, ego, and superego; anxiety and defense mechanisms; repression, displacement, and rejection; and the libido and death instinct. His therapeutic approaches include dream analysis, free association, and transference. Indeed, Freud even made the terms *hysteria* and *penis envy* household words, but today criticism of his unorthodox research methods and emphasis on sexuality makes his practices less relevant. Currently, one in four American adults seeks professional psychological advice some time during his or her life for services ranging from treating severe depression to counseling on life strategies. The stigma is gone. New disorders, some consider fads, are continually being defined, including the seemingly pervasive attention deficit hyperactivity disorder (ADHD). In 1995, 2.5 million American children were on Ritalin. In the 1980s multiple personality disorder (MPD) became epidemic. In essence, critics claim personality traits formerly seen as eccentric or troublesome are being pathologized, causing the field of psychiatry to grow. Again, for better or for worse, in recent times drug therapy—even with its side effects—continues to replace lengthy patient-oriented talk sessions as the gold standard of care.

Because the history of mental illness reaches back as far as the written word, this abbreviated version provides merely a snapshot illumination of specific issues in *Cuckoo's Nest*. Age-old attempts to treat madness seem from our perspective today, cruel and unusual. Besides, with pathology poorly defined, odd behavior alone would be cause for confinement. Today, while new methods advance understanding and care, a significant part of the future of mental illness diagnosis may lie in constant revelations arising from brain imaging and the deciphered genome, with the promise of targeted treatments. Nonetheless, even with vast knowledge of the human body, Edward Shorter adds, "Science wanders astray easily in the world of quotidian anxiety and sadness, in the obsessive traits of behavior and the misfiring personality types that are the lot of humankind. Here the genetic trail grows dim and the neurotransmitters evaporate. Biology counts for little, culture and socialization for lots" (*A History of Psychiatry*, 288). The nature versus nurture debate is very much alive.

LITERARY ANALYSIS

One Flew Over the Cuckoo's Nest, one of the most influential novels of the twentieth century, derives from Ken Kesey's observations at a mental institution. Although it is a popular myth that *Cuckoo's Nest* sprung full-blown from Kesey's drug-induced state, he admits only some of it was inspired that way. Written during the post–World War II era of the psychedelic 1960s, when the U.S. faced a Communist threat, he wanted his black satire's good versus evil plot, rich with symbols, literary allusions, and bioethical and medical issues, to show how individuals must stand up to authority so their rights are not quashed by government control. As a prototypical depiction of mental illness, *Cuckoo's Nest* describes how the mentally ill were treated, and this analysis focuses on the effects of the therapies applied at the time.

Chief Bromden's observations as narrator make him the most important character in the novel. The "deaf and dumb" American Indian, who has seen his lands taken away to build a hydroelectric dam and his family destroyed, tells the story, at first in a flashback sequence and then in hallucinatory visions. It is possible to trace throughout the novel his self-evolving passage out of the fog of schizophrenia. The action centers on the free-spirited Randle P. McMurphy (Mack), who of course personifies the counterculture Beat Generation. He "was a giant come out of the sky to save us from the Combine," the Big Chief believes. Mack faces off against Nurse Ratched, who personifies governmental authority and repression and in whom the Combine (evil government forces seeking conformity) culminates. The Combine includes Ratched's network of handpicked and personally trained nurses, doctors, and aides. Mack, "crazy like a fox," has capitalist intent in feigning mental illness to leave a prison work farm. However much of a charming con man he appears to be, though, in setting up gambling opportunities, his antiauthoritarian rebelliousness makes him an imperfect antihero. Because he has been involuntarily committed by the prison, Ratched has absolute power to hold him until she deems him cured. But most of the other Acute patients who are deemed hardcore and seek institutional discipline can release themselves. In his battle with his nemesis, Nurse Ratched (symbolically a ratchet, a tool controlling by degree), he appears to be both a classic psychopath and a cocky comic book figure. Regardless of the impurity of Mack's self-serving hustling instincts, his antagonizing Ratched allows him to grow and the other patients to be liberated. Considering the complexity of mental states, it is ambiguous whether he extended his stay (breaking the nurses' station window twice) for his greed or for solidarity with the patients. Is he the victim of an ill-conceived plan or a martyr?

While Mack "walks out of step; hears another drum," a literary reference to Henry David Thoreau that is a leitmotif symbolizing individualism, the Chief stands for the vanishing American Indian, an invisible man diminished by white society. Kesey goes into great detail about how the Chief's disintegrating culture has paralyzed him into catatonia, effecting a split personality and sporadic loss of reality. The Chief has been on the ward the longest; Mac is the new patient. Each is putting on an act: the Chief's hallucinatory insights on hospital activities reflect his silent savvy; Mack's noisy bravado either agitates or rallies patients by challenging Ratched's matriarchal authority. Kesey's contrasting the Chief and Mack causes interest. But, the ingenious part of the novel is the ability to trace Mack's influence on the Chief. Inextricably linking mental prowess and physical size, the Chief in his mind's eye appears to grow physically bigger as he becomes mentally released from his schizophrenic fog. In an example of the complexity of Mack's motives, he uses the Chief to lift the control room panel as the basis of a bet, but at the same time it empowers the Chief.

The mental institution culture in *Cuckoo's Nest* reveals how the lines between sanity and insanity are often blurred. It describes many types of illness, divided between the Acutes and the Chronics, and includes the obsessive-compulsive disorder (OCD) patient who cannot get dirty, two epileptics with opposing drug administration problems, cowering depressives, self-mutilating passive-aggressives, hallucinating schizophrenics, and troublemaking psychopaths. In a group therapy meeting Mack sets out to challenge authority by persuading most of the patients to vote to watch the World Series during their work detail. Although a democratic vote is taken—modeling the type of behavior needed on the outside—Ratched wields her authority and cuts the power to the set. The patients then gather in front of it in a rebellious sit-in. The Chief tacitly observes they would all appear crazy to an outsider. Talk therapies based on ward log entries are run like confrontational pecking parties, with the patients acting like scared rabbits. Harding and others fear Ratched, viewed as a surrogate wife and mother, and want her to keep them in their place. Throughout the novel women are mostly portrayed as dominating "ballcutters" or submissive pleasure-givers.

Dale Harding, symbolizing the voice of reason as president of the Patients' Council, explains the system and treatments like electroshock therapy and lobotomy. What may be inexplicable, though, is the therapeutic role of nature and the healing power of laughter seen throughout the novel. In a classic road literature scenario, Mack and the other patients on a fishing trip learn and grow along the way as they face challenges and overcome obstacles. Mack laughs at fishing trip mishaps, the Chief tells us,

> Because he knows you have to laugh at the things that hurt you just to keep yourself in balance, just to keep the world from running you plumb crazy. He knows there's a painful side; he knows my thumb smarts and his girl friend has a bruised breast and the doctor is losing his glasses, but he won't let the pain blot out the humor no more'n he'll let the humor blot out the pain.

The contagious laughter pumped the men up, as it "rang out on the water in ever-widening circles." Laughter, in fact, as a proponent of the holistic mind-body-spirit approach to health and healing, may relieve pain and renew hope. In 1964 Dr. Norman Cousins, diagnosed with the crippling and degenerative disease *ankylosing spondylitis*, with his doctor's permission removed himself from the clinical environment and checked into a hotel for combination therapy comprised of belly laughter (watching Marx Brothers films) and taking massive doses of vitamin C. His disease went into remission. He did not necessarily reject scientifically, Western medicine that documents how positive emotions affect the adrenal glands and the endocrine system, and how the placebo effect increases the mind's willpower over matter. Cousins, in writing up his account in *Anatomy of an Illness* (1981), answers critics and leaves others to speculate about his alternative therapy: "Laughter may or may not activate the endorphins or enhance respiration, as some medical researchers contend. What seems clear, however, is that laughter is an antidote to apprehension and panic." He was, in effect, retaking control of his life. Since Cousin's classic book, others have espoused hope, faith, and love as therapeutic values, such as Bernie Siegel's *Love, Medicine & Miracles*. Nonetheless, when considering alternative or holistic approaches to medicine, it is wise to beware of age-old quackery.

Mack's therapeutic role—if it can be called such—demonstrates the importance of levity as well as of maintaining some self-respect in institutional living. Unfortunately, in Ratched's therapeutic community her dehumanizing and belittling ways "ballcut" all men, including Dr. Spivey. Contrary to today's conventional wisdom, she controls the population by diminishing the men's self-esteem. She also administers narcotic drugs daily. Her threats of using electroshock therapy and lobotomy as punishment would now be seen as unethical, at the least. Mack progressively builds up their masculine confidence. But then he lets them down, until in one last hurrah he puts his personal interests aside when he and the Chief protect George in a fistfight with the black aides who try to give him an enema. Although Ratched gives Mack a chance to get out of ECT as punishment by admitting he has been wrong, in a pivotal show of selfless solidarity, he refuses, feeling it would be the same as confessing to a "plot to overthrow the government." As he undergoes a series of ECT in the Disturbed Ward, his bravado creates a heroic legendary status that Ratched fears. In a psychological ploy to regain control, she brings him back to the ward where she can watch him—and plot.

Sexuality is also a part of life—even in an institution. Mack arranges for Billy Bibbit, 31 but mentally an adolescent controlled by his mother, to lose his virginity to a smuggled-in prostitute during a drunken evening on the ward. Mack's attempt to restore a manly independence in the men may release some from psychosomatic illness; however, for Billy, things are not that simple. Ratched, in her zeal to keep things under control, shames him into extreme guilt. Fearful of his mother, he commits suicide. At this point *Cuckoo Nest*'s rich literary references to Melville culminate in *Moby Dick's* good versus evil overtones and in a suggestion of *Billy Budd's* stuttering, innocent protagonist. Applying Darwinian reasoning to the pecking order of the mental ward, Ratched's "ballcutting" approach mandates that only the fittest survive. So Mack viciously attacks Ratched for Billy's suicide, leading to her final retaliation: his lobotomy. What makes Kesey's dramatization so compelling, however, is the way Christian imagery used throughout the novel coalesces into his final redemption: Mack is the martyred Christ who has compromised authority and released the patients from the Combine's control of them. In fact, *Cuckoo's Nest*'s grotesque description is so compelling it took lobotomy as therapeutic psychosurgery underground, until today when updated versions of it are deemed acceptable, beneficial treatments. In the end, the Chief's releasing Mack from his vegetative state and escaping out into a new life show the healing power of individuals. Nonetheless, life is messy, and Kesey's ambiguous conclusion causes speculation that the Combine, bigger than Nurse Ratched and her mental institution, cannot be so easily defeated.

The allegorical title, *One Flew Over the Cuckoo's Nest,* comes from a nursery rhyme the Chief recites in part 4:

> Ting. Tingle, tingle, tremble toes, she's a good fisherman, catches hens, puts 'em inna pens . . . wire blier, limber lock, three geese inna flock . . . one flew east, one flew west, one flew over the cuckoo's nest . . . O-U-T spells out . . . goose swoops down and plucks *you* out.

The cuckoo's nest is the mental hospital; Ratched "tremble toes" pecks at the men; the Bull Goose Loony Mack "plucks out" the Chief, who embodies Mack's spirit as he makes his hopeful escape into the moonlight. Kesey's cautionary tale, a metaphor for how society socially constructs its attitudes toward mental illness, makes us question, conversely, how mental illness derives from culture as well as from disease. What is more clearly understood, however, is that views of insanity change in our culture and that therapies go in and out of fashion. *Cuckoo's Nest* makes us wonder how we should balance mental health care's need to control and to conform with maintaining individual rights. In Kesey's novel, the psychiatric staff are not always the good guys, and the patients often are more complicated than they first appear. With generational fluctuations in psychiatric perception, it is necessary to ask, by whose idea of normal should we be measured?

SYNOPSIS OF THE NOVEL

An Oregon state mental institution in the 1960s is the scene for a contest of wills between the staff and the inmates. The catatonic Native American Chief Bromden (Chief Broom) narrates *One Flew Over the Cuckoo's Nest* even though he appears deaf and mute. Diagnosed with delusional paranoia, while in a fog and feeling helpless, he fears the Combine controls everything. The driving force in the mental institution is the militaristic Nurse Ratched (the Big Nurse), who wields her authority severely over everyone, including the professional medical staff, the black boy aides, and the patients. The new patient, Randle P. McMurphy (Mack), whom the court ruled a psychopathic prisoner, has feigned insanity to be transferred from Pendleton Work Farm. In his cocky, in-your-face manner, he introduces himself as "a gambling fool" to other asylum inmates. Using his charm, he craftily sets them up as pigeons to pluck in card games. The patients are divided into the incurable Chronics like the big half-breed Chief, who is a flawed product of the Combine, and the curable Acutes who Nurse Ratched eggs on, attacking them where they are most vulnerable. A patient may come in as an Acute and then be turned into a robotic Chronic (Walker, Wheeler, or Vegetable) after being punished in the Shock Shop with electroshock treatments or with the permanent disfiguration of psychosurgery (lobotomy). Threats with these therapies enforce cooperation while keeping the two groups separated. Ratched has already assessed Mack as a troublemaker who will manipulate the system and disrupt the mental ward. She runs a tight ship, shunning outside disturbances to keep the precision asylum machinery (the Combine) humming. Her ideal medical staff, the Chief tells us, has been hand-picked and after years of training molded to suit her needs, staying "in contact on a high-voltage wavelength of hate." She taught them her way to get inmates into shape was to patiently "wait for a little advantage . . . then twist the rope and keep the pressure steady."

Through the fog of his schizophrenia the Big Chief keenly watches the new admission, McMurphy, in the group psychotherapy meeting. Ratched begins the discussion from a topic logged in the ward book having to do with Dale Harding's promiscuous, well-endowed young wife, his feelings of inferiority, and resultant sexual dysfunction. He is a probable case of situational madness resulting from his wife's emasculating nature. Mack had initially challenged Harding, the effeminate, college-educated president of the Patients' Council, for the role of the Bull Goose Loony or the alpha male, but they soon become friendly when Harding proves a valuable source of information. Mack garners the most interest in the meeting, however, when Ratched introduces him as a recipient of the Distinguished Service Cross in Korea for leading a Communist prison camp escape. Subsequently, he was dishonorably discharged for insubordination and later arrested for drunkenness, gambling, assault and battery, and statutory rape. Mack refutes only the latter. Dr. Spivey, the ward doctor, misaddresses him as "Mr. McMurry"—Ratched's attempt to demoralize Mack through improperly pronouncing his name—and looks into his file, reading the diagnosis: "repeated outbreaks of passion that suggest the possible diagnosis of psychopath." In retaliation, Mack tries to intimidate Ratched. Meanwhile, Dr. Spivey explains the group meeting protocol and why a democratic therapeutic community, as a prototype of the outside world, requires conformity that will allow them to return to the outside. The patients in group therapy are encouraged to discuss and confess, revealing the secrets of the subconscious. Rather than being Freud-inspired talk therapy, though, it turns out to be a Ratched-led pecking party, and this time Harding is unmercifully grilled and shamed. Hearing all this and watching an agitated patient receive a subduing hip shot, Mack, in the end, thinks it might be smart to carefully assess the situation before he "makes any kind of play." He enters into a lengthy dialogue with Harding and others about Ratched's role in emasculating them, culminating in a bet that he will "get her goat" within a week.

Mack's rebellious nature takes over as he begins rallying the patients and gaining hero status by challenging Ratched's authority and by procuring special favors for them. For example, in the shower room Mack complains to a black orderly about the ward policy that he can brush his teeth at only a certain time, and when Ratched comes in, he tells her his clothes were taken and threatens to drop his towel. Ratched angrily calls for new clothes. Further taunting Ratched, Mack complains about loud ward music overriding his conversation while gambling for cigarettes; however, Ratched says it consoles the hard-of-hearing older patients. Mack then presses to move his game to the old tub room, no longer in use because drugs have replaced hydrotherapy. She refuses, but Mack persuades Dr. Spivey to change the venue. Mack continues to break the rules by using real money (not cigarettes) to play Monopoly. He takes bets on the World Series. In a key vote to watch the World Series, Mack gets the Big Chief to raise his hand. Ratched balks at the schedule change, and the Acutes do a sit-in protest in front of the TV set. With each loss of authority Ratched patiently, coldly waits: "she has all the power of the Combine behind her."

In part 2 Ratched is suspicious of the Big Chief's new cognitive responsiveness, and even though he still exhibits paranoia, his schizophrenic fog may be lifting. In a staff meeting, the question arises whether Mack is a clever con man or a violent psychopath. Ratched convinces others that sending Mack to the Disturbed Ward would only enhance his hero status; therefore, she favors keeping him in the general population where, before long, he will show his own avarice and cowardice. The Chief, in his narration, theorizes Mack truly is an extraordinary man, capable of resisting the Combine. Noting aberrant staff actions, however, he questions who in the mental institution is completely sane. Mack's leadership continues to embolden the Acutes. He has given them a reason to wake up, and they now question ward policies, such as on rationing cigarettes. Then Mack, in a catch-22, backs off when he realizes, as an involuntarily committed patient, Ratched decides if he is cured or not (released or not). By failing to rally forces against Ratched, he disheartens the patients, possibly leading to Cheswick's suicide. Ward privileges are revoked, and therapy sessions return to silence.

Mack witnesses an epileptic seizure, learning about the side effects of the drug that may prevent it, as well as the staff wielding its power through using electroshock therapy ("brain burning"), which, ironically, is actually the induction of a seizure. Mack is shocked to learn that Harding, Billy, and others have voluntarily committed themselves, and they are free to leave at any time. It is only their fears of the outside world that keep them there. Ratched, feeling her control returned, smugly informs the men that they must have the privilege of using the tub room for card playing taken away as punishment for their insurrections and that having a sense of order and discipline will help them adjust to societal rules in the outside world. Convinced she had the final victory and control over Mack, Ratched is startled to see him plunge his hand through the glass window of the nurses' station, extracting one of his own cigarettes. She does not retaliate but bides her time.

In part 3 sports are introduced, causing the men to renew their muscle-flexing and to build self-esteem. Being denied day passes, Mack again puts his hand through Ratched's glass window. Tension builds as Mack's rebelliousness increases. At this time, he recruits the patients to go on a supervised deep-sea fishing trip, but Ratched frightens the men. Chief Bromden really wants to go but knows he will blow his cover by indicating so. Acting deaf has allowed him to hear. It started as a child when outside people who saw an American Indian as invisible quit listening to him. When Indian land was seized to make a hydroelectric dam, the government had his white mother, instead of his chief father, sign the deal. Chief Broom begins to emerge from his silence one night when Mack offers him some gum, and he replies, "Thank you." A conversation ensues, and Mack works on the Chief's ego to convince him to throw the tub room control panel out the window for escape.

Mack pushes to arrange a deep-sea fishing trip, signing up the Chief as the only Chronic going. With great effort, because Ratched had tried to "damp the man out of them," Mack gets the quota needed for the trip. But, when only one chaperone shows up, the prostitute Candy Starr, Dr. Spivey must step forward as the second chaperone. All the way to the dock, the men show bravado and courage, and instinctively a manliness once derailed returns. They surpass many obstacles on their road trip to the sea; in the end, without a properly signed waiver, they even hijack a boat. The fishing trip, complete with victorious fishing and hearty camaraderie, has returned a natural masculinity to formerly emasculated men. And laughter "started slow and pumped itself full, swelling the men bigger and bigger." Mack watches as the men appear to slowly take back their lives. Billy and Candy become smitten, and Mack invites her to the mental institution on Saturday.

Back at the mental institution in part 4, Ratched plots to discredit Mack by disclosing to the patients how much money he is making on them from gambling and arranging games and trips. Her ploy seems to be working, until Mack and Chief Bromden defend George Sorenson in a fistfight with the black orderlies. As punishment, they receive EST in the Disturbed Ward, which Mack compares to electrocution. Because he will not relent, but rather acts heroically, Ratched orders more EST for Mack. When he begins to attain legendary status, Ratched brings him back to her ward where she works on making him appear weak. Still rebellious, Mack arranges for Billy to lose his virginity to Candy during a drunken night on the ward. The other patients urge Mack to escape rather than face further repercussion from Ratched. But, drugged and drunk, he falls asleep. In the morning, Ratched takes it all in and threatens to tell Billy's mother about his encounter with Candy. When Billy cuts his throat, Mack attacks Ratched. In retaliation, she has him lobotomized. Bromden humanely releases Mack from his vegetative state by suffocating him, and he escapes back out into his life.

TOPICS FOR ORAL AND WRITTEN DISCUSSION

1. What role did the rebellious Merry Pranksters have in defining the counterculture in which *Cuckoo's Nest* is set?

2. What psychological characteristics make Chief Bromden an effective narrator?
3. How does the individual versus the Combine encapsulate the allegorical book's conflict?
4. Through scene analysis, define incidents of insanity as well as gender and racial bias.
5. How is the fishing trip therapeutic for the patients?
6. As seen through the eyes of Chief Bromden, whose mental illness may derive from a cultural schism, relate Christian imagery to Mack as he goes from maverick to self-sacrificing saint.
7. Describe Ratched's ward in totalitarian terms, incorporating a discussion of her authoritarian ways and the patients' loss of civil liberties.
8. Discuss the psychological effect of domineering women in *Cuckoo's Nest*.
9. In the black satire *Cuckoo's Nest* would the electroshock therapy and lobotomy administered as therapy and/or punishment be ethical now?
10. Throughout the novel, trace Mack's influence on the Chief's passage out of the fog of schizophrenia.

BIBLIOGRAPHY

Cousins, Norman. *Anatomy of an Illness: As Perceived by the Patient*. New York: Bantam, 1981.

Fink, Max. *Electroshock: Restoring the Mind*. New York: Oxford University Press, 1999.

Freud, Sigmund. *Introductory Lectures on Psycho-Analysis*. Trans. James Strachey. New York: Norton, 1966.

Friedberg, John. *Shock Treatment Is Not Good for Your Brain*. San Francisco: Glide Publishing, 1976.

Gilman, Charlotte Perkins. *The Yellow Wallpaper*. New York: Feminist Press at the City University of New York, 1973. Also: www.pagebypage books.com.

———. "Why I Wrote 'The Yellow Wallpaper'." World Wide School Library. http://www.worldwideschool.org/library/books/lit/socialcommentary/yellowwallpaper/chap2.html.

Kerouac, Jack. *On the Road*. New York: Viking, 1957.

Kesey, Ken. *One Flew Over the Cuckoo's Nest*. New York: Viking, 2002.

Robinson, Mary Frances, and Walter Freeman. "Glimpses of Postlobotomy Personalities." In *Psychosurgery and the Self*, 15–32. New York: Grune, 1954.

Shorter, Edward. *A History of Psychiatry*. New York: Wiley, 1997.

Siegel, Bernie. *Love, Medicine & Miracles*. New York: Harper, 1986.

Wolfe, Tom. *The Electric Kool-Aid Acid Test*. New York: Farrar, 1968.

SUGGESTED FURTHER READING

Chekhov, Anton. "Ward Number Six." In *Ward Number Six and Other Stories*. Trans. Ronald Hingley. New York: Oxford University Press, 1974. Written in 1892, this attack on involuntary mental hospitalization shows the darker side of psychiatric history.

Donley, Carol, and S. Buckley, eds. *What's Normal: Narratives of Mental and Emotional Disorders*. Kent, Ohio: Kent State University Press, 2000. Exceptional anthology.

Grandin, Temple. *Thinking in Pictures and Other Reports from My Life with Autism*. New York: Vintage Books, 1996. The increasingly diagnosed high-functioning autism blurs the lines between normal and abnormal.

Green, Hannah. *I Never Promised You a Rose Garden*. New York: Holt, 1964. The anguish and hope, in the first person, of a schizophrenic mental patient.

Jamison, Kay Redfield. *An Unquiet Mind: A Memoir of Moods and Madness*. New York: Knopf, 1995. A clinical psychologist suffers from manic depression.

————. *Night Falls Fast: Understanding Suicide*. New York: Vintage, 1999.

Kesey, Ken. *The Further Inquiry*. New York: Viking, 1990. Screenplay about the 1964 bus voyage.

Sheehan, Susan. *Is There No Place on Earth for Me?* Boston: Houghton, 1982. The author's firsthand account of life as a schizophrenic woman.

Styron, William. *Darkness, Visible: A Memoir of Madness*. New York: Vintage, 1992. First-person account of severe depression.

ALICE WALKER'S *POSSESSING THE SECRET OF JOY* (1992)

There are those who believe Black people possess the secret of joy and that it is this that will sustain them through any spiritual or moral or physical devastation.

—Alice Walker, epigraph, *Possessing the Secret of Joy*

HISTORICAL CONTEXT

While Kesey's *One Flew Over the Cuckoo's Nest* and Walker's *Possessing the Secret of Joy* are both cultural representations of mental and

---

Note to teachers: This novel contains mature subject matter. Please see appendix D.

physical illnesses, they are as diverse in time, setting, and characterization as the backgrounds of their authors. Alice Walker (born 1944), the first black woman to win both the Pulitzer Prize and the American Book Award, for *The Color Purple* (1983), was born to poor sharecropper parents in Eatonton, Georgia, the last of eight children. Her mother's grandmother was mostly Cherokee Indian. At the age of nine, Walker was blinded in the right eye with a BB gun pellet and facially disfigured while playing cowboys and Indians with her brothers. She retreated into books. Walker excelled despite the partial loss of eyesight, and at her high school graduation in 1961 she was valedictorian and prom queen. She received a scholarship to Spelman College in Atlanta, Georgia, but before she left her mother wisely gave her three gifts: "a sewing machine for self-sufficiency, a suitcase for independence, and a typewriter for creativity." While in Atlanta, Dr. Martin Luther King, Jr. invited her to his home, and later Walker attended the Youth World Peace Festival in Helsinki, Finland. These two events immersed her in the civil rights movement and gave her greater understanding of other cultures. In 1963 Walker took part in the March on Washington for Jobs and Freedom, where she heard Dr. King's "I Have a Dream" speech.

After two years at Spelman, Walker received a scholarship to attend the prestigious Sarah Lawrence College in Bronxville, New York. During her senior year she became pregnant and consequently suffered from suicidal thoughts and depression. She poured her feelings into poetry and a short story, "To Hell With Dying," which was published after receiving the endorsement of the famous poet Langston Hughes. With the help of classmates, Walker arranged to safely abort the pregnancy, which was illegal at the time. Following college graduation in 1965, Walker increased her civil rights activism by the door-to-door registering of poor voters in Georgia. Later she met and married Mel Leventhal, a Jewish law student in New York City, who later worked for the NAACP. They moved to Mississippi where threats of violence tested their interracial marriage. Walker got pregnant again, but lost the baby during the frenetic time following King's assassination. She later delivered a healthy daughter. After receiving a number of grants and fellowships, Walker taught at Wellesley College in Massachusetts, one of the colleges that in the nineteenth century championed women's rights (a movement born out of abolitionism), including voting and property rights, education, and health reform. While there, Walker created one of the first women's studies courses. In the mid-1970s she and Leventhal divorced.

After Walker finished her most famous work, *The Color Purple*, she traveled to Africa to research the oppressive practice of female genital mutilation (FGM), which also occurs in the Middle East and in part of the Western Hemisphere. Her work on the topic turned into *Possessing the Secret of Joy*, which focuses on one woman's traumatic experience with FGM. Later with collaborator Pratibha Parmar she filmed a documentary with a companion book, *Warrior Marks* (1993). Walker draws from a deep reservoir of personal experiences to write realistically about many issues in her novels and poetry. For instance, she cares very much about poverty, racism, and the health issues that emanate from global violence against women. Her works dramatize the oppression of women, in particular, and lately have addressed bisexual and father-daughter relationships. As a former teacher, she hopes to educate her readers on the brutality of misogyny, the dangers of silent taboos, and the effects of rituals. Her activism, which started during her college days at Spelman, now addresses other causes such as protecting indigenous cultures in their natural environments. Walker, a California resident, continues to write and to lecture.

The main topic Walker addresses in *Possessing the Secret of Joy* is how the female genital mutilation ritual in a specific African tribe affects the mind, body, and spirit of its bicultural protagonist, her family, and her countries. However, it is necessary to note that Walker's literary representation of FGM applies to only a small percentage of African tribes and that the surgical ritual is conducted in many different ways, in hospitals as well as in huts, for many different reasons. For these general purposes, the procedure is more descriptively called female genital cutting (FGC) because, by degree, it ranges from a slight ceremonial nicking of the clitoris to draw blood to the more radical excision (removing some or all of the outer genitals) and infibulation (sewing up the vagina and leaving a small opening for urination and menstrual flow). The ritual's end result spans the gamut from a proud youth who has experienced a spiritual initiation into adulthood and elevated tribal status to a scared young girl's agonizing pain and lingering death. A woman who has had the more radical procedure often has very painful intercourse and child delivery. Even the newborn may be harmed mentally and physically from passing through the narrow opening. After childbirth, the woman is reinfibulated, or sewn back up.

The origin of FGC goes back as far as Aristotle's thinking that women were unfinished men; consequently, the malformed and unclean female parts needed altering. It is believed Queen Cleopatra of Egypt had undergone pharaonic circumcision to, theoretically, ensure a union that could extend her realm's interests. Historically, only a virgin who could protect the paternal bloodline was marriageable, and therefore FGC (euphemistically "having a bath" or "cutting the rose") effected a sort of chastity belt. It became a mother's duty to keep her daughter pure until marriage, and therefore a prospective bride's excised and infibulated vagina became aesthetically desirable. In addition, a desexed girl was more likely to keep chaste until and during marriage. For these reasons, African mothers who force FGC on their daughters help maintain their status and that of their daughters. In 2003, a 32-year-old unwed pregnant Nigerian mother, charged with adultery, was sentenced to death by stoning in a case where global human rights activists debated fundamentalist Islamic law. Because of international attention she was found not guilty by an Islamic appeals court. Thus, a mother who takes extreme measures to keep her daughter chaste could even protect her life. Contrary to popular belief, the rite of passage tradition in some cultures does not derive solely from male dominance; rather, it gives the girls who prove their bravery by transcending physical pain more control over their tribal lives. In fact, some describe their experience as spiritual ecstasy. Those who show cowardice ("crying the knife") are socially ostracized. The tradition in a few tribes includes boys who vie for tribal leadership by a test of their courage. They must be stoic while, without anesthesia, their penises are circumcised and ritually mutilated.

Putting FGC into its cultural context and comparing it with other rituals, taboos, and practices is helpful. Christian missionaries were trying to eradicate FGC in Africa at the same time Puritan moralists in America believed clitoridectomy was a necessary surgery to control nymphomania and masturbation and to cure hysteria and melancholia. While some argue that there is no sound medical reason for male circumcision, in the Western world and elsewhere it is still done both for hygienic purposes and as a powerful religious ritual. However, for males, circumcision (the removal of the foreskin) is relatively trivial—unless it goes awry—compared to its female counterpart (clitoridectomy, at its worst), in which sexual pleasure is replaced with pain. Other related myths, taboos, and practices shed light on how FGC is culturally represented. Historically, menstruation and menopause myths declaring women unclean or undesirable, respectively, have mandated isolation and subjugation. Ancient Chinese foot binding hobbled women into a helpless desirability, while recent headlines report female infanticide where sons are desirable.

Whether rituals, traditions, and practices are considered heinous or not is a matter of perspective, though, because to many around the world the American death penalty (an ancient form of justice stemming from the philosophy of an eye for an eye) is considered barbaric. A hot contemporary issue in the United States is the sexual reassignment of hermaphrodites or intersexuals (one in 2,000 births, or 0.5 percent of the population) whose genitals do not fit into the culture's binary notions. Cheryl Chase, born with ambiguous genitals, argues in "'Cultural Practice' or 'Reconstructive Surgery'? U.S. Genital Cutting, the Intersex Movement, and Medical Double Standards" that it is a double standard to call FGM a barbaric ritual and sexual reassignment surgery a scientific necessity exempt from the federal law banning FGM. Chase asserts that in sexual reassignment cases, done since the 1950s, surgeons perpetuate violence against intersexuals by trying to transform "transgressive bodies into ones that can safely be labeled female and subjected to the many forms of social control with which women must contend" (Chase, 145). Doctors said Chase, born with a micropenis, undescended testes, hypospadias, and other abnormalities, could not function as a male in society, so he was surgically and hormonally altered to appear female but is nonorgasmic and infertile, something s/he is not emotionally comfortable with. U.S. surgeons reconstruct intersexuals' genitals to fit into a narrowly defined psychosocial system, just as mothers who force FGM onto their daughters consider their social well being in the particular tribal culture. Whether it occurs in the United States or in Africa, Chase asks, is not genitally mutilating children who cannot give informed consent child abuse?

Anthropologists and missionaries have known about FGC for many centuries. It was brought to the popular consciousness, though, in a 1980 *Ms. Magazine* article by Gloria Steinem and Robin Morgan titled "The International Crime of Genital Mutilation." Later Democratic Representative Patricia Schroeder of Colorado shocked Congress with the reality of FGM, and eventually it passed the Federal Prohibition of Female Genital Mutilation Act in 1996, making it a federal crime punishable by up to five years in prison. Intersex reassignment surgeries are exempt. Alice Walker, who fictionalized the issue in *Possessing the Secret of Joy,* and others who wrote about their private ordeals have horrified Americans. What followed these revelations was a Western media blitz on national news and talk shows. Claire C. Robertson, interested both in diminishing FGC and in eradicating poverty, writes in "Getting Beyond the Ew! Factor" that she is concerned about these "tendencies toward sensationalism and polemics," saying First World feminists seem arrogant and Americans voyeuristic with prurient tendencies when "All issues were being subsumed into this one and African women [were] being reduced to their genital status" (Robertson, 54–5). Can we claim moral superiority in a country where increasing incidents of rape, sexual assault, wife battering, and sexual harassment against women made it necessary for us to pass the Violence Against Women Act in 1994?

Whether or not First World countries can claim moral superiority, it is going to take the hard work of an international community, including the support of Amnesty International, the World Health Organization, and the United Nations, as well as local and international human rights and women's organizations, to debate the violation of human rights and health issues. The polar positions taken are: 1) extreme cultural relativism—FGC practiced on girls is tied up with national identity, and we cannot judge another country's morals and interfere, or 2) we should withhold aid from countries practicing FGC. With the consequences of FGC stirring the public conscience, it is not that easy to remain uninvolved as evidenced in the action our government took in AIDS funding. In 2003 former South African president and Nobel Peace Prize laureate Nelson Mandela praised President George W. Bush for pledging $15 billion to fight AIDS, a disease expected to kill 20 million more Africans by the end of the decade. The urgency of addressing the AIDS pandemic hit home when Mandela's own son, Makgatho, died of AIDS on January 6, 2005. About 5 million South Africans have the virus. The United Nations estimates that 45 million worldwide are HIV-infected. The world community continues to interfere in domestic human rights issues by condemning slavery, genocide, and infanticide, while it educates and provides other basic needs, such as food, clean water, and urgent health care. The two million girls every year who undergo FGC, and especially infibulation, risk a myriad of mental and physical health problems, including shock, trauma, hemorrhage, bacterial and HIV infections, incontinence, menstrual problems, sterility, frigidity, and childbirth problems. Many will die. Compared to the difficulty of eliminating the culturally entrenched habit of smoking, which annually kills 440,000 Americans and 4.9 million worldwide, the World Health Organization says it will take educating three generations and many more years to eradicate FGC.

Part of the world feels it is contentious to call their venerable female circumcision rite "mutilation"; nevertheless, for most Americans Secretary of State Madeleine Albright put it best: "When people are mutilated, it is criminal, not cultural."

LITERARY ANALYSIS

In *Possessing the Secret of Joy* the black liberal feminist Alice Walker dramatizes how her main character, Tashi, in an act of tribal allegiance, gets facial scarring and circumcision "because she recognized it as the only remaining definitive stamp of Olinka tradition." The tribe's leader, who is compared to Nelson Mandela and even Jesus Christ, has instructed the people "not [to] neglect ancient customs." He has been imprisoned by the white regime. Walker explores the effects of FGM in a dazzling style that simultaneously seems to contrast and to transcend cultural differences. The various viewpoints are artfully integrated into dialogue and flashbacks, intermixed with myths, symbols, and psychology. Walker uses the narrative device of renaming Tashi relative to her changing cultural and psychological state of mind; for example, when referring to her evolving American self she is "Tashi-Evelyn." In this way, Walker conveys the essence of Tashi's journey. However, Tashi is not described sympathetically because she was circumcised against the wishes of her Christian mother whose other daughter died as a result of FGM. Furthermore, because Tashi was sexually responsive with Adam, she knows the operation will result in a loss of pleasure. Even after Tashi's sparkling youthfulness turns into a flat-eyed passivity, Adam marries her, and she emigrates with him to America. Only then does she understand her physical and emotional loss and explode into rage. This analysis focuses on Walker's literary achievement in *Possessing the Secret of Joy* in which she creates a bicultural lens through which we can examine Tashi's African soul and warring American consciousness.

The title, *Possessing the Secret of Joy,* reflected in the first epigraph, derives more fully from a passage in Mirella Ricciardi's 1982 memoir *African Saga*. Ricciardi was a French Italian woman born and raised on a farm in Kenya, then a colony in British East Africa, who wrote, "Black people are natural, they possess the secret of joy, which is why they can survive the suffering and humiliation inflicted upon them. They are alive physically and emotionally, which makes them easy to live with. What I had not yet learned to deal with was their cunning and their natural instinct for self-preservation" (Ricciardi, 147). The condescending tone of Ricciardi's colonial remembrance highlights how nationalistic backlash plays into Tashi's mindset when she undergoes FGM. In *Possessing the Secret of Joy*'s scenario, a First World organization's attempts to change a Third World culture cause defiant anticolonial acts. Walker's second epigraph/proverb further sets the story into its bicultural context, prophesying Tashi's state of being torn apart from within: "When the axe came into the forest, the trees said the handle is one of us." Walker's plot borrows further from Ngugi wa Thiong'o's novel *The River Between* (1965), in which two lovers living across the river from each other play out the drama of Christian converts clashing with African traditionalists. Like *The River Between*, Walker's theme in *Possessing the Secret of Joy* argues that female circumcision destroys not only individual women but their country as well. Tashi endures pain to prove her devotion to tribal heritage; she symbolizes ritual sacrifice and the ultimate hope for change. Conversely, the circumciser M'Lissa, a "monument," symbolizes ancient beliefs and keeping the old ways.

Possessing the Secret of Joy is a vehicle for Walker's own feminist agenda. By putting Tashi into a particular context, Walker is able to develop her human rights and health issues as well as argue for political change. Tashi's story becomes part of Walker's own. For instance, the autobiographical elements are clear when Walker refers to FGM as "sexual blinding," a reference to her brothers shooting her in the eye and swearing her to silence. Both Walker and her character Tashi aborted a pregnancy and bridged cultures in search of an identity. They are storytellers whose myths teach lessons, filling the novel with stories of repression, of struggles, and eventually of self-actualization. Walker's strong female character, Adam's lover Lisette (Walker's alter ego), is an altruistic white woman who, as the voice of reason, contrasts with the emotional Tashi. As a youth Lisette had visited Olinka with a church youth group, and her family were colonists in Algeria. As an adult she is a high school French teacher in Paris who studies her "co-wife" Tashi from afar. The novel's opening parable of the panther foreshadows the Tashi-Adam-Lisette love triangle and even foretells the outcome. Adam's child with Tashi, the American-born retarded Benny, is born doing what turns out to be a painful sideshow for Western doctors; his child with Lisette, the Paris-born precocious Pierre, is the result of a natural, orgasmic home birth. The autonomous Lisette starkly contrasts with the fractured Tashi.

After Lisette dies from cancer, Pierre "continues to untangle the threads of mystery that kept [his stepmother Tashi] enmeshed." He reports that FGM may have been a reaction to "the Hottentot apron," or, as described by early European anthropologists, the unusually elongated labia on uncircumcised Khoisan women with enlarged buttocks (steatopygia). The bisexual and biracial Harvard-educated Pierre explains how some tribes eventually decided a woman's dual genitalia needed modifying because she could not perform both female and male roles. Continuing on Tashi's journey to self-knowledge, Olivia takes her sister-in-law to her first "shrink," a white "son of Freud" couch analyst who gawks at her as a publishable case history. He simplistically declares that healing is impossible because Africans cannot blame their mothers. Tashi's next analyst is Lisette's uncle, the Old Man or Mzee. Clearly, as Walker references in her afterword, her Old Man character is Carl Jung (1875–1961), the Swiss analytical psychologist who opposed Freud's idea that the libido (sexual instinct) alone drives life. Jung differed from Freud by espousing an interest in the opposites in nature (the divided self), even expressed in the way Jung, unlike Freud's couch analysis, sat in a chair opposite his patient to actively engage in dialogue.

Applying the Old Man's Jungian psychology to the bicultural and divided Tashi, she must reconcile her conscious ego with her unconscious, repressed experiences through interpreting her dreams, stories, and art. For example, during art therapy, after Tashi draws a large, evil rooster ("a humongous feathered creature"), she felt she was "seeing the cause of [her] anxiety itself for the first time, exactly as it was." It was a beast-sized indication of her psychosis, the "[e]motions that had frightened her insane." All at once Tashi remembered hiding in the grass and witnessing her sister's murder: "No longer would my weeping be separate from what I *knew*." The insidious tribal taboo demanding silence and repression had subverted her childhood memory. In *Possessing the Secret of Joy* Walker applies to Tashi's recovery the Jungian analysis she herself underwent. Jung's archetypal elements of the ego (central consciousness), shadow (unpleasant unconscious—Dr. Jekyll to Mr. Hyde), animus (Tashi's masculine unconscious mind), and Self (whole regulating center of the psyche, transcending the ego) help identify Tashi's psychological process toward wholeness or individuation. More simply put, Walker equates Jung's psychic ideal—harmonizing the conscious and unconscious, decentralizing the ego, and acknowledging the shadow and animus—with Tashi's coming to terms with her past, at last bringing her discovered Self spiritual peace. Even Walker's final chapter title, "Tashi Evelyn Johnson Soul," cues the reader that Tashi's fragmented mental state is at last reconciled.

After the Old Man dies, Tashi's new analyst, the black American feminist Raye, only understands Tashi's physical pain after having her own periodontal surgery. Tashi opens up to her, breaking her silence and referencing her shadow, or dark self, and self-acceptance follows. Raye and Pierre analyze Tashi's dream of being the queen termite imprisoned in a dark tower with broken wings. In African culture, the protruding termite hill symbolizes an elevated clitoris barring male entry; the hill being cut down symbolizes the ritual desexing. Because the girl's male soul is in the clitoris, it must be excised to rid her of the dangerous duality. Nonetheless, Tashi's personal anguish cannot be assuaged by Pierre's anthropological facts, the Old Man's analytical psychology, or Raye's empathy alone, so she premeditates killing the old circumciser M'Lissa. Tashi returns to Africa with a banner that reads, "If you lie to yourself about your own pain, you will be killed by those who claimed you enjoyed it." Ironically, M'Lissa is disdainful about her ancient practice, unfeelingly excising and infibulating the Olinkan girls, and even expects to be martyred, robbing Tashi of complete satisfaction. Walker, as embodied in *Possessing the Secret of Joy,* speaks more to the tribal mothers who she believes subject their daughters to perpetual lies, familiar tortures, and to the numerous murders of the spirit.

Walker's novel, detractors say, is overwrought sensationalism and polemics and should not be read as a fact-based anthropological study of FGM, in decline since 1920. Nevertheless, Walker's feminist ideology in *Possessing the Secret of Joy* has had an impact on FGM legislation here and cultural interventions abroad. But it tends to subsume the myriad of issues facing African women into the reductionist's view they are only mutilated genitals. Hence, the "yuck factor" eclipses productive debate. On the other hand, the cultural relativists believe tribal customs are an integral part of each society and should be observed but not interfered with. In the mid-twentieth century their controversial views superseded the late-nineteenth-century Social Darwinians who classified societies on the basis of race. Regrettably, when First World organizations attack tribal practices perceived as objectionable, nationalistic backlashes occur. Moreover, the notion of women as oppressed victims of men becomes questionable in some cultures where the social interaction in FGC builds sisterhoods and elevates their tribal status, says Efua Dorkenoo in *Cutting the Rose.* Critics contend that Walker's *Possessing the Secret of Joy* created an explosive topic with some misrepresentation and started a mass media trend toward First World voyeurism, leaving to be desired practical approaches to address human rights and health issues.

Possessing the Secret of Joy is about one woman's struggle with her African heritage and her right to self-determination beyond cultural constraints. It is not a factual anthropologist's case study but rather has the emotional power of literature. Even as sensationalized cultural criticism, it has added to the general dialogue on human rights and health issues. In principle, it foregrounds a number of issues of cultural, medical, and legal importance. It shows women complicit in a world run by male ideologies, culture intersecting with gender and health issues, and Walker's ethical basis for a controversial worldwide stance. In a postscript Walker addresses her reader, saying she does not know where her African ancestors came from, but she claims Tashi as her sister. While *Possessing the Secret of Joy* powerfully addresses FGM and highlights AIDS, for some her Western feminist approach remains problematic. In the end, Tashi's friend Mbati reflects on the colonialist memoir, Ricciardi's *African Saga,* underscoring Walker's interpretation of possessing the secret of joy: "Oh, I say. These settler cannibals. Why don't they just steal our land, mine our gold, chop down our forests, pollute our rivers, enslave us to work on their farms, fuck us, devour our flesh and leave us alone? Why must they also write about how much joy we possess?" At Tashi's execution, her friends and family hold a sign: "RESISTANCE IS THE SECRET OF JOY!" And only after dying, when her divided selves unite into her whole Self, has Tashi resisted what is evil (the power over her) to possess the secret of joy.

SYNOPSIS OF THE NOVEL

In Walker's *Possessing the Secret of Joy* there are seven main characters, and every few pages the viewpoint changes with each new speaker. Tashi, who is a peripheral character in *The Color Purple,* has shown allegiance to her Olinkan people by having the tribal marks cut onto her face and by having the female genital cutting ceremony. The book begins in a flashback when the imaginative Tashi, who is now an American, reflects on what her life has become. Telling the parable of the panthers, Tashi sets the tone for the whole book, and she moves the plot along by intermittently telling myths and stories. Raised in Olinka, Tashi's sister, Dura, died after a ceremonial genital cutting ritual. The African American missionary's children, Olivia and Adam, befriend Tashi. Adam becomes her lover, breaking tribal taboos. Adam also meets Lisette, a white French Algerian missionary, with whom he shares stories of the Olinkan culture. Tashi, in the name of Olinkan pride, has the circumciser M'Lissa excise and infibulate her, above the protests of her Christian mother, Adam, and Olivia. By doing this, she intends to join in solidarity with the other women, whom she envisions as completely strong and invincible African women. Days after the operation, Tashi is told to sit up and walk a few steps—her own proud walk has become a permanent shuffle. It takes 15 minutes to urinate now. Her menstrual cramps last half the month because it is nearly impossible for flow to pass through so tiny an aperture. The residual flow that does not find its way out and is not reabsorbed into her body has nowhere to go; so the odor of soured blood follows her around. Tashi's friend Olivia observes, "That her soul had been dealt a mortal blow was plain for anyone who dared look into her eyes."

Adam marries his friend, the once proud and lively Tashi, who is now heartbreakingly slowed by pain, and he takes her back to the United States. Living biculturally, Tashi cannot rationalize the emotional anguish she experiences daily in the name of her tribal leader's call for Olinkan pride, so she sees several psychiatrists. The first one tells her Negro women cannot be cured "because they can never bring themselves to blame their mothers." Tashi still thinks of herself as an African woman, not an American Negro. Another psychiatrist, Lisette's white uncle (the Old Man or Mzee), tries to help Tashi in Switzerland with art therapy and by analyzing her dreams, which she cannot share with her husband. When the Old Man dies, the black feminist Raye becomes her therapist. Tashi explains to her how their African leader mandated FGM from one generation to the next through a sacred tribal code, there being a strong cultural taboo against speaking of it to outsiders. The act was designed to keep the female body pure by cutting out the dual female soul that interferes with male domination. If a woman is not circumcised, the myth goes, her unclean parts will grow long and touch her thighs. Unremedied, warn the elders, who act as if they have recently witnessed this evil, no man can enter this masculine woman, who arouses herself. The circumcised women do not remember having vaginal lips or a clitoris, so they laugh and jeer at the monstrous "tail"; circumcised girls run from "the demon." The tribe passes on unverified beliefs because the old ways must be kept. Tashi, who had been a young orgasmic girl with Adam, gave up her sexuality to preserve the old ways.

In America, Adam and Tashi have a son, Benny, born retarded from passing through the birth canal narrowed by FGM. Unable to bear further pain, Tashi then aborts a subsequent pregnancy. Adam later becomes reacquainted with the free-spirited Lisette, and they become lovers, seeing each other on his biannual visits to Paris. Together they have a child, Pierre, which enrages the dispirited Tashi. Pierre, unlike Benny, is bright and inquisitive; he studies black American literature and decides to go to school in America. His mother has died, and he wants to become closer to his father. Tashi feels threatened and attacks

Pierre. Tashi returns to Olinka when she reads about M'Lissa's becoming a venerated symbol of Olinkan pride. In an elaborate scheme, the tortured Tashi, now in advanced middle age, plots her revenge. She seeks an audience with the venerated circumciser M'Lissa, and over a period of several weeks they talk. Tashi ritually washes her intended victim, who taunts her for foolishly submitting to circumcision. M'Lissa is prepared to become a martyr, and Tashi smothers her with a pillow as she attends her. She is indicted for murder.

Tashi is imprisoned in Olinka and put on trial for killing M'Lissa. Her family and friends are there to support her, and Adam reflects on how he has witnessed his wife's hell on earth. The prison also houses a whole floor of AIDS patients waiting to die. Many believe they contracted AIDS in an experiment, like the Tuskegee Syphilis Study, when scientists vaccinated them for polio. In the end, Tashi grows weary of the plodding trial and confesses to the murder; nevertheless, the trial, a media circus, goes on. At her execution by firing squad on the soccer field, Tashi is released from her tortured soul for "killing someone who, many years ago, killed me." Adam, Olivia, Benny, Pierre, Raye, and Mbati hold a banner: RESISTANCE IS THE SECRET OF JOY!

TOPICS FOR ORAL AND WRITTEN DISCUSSION

1. Compare and contrast Kesey's Big Chief and Walker's Tashi as examples of how mental and physical illness derive from a specific culture as well as from disease. How have *One Flew Over the Cuckoo's Nest* and *Possessing the Secret of Joy* had the power to change the system?

2. With increasing global awareness of human rights violations effected through literature and organizations such as Amnesty International, the World Health Organization, and the United Nations, why do certain cultural practices like FGM and stoning continue? What are cultural relativism and Social Darwinism? Relate the culturally entrenched habit of smoking (also called the "brown plague") to FGM.

3. Reflecting on Tashi's painful physical abnormalities, describe how it affects her mental state as she describes it to her various mental professionals. How in particular does the Jungian analytical psychologist work with her to ultimately achieve her Self?

4. While the Olinkan male leader appears to mandate FGM, how and why are the tribal women complicit in maintaining the ritual?

5. Compare and contrast the tortured Tashi and the free-spirited Lisette. How do these two women interrelate?

6. Discuss how Pierre and Benny represent their respective mother's autonomy and inadequacies.

7. How does Walker, an imaginative storyteller, use symbols (Tashi, M'Lissa, termite hill, clay), parables, and myths to tell Tashi's story and to teach a lesson?
8. As highlighted in *Possessing the Secret of Joy*, how has the Tuskegee Syphilis Study impacted the question of trust in treating AIDS in Africa?
9. What is M'Lissa's perspective on FGM and her actions, as told to Tashi before her death?
10. On Tashi's journey toward wholeness, what is her resistance to in teaching us about possessing the secret of joy?

BIBLIOGRAPHY

Amnesty International. Universal Declaration of Human Rights (1948). http://www.amnestyusa.org/udhr.html.

Baartman, Saartjie. *Tragic Venus*. Special South Africans. http://www.zar.co.za/baartman.

Chase, Cheryl. "'Cultural Practice' or 'Reconstructive Surgery'? U.S. Genital Cutting, the Intersex Movement, and Medical Double Standards." In *Genital Cutting and Transnational Sisterhood: Disputing U.S. Polemics*, ed. Stanlie M. James and Claire C. Robertson, 126–51. Champaign: University of Illinois Press, 2002.

Dorkenoo, Efua. *Cutting the Rose: Female Genital Mutilation, the Practice and Its Prevention*. London: Minority Rights Group, 1994. Emphasizes cultural context.

Gilman, Charlotte Perkins. *The Crux*. In *The Charlotte Perkins Gilman Reader*, ed. Ann J. Lane. Charlottesville, Va.: University of Virginia Press, 1999.

Jung, Carl. *Man and His Symbols*. New York: Dell, 1968.

National Research Council. *Understanding Violence against Women*. Washington, D.C.: National Academy Press, 1996.

Ngugi wa Thiong'o. *The River Between*. Portsmouth, N.H.: Heinemann, 1965.

Ricciardi, Mirella. *African Saga*. London: Collins, 1982.

Robertson, Claire C. "Getting Beyond the Ew! Factor: Rethinking U.S. Approaches to African Female Genital Cutting." In *Genital Cutting and Transnational Sisterhood: Disputing U.S. Polemics*, ed. Stanlie M. James and Claire C. Robertson, 54–86. Champaign: University of Illinois Press, 2002.

Walker, Alice. *Possessing the Secret of Joy*. New York: HBJ, 1992.

Walker, Alice, and Pratibha Parmar, eds. *Warrior Marks: Female Genital Mutilation and the Sexual Blinding of Women*. New York: Harcourt, 1993. Book and video.

World Health Organization. Female Genital Mutilation, June 2000. http://www.who.int/mediacentre/factsheets/fs241/en/.

SUGGESTED FURTHER READING

Atwood, Margaret. *The Handmaid's Tale*. New York: Fawcett, 1986. Power relations, science and sexuality, women's health.

Chopin, Kate. *The Awakening*. New York: Bard-Avon, 1972. A desperate woman swims out to sea.

Conrad, Joseph. *Heart of Darkness*. 1901. New York: Penguin, 1999. Also: The Literature Network, http://www.online-literature.com. Marlow travels to the dark interior of the Congo searching for his European self in Mr. Kurtz.

Eugenides, Jeffrey. *Middlesex*. New York: Farrar, 2002. Won the Pulitzer Prize.

Hemingway, Ernest. "Hills Like White Elephants." In *On Doctoring*, ed. Richard Reynolds and John Stone. New York: Simon & Schuster, 2001.

Kassindja, Fauziya. *Do They Hear You When You Cry?* New York: Delacorte, 1998.

Klass, Perri. "Invasions." In *A Not Entirely Benign Procedure*. New York: Signet, 1988.

Selzer, Richard. "Abortion." In *Mortal Lessons*. New York: Simon & Schuster, 1987.

Thiam, Awa. *Speak Out, Black Sisters: Feminism and Oppression in Black Africa*. London: Pluto, 1978. Graphic descriptions of FGM; cultural perspectives.

Walker, Alice. "Abortion." In *You Can't Keep a Good Woman Down*. Orlando, Fla: Harcourt Brace and Jovanovich, 1988.

———. "Advancing Luna—and Ida B. Wells." In *You Can't Keep a Good Woman Down: Short Stories*, 85–104. New York: Harvest-Harcourt, 1981. A white woman raped by a black civil rights leader remains silent to advance the cause.

———. *The Color Purple*. New York: Washington Square Press, 1982.

Whitney, Ruth Linnea. *Slim*. Dallas: Southern Methodist University Press, 2003. Novel about AIDS in Africa.

5

End of Life—Disease and Death: An Analysis of John Updike's *Rabbit at Rest* and Margaret Edson's *Wit*

INTRODUCTION

Ken Kesey, Alice Walker, John Updike, and Margaret Edson all write stories in which culture plays a significant role. In each of their featured works a particular gender, ethnic, social, and professional group can be observed through the main character's eyes. Indeed, each story incorporates clashing cultural extremes. While chapter 4 clearly shows these profound human differences, chapter 5 focuses more on our commonality of moving inexorably toward death. The quality of our passage may depend on how we care for our bodies, minds, and spirits. John Updike chronicles his main character's lifestyle and its consequences in a quartet of famous novels: *Rabbit, Run* (1960), *Rabbit Redux* (1971), *Rabbit is Rich* (1981), and *Rabbit at Rest* (1990). By updating Rabbit's life every decade—from his twenties to his sixties—Updike portrays his high school basketball star's turning into a self-indulgent car salesman. Updike's everyman lives through the 1960s "decade of discontent," the 1970s "Me Decade," and the AIDS-plagued 1980s, emphasizing the health consequences of the sexual habits of the time. Years of self-abuse lead to Rabbit's rapid decline during the last years of his life, leaving him little reason to live.

In *Rabbit at Rest* Updike artfully dissects middle-class dysfunctional life, giving a powerful cultural critique of America. He juxtaposes technical and metaphorical language to describe Rabbit's various diseases, symptomatically expressed as morbidly depressed, chest pains, and a bloated body worn "like a set of blankets the decades have brought one by one," all leading to a fatal heart attack. *Rabbit at Rest* illuminates specifically how untimely deaths occur when contemporary medicine records life expectancy at an all-time high. Other topics it covers are cocaine addiction, patient experience, family relationships, and American hedonism.

Dr. Vivian Bearing's courageous and protracted death from cancer in Margaret Edson's play *Wit* counters Rabbit's self-inflicted early demise from heart disease in John Updike's *Rabbit at Rest*. In the Pulitzer Prize-winning play, poetry, science, and death interrelate for Bearing, a John Donne professor and stage 4 metastatic cancer patient. She becomes a research subject to contribute to knowledge, even without therapeutic value for her. During eight months of chemotherapy the dedicated scholar turns from erudite to vulnerable. She has only one hospital visitor, having valued ideas over personal relationships. Special insights on the medical professional-patient relationship come through two supporting characters: the compassionate nurse who knows how to emotionally nurture and the unfeeling young research doctor with so-called detached concern. Since increasing technology and managed-care time constraints tend to distance doctor and patient, the play redefines the terms *empathy* and *compassion*. It asks, how do you treat the dying patient? What do you say to soothe rather than to add insult to injury?

Edson, by looking at doctor paternalism, patient autonomy, and human rights in clinical trials, puts the American medical system on trial in *Wit*. She shows, in the art of medicine, how hope, kindness, and a sympathetic touch can interface with research ethics. In a layered approach using metaphysical poetry to shed light on twenty-first-century medical research, *Wit* also ponders serious philosophical and religious questions, asking how can we live a fulfilling life by giving and receiving love? Furthermore, in our medicalized system of dying, how can we realize a good death? *Wit* dramatically evokes a spirituality to bring catharsis: "And death shall be no more, Death thou shalt die" (John Donne, *Devotions upon Emergent Occasions,* London, 1624). Notwithstanding the poetic revelation that everlasting life follows death, the play's themes underscore the present-day need for better trained end-of-life and palliative-care medical professionals. Lastly, *Wit,* by evoking laughter and tears, allows us to take an unflinching look at disease, dying, and death.

JOHN UPDIKE'S
RABBIT AT REST (1990)

Food to the indolent is poison, not sustenance.
—*Life and Times of Frederick Douglass*
(*Rabbit at Rest* epigraph)

HISTORICAL CONTEXT

John Hoyer Updike was born in Reading, Pennsylvania, in 1932 but grew up in nearby Shillington. At 13 he moved to an isolated family farmhouse near Plowville, Pennsylvania. His mother, an unpublished writer, encouraged him to read and to write; his father was a math teacher. In youth Updike suffered from an embarrassing stutter and disfiguring psoriasis, the latter about which he subsequently wrote in "From the Journal of a Leper." In this gripping autobiographical story Updike in finely wrought prose chronicles his young adult character's humiliating life, feeling "lusty [but] loathsome to love" (*Problems*, 203). After he undergoes modern medical treatments, his skin is cured but his new perfection causes him to become narcissistic. Ironically, he loses the things he had valued most: a lover and his artistic ability as a potter.

Updike, president and covaledictorian of his Shillington High School class of 1950, said he entered Harvard "a true tabula rasa," absorbing whatever it offered (*New York Times*, 4 July 1965). He wrote, edited, and drew cartoons for its famous humor magazine, the *Harvard Lampoon*. After he graduated with an English degree in 1954, he and his wife, Mary Pennington, moved to Oxford, England, where Updike studied art at the Ruskin School of Drawing and Fine Arts. In 1955 his first job was as a staff writer for the prestigious *New Yorker*. Two years later Updike became a full-time writer, moving to Ipswich, Massachusetts. His first book, *The Carpenter Hen and Other Tame Creatures*, a collection of poetry, was published in 1958. The next year he published his first novel, *The Poorhouse Fair* (1959). During the 17 years Updike lived in Ipswich, he keenly observed its suburban couples, writing about their sexual antics in *Couples* (1968). Adultery and divorce continued as a theme in his *Rabbit* tetralogy, which he confessed in a 1996 talk at Franklin and Marshall College in

Lancaster, Pennsylvania, was inspired out of jealousy for Jack Kerouac's popular *On the Road*. Updike, however, rather than motivating readers to "hit the road," told the audience his novels illustrate that "the road has problems, too" (Knapp).

The prolific John Updike has published more than 50 volumes, including poetry, essays, novels, and short stories. He writes literary criticism and reviews and has written drama and a libretto. Although he uses mythology and rewrites ancient history, Updike constantly scrutinizes contemporary American culture, asking readers to recon-sider preconceptions of human values, especially those relating to sex, art, and religion. Updike's eloquent rendering of his characters' flaws simultaneously connects the reader to humanity and affirms its worth. He continues to write autobiographically, as most authors do, and has received many honors and earned many national awards, including two Pulitzer Prizes for fiction, for *Rabbit is Rich* (1982) and *Rabbit at Rest* (1991). In 2003 Updike was honored with the National Humanities Medal for his significant contribution to the humanities in America. Besides paralleling Harry (Rabbit) Angstrom's life for more than 40 years, Updike also maintains an alter ego in his series on the Jewish American novelist Harry Bech. After Updike and his first wife, Mary Pennington, divorced, he married Martha Bernhard in 1977. He is the father of four grown children and lives with Martha in rural Mas-sachusetts, near Boston.

Updike gives a powerful cultural critique of American life in *Rabbit at Rest*. The specific medical issue it addresses is how his everyman protagonist, Harry "Rabbit" Angstrom, has abused his body, mind, and spirit for most of his life, culminating in a fatal heart attack. Up-dike's keen language documents the events contributing to Rabbit's heart disease, leading to his death at the age of 55 when the average life expectancy exceeds 82 (IRS table 1). In fact, geriatric experts once viewed over age 85 as the genetically programmed "old of the old," but twenty-first-century records exceed 120, with centenarians being the fastest growing segment of the population. To understand how Rabbit diminished his potential life expectancy, study the amazing hu-man heart. Simplistically put, the four-chambered heart, with a com-plex of arteries, veins, and valves, is a dynamic double-pump-action organ with an all-important pacemaking sinoatrial node. In 100,000 rhythmic beats each day the right side reoxygenates the blood in the lungs, then the left side returns 14,000 pints of blood daily to the entire body from head to toe. Indeed, a healthy heart, looking like a valentine, is a masterwork of nature that humans relate to feelings, often referring to it as the seat of the soul. Even more poetically, in the words of Yale doctor-writer Richard Selzer, "The heart is purest theatre . . . throbbing in its cage palpably as any nightingale. It quickens in response to the emotions. Let danger threaten, and the thrilling heart skips a beat or two and tightrope-walks arrhythmically before lurching back into the forceful thump of fight or flight. And all the while we feel it, hear it even—we, its stage and its audience" (Selzer, *Mortal Lessons*, 63). Ah, the heart. It's a marvel!

However, when the heart for any number of reasons fails to deliver its oxygen-laden and nutrient-rich blood all over the body, including to the lungs, liver, kidneys, and the brain, it causes a number of systems' failures. In particular, when the brain has been deprived of oxygen for as little as two to four minutes, brain death occurs, as partly determined by an electroencephalogram (EEG) reading. Brain death, pronounceable by a doctor, is also a legal term (*see* chapter 2, *Coma*, on transplantations). Conscientious people who heed the age-old warning *memento mori* can do a number of things to maintain heart health and to extend life expectancy. Simply put, the quality and length of life may depend on managing diet, exercise, and stress. The American Heart Association's (AHA) specific recommendations for monitoring heart health include taking periodic blood pressure, cholesterol, and electrocardiogram (EKG) readings. On October 28, 2003, *Circulation* reported that a new blood test measuring apolipoprotein B (ApoB) may be a better indicator of heart attack risk factors than taking LDL cholesterol levels. Heart attack (acute myocardial infarction, or MI), to paraphrase the AHA's definition, occurs when there is a blockage in the heart's arteries that reduces or completely cuts off blood supply to a portion of the heart, causing a clot to form that totally stops coronary artery blood flow. To prevent irreversible heart muscle damage, medical help must be called immediately; therefore, it is important to know these AHA heart attack warning signs:

- Uncomfortable pressure, fullness, squeezing, or pain in the center of the chest lasting more than a few minutes.
- Pain spreading to the shoulders, neck, or arms. The pain may be mild to intense. It may feel like pressure, tightness, burning, or heavy weight. It may be located in the chest, upper abdomen, neck, jaw, or inside the arms or shoulders.
- Chest discomfort with lightheadedness, fainting, sweating, nausea, or shortness of breath.
- Anxiety, nervousness, and/or cold, sweaty skin.

- Paleness or pallor.
- Increased or irregular heart rate.
- Feeling of impending doom.

The signs may come and go, as Updike chronicles in *Rabbit at Rest*, and not all of them may appear in every attack. Because they seem to manifest in men and women differently, symptoms specific to women should not be overlooked. If there is no breathing or pulse (cardiopulmonary arrest), cardiopulmonary resuscitation (CPR) must be started immediately and 911 emergency help called. If an automated external defibrillator is nearby with a trained operator, it should be used immediately to restart the heart. Only a doctor will make the actual diagnosis of a heart attack after a physical examination including patient medical history, an EKG that ascertains heart abnormalities, and a blood test detecting abnormal enzyme levels. Current hospital practice for a patient who has suffered cardiac arrest and for whom oxygen has been temporarily cut off is to cool down the body to 89.6 to 93.2 degrees Fahrenheit after the heart has started beating again. This act helps preserve brain function by lowering inflammation. Research is under way to develop a high-density lipoprotein (HDL) therapy for removing arterial cholesterol, referred to as sort of a "liquid Drano," reports the *Journal of American Medical Association* (4 November 2003).

In *How We Die* Sherwin B. Nuland, Yale surgeon and professor of the history of medicine, portrays how 40 years earlier the "patterns of living that we now know are suicidal" had seduced a construction executive into a classic heart attack. Smoking, "great slabs of bacon," and a sedentary lifestyle led to his patient's hospital arrival one hot and humid evening, "complaining of a constricting pressure behind his breastbone that seemed to radiate up into his throat and down his left arm." After a heavy dinner, a few smokes, and an upsetting phone call from his youngest child, the patient had turned ashen and sweaty with an irregular pulse (Nuland, 3–4). An EKG revealed an infarction (damage to the heart) but the patient appeared stabilized and was admitted for observation. When Nuland, then a third-year medical student, went to take his new patient's history:

> [H]e suddenly threw his head back and bellowed out a wordless roar that seemed to rise up out of his throat from somewhere deep within his stricken heart. He hit his balled fists with startling force up against the front of his chest in

a single synchronous thump, just as his face and neck, in the flash of an instant, turned swollen and purple. His eyes seemed to have pushed themselves forward in one bulging thrust, as though they were trying to leap out of his head. He took one immensely long, gurgling breath, and died. (Nuland, 5)

Dr. Nuland subsequently tried to revive his patient with an extreme intervention, unsuccessfully. His dramatic and concise description of cardiac arrest contrasts, however, with the considerably more methodical and extensive ways to diagnose and means to treat heart disease. For example, the Framingham Heart Study, following 4,000 Massachusetts men for more than 40 years, learned that 25 percent of its subjects' heart attacks went undetected until an annual EKG discovered heart damage. Generally in these so-called silent heart attacks arteriosclerosis (arteries progressively narrowed by cholesterol plaque) causes a chronic oxygen and nutrient shortage to the heart, generating a protest from the heart or crushing angina pain. A damaged heart can lead to disabilities such as congestive heart failure or irregular heartbeat arrhythmias. Risk factors for coronary artery disease that usually can be managed include high blood pressure and cholesterol, diabetes, smoking, lack of exercise, and obesity. Someone dies every 33 seconds from heart disease, and Americans suffer 1.1 million heart attacks every year. In 2003, cardiologists in Los Angeles at Cedars-Sinai Medical Center and their colleagues in Sweden reported that they were conducting research to develop a vaccine, administered routinely to children, against coronary artery disease (arteriosclerosis). It works by triggering an antibody to control infection and inflammation caused by plaque buildup as well as blood clot formation leading to heart attacks and strokes.

The additional good news is that studies of centenarians provide a powerful tool for learning how to extend longevity. Both the Living to 100 Life Expectancy Calculator and the Alliance on Aging relate practical approaches to a healthier, longer life. Preventive measures include keeping an optimistic attitude to manage stress, avoiding tobacco and excessive alcohol, and maintaining an ideal weight. Formerly called the "silent epidemic," obesity is defined as 20 percent above ideal weight or a body mass index of 30 or more. According to the CDC, in 2003 obesity affected more than 20 percent of American adults and 25 percent of children. Even one in four pets is overweight. Harvard surgeon Atul Gawande's essay "The Man Who Couldn't Stop

Eating" describes the soaring popularity of a radical procedure to lose weight. He observed a patient, housebound and in failing health, who underwent a Roux-en-Y gastric-bypass operation "intended to control a person's will—to manipulate a person's innards so that he will not overeat again." Paradoxically, general anesthesia put the obese patient at further risk, including possible respiratory failure and heart attack, wound infections, hernias, and even death might ensue. In the two-hour operation, the patient's stomach was reduced from holding a quart-sized meal to holding an ounce-sized meal. For this particular 54-year-old, 428-pound, 5'7" patient, recovery from anesthesia was difficult. He became delirious, and his kidneys stopped working. Three weeks later Gawande visited him at home: he had lost 40 pounds, but he wheezed and eating a spoonful of scrambled eggs "made him so full it hurt, he said, really hurt . . . 'like something was ripping,' and he threw it back up." Before the surgery the patient had high blood pressure and cholesterol as well as diabetes. Life for him had become nonexistent because sleep apnea deprived him of a good night's sleep; and skin folds, boils, and infections made good hygiene and sexual relationships impossible. He was no longer able to earn a living for his family. Why did he eat so much, Gawande asked him? "Eating felt good instantaneously," replied the patient whose worst habit involved eating enormous quantities: "I was never hungry" (Gawande, 162–5).

The American Society for Bariatric Surgery estimates more than 100,000 patients will have gotten obesity-related operations in 2003, mostly gastric-bypass procedures despite the conservative statistic that 300 of them will die within three months (International Bariatric Surgery Registry). Incredibly, as many as one in five bariatric surgery patients will cheat the operation, eating numerous small, high-calorie meals to regain the weight. It is not an easy fix. Long-term lifestyle changes may be more effective. Fifteen million Americans are morbidly obese, and overeating is a hard habit to break—even when it is done to its painful conclusion of "dumping" or vomiting. Gawande reports that research shows while it is hard for adults to break bad eating habits, obese children from age six to 12 who receive behavioral training are more successful. In 2003 the CDC declared obesity the number two preventable health threat facing Americans, following smoking.

Americans are not only getting heavier, they are getting older. Demographic studies indicate that by 2030 there will be 70 million Americans over age 65—that is one in five. Because of better preventive care and new medical treatments, the fastest-growing segment of the population is over age 85. Regardless of this achievement, the Alliance for

Aging Research says many of these patients will have several chronic medical conditions—diabetes, arthritis, and heart disease—requiring numerous medications. Medical schools heeding these demographic studies are revamping their core curricula to serve the mental and physical needs of the geriatric, diseased and dying patient.

Rabbit at Rest describes one man's late-twentieth-century lifestyle and consequential health problems, thereby giving a powerful cultural critique of American medical issues. By portraying Rabbit's bad lifestyle choices the novel clearly shows how individuals can improve their chances for a healthier, happier life. In the end, especially with the health-care needs of baby boomers flooding the system, it is urgent to ask: Are our medical professionals and institutions adequately prepared to meet all the demands? A 2003 opinion poll reflects the public's growing unease with a health-care system in critical condition that fails to provide adequate services, especially to the one in 10 uninsured children. Although $1.6 trillion went to health care annually, more than half of Americans favored moving toward a universal governmental policy covering everyone as opposed to the single- or employer-paid system. On December 8, 2003, President George W. Bush signed the historic Medicare bill into law, calling it "a great achievement of a compassionate government" to benefit 40 million elderly and disabled Americans with revamped prescription-drug coverage.

The purpose of this medical context is to provide useful background information focused specifically for discussing *Rabbit at Rest*. Therefore, the nature of this material is limited. Because medical practices and policies change rapidly, it is recommended that readers wanting additional information seek medical references for further study or consult their medical professionals, from whom they may obtain current and comprehensive material.

LITERARY ANALYSIS

Larry "Rabbit" Angstrom, the fictional antihero in the *Rabbit* quartet, and John Updike, his creator, led parallel lives. Both were born in the early 1930s and grew up around Reading, Pennsylvania. There, however, the similarities end. While Rabbit was a "beautiful brainless guy" whose glory days peaked at 18, Updike became a world-famous author, an ability seeded in a Harvard education. The *Rabbit* series derived from Updike's early blank verse poem "The Ex-Basketball Player," in which the speaker mocks the title character with no appreciable talents to transfer into the bigger world. The ex-jock Flick Webb accepts his mediocre fate as a small-town gas station pump-jockey. The townspeople who once lived vicariously through his high school accomplishments now give him only fleeting affirmation. Updike's skillful use of figurative language and images builds the contrast between Flick's lackluster adult life and his short-lived fame. The poem, replete with sports analogies, correlates Flick's cut-off, bleak future with having never learned a trade—the idiot just exists. After Updike wrote the poem in the 1950s, he imagined Flick's life further into the future, becoming the *Rabbit* quartet.

This analysis focuses on how Rabbit, an everyman middle-class, white Protestant male, reflects late-twentieth-century American culture and its growing medical issues. Rabbit experienced adolescent and young adult sexuality during the postwar boom of the mid-1940s through the 1950s. He was a married man and adulterer with a family during the hippie 1960s and the feminist 1970s (also called the age of discontent). In fact, author Tom Wolfe coined the term the "Me Decade" to describe the selfish seventies mentality, which Updike applied to the impulsive, sexually obsessed Rabbit who shirked commitment. By the time we catch up to Rabbit in *Rabbit at Rest,* it is now the AIDS-plagued 1980s, foreshadowing Updike's deep theme, "the blossoming and fruition of the seed of death we all carry inside us" (Oates, 449). The novel, covering the last nine-month period in the life of the racist, xenophobic, misogynist, and homophobic Rabbit Angstrom, is written in three chapters titled after his states of being: "Florida," "Pennsylvania," and "MI" (myocardial infarction).

In the first chapter the 6'3" Rabbit is 55 years old and 40 pounds overweight, making him late middle-aged and obese. He and his long-suffering wife Janice are semiretired in Florida. From the time they pick up their estranged son and his family at the airport "a sense of doom regrows its claws around his heart." Thereby, right from the beginning at their unpleasant and stressful family reunion, Updike artfully interweaves into the scene a classic symptom of heart disease, following it with a description of the gluttonous lifestyle supporting it. That is, Updike's omniscient narrator speaking for the brooding Rabbit fully orients descriptions of his stress, overeating, and depression to his angina pains, bloated body, and the frightening sensation there is "nothing under you but black space." Furthermore, Rabbit, insensitive to blacks, foreigners, women, and gays, becomes a focal point around which an understanding of an era develops. Having lived through the Cold War, Rabbit's burgeoning anticommunist ideology bursts when President Ronald Reagan tears down its symbol, the Berlin Wall. Young readers who see Presidents Bush and Putin embrace in solidarity in the twenty-first century are fascinated to hear parents describe their duck-and-cover desk drills during an age of nuclear bomb threats. Rabbit also lived into the war on drugs, unsafe sex, and AIDS concerns, leaving him with a sense of impending doom. Foretelling the age of terrorism, the novel references many air disasters, including the explosion of Pan Am 103 over Scotland. Like *Cuckoo's Nest*'s sexually promiscuous antihero Mack, Rabbit reflects the free-love culture by acting instinctually.

Updike weaves many cultural threads into *Rabbit at Rest*, namely historical, political, economical, religious, and social; but this analysis puts specific emphasis upon Rabbit's lifestyle with its consequential medical issues. In particular, Rabbit is best understood by looking at what he relates to the most: food, sex, and sports. He was an admired high school athlete who ate and had sex as much as he could. He is now an indolent aging junk-food addict who resides in the sex-phobic AIDS era. Rabbit is fixated on sports heroes who vicariously revive his glory days, such as football-baseball player Deion "Prime Time" Sanders who needs to be the star of the show. Then, in the Spring, Rabbit's egotism transfers wholly to baseball, as American as apple pie and heart disease. The Philadelphia Phillies all-star third baseman Mike Schmidt, whom the media calls a has-been, momentarily invigorates Rabbit by rallying to hit two home runs in the first two games of the season. Reflecting on his own 1950s glory days, Rabbit is not sustained for long, however, especially after the injured Schmidt retires at age 39.

In addition, the Pete Rose fiasco agitates Rabbit. Baseball Commissioner Bart Giamatti imposed a lifetime ban from baseball on Rose for gambling on his own team. Rabbit, whose "wasting muscles and accumulating fat" cause a serious health risk, parallels the deleterious diet-stress lifestyle that causes Giamatti's massive heart attack death. After an angioplasty following a first warning heart attack, Rabbit does not curb his insatiable eating habit, reduce his stress, or exercise. Rather, he rationalizes that unlike Giamatti *he* is a non-smoker. Adding insult to injury, his son, Nelson, removes the old blown-up Rabbit basketball photos at Springer Motors (the slender thread by which Rabbit's fragile ego was tethered). Later, after seeing his former lover Thelma, Rabbit soon returns to "a mood of stirred-up unsatisfied desire at whose fringes licks the depressing idea that nothing matters very much, we'll all soon be dead." By personifying depression, Updike's choice of just the right word *(le mot juste)* brings acute understanding of Rabbit's chronically down state of mind and wilting ego.

Each successive novel in the *Rabbit* tetralogy informs the next, making the series recommended reading to trace Rabbit's lifestyle and its consequences. Nonetheless *Rabbit at Rest* read alone fascinates by showing Rabbit and the century winding down together. Like his progenitor in "The Ex-Basketball Player," Rabbit's failure to upgrade his education and skills causes him to unconsciously ride cultural tides until his energy gives out. He is "too old for flux." He is also too close to his own predicaments for self-awareness and too shortsighted to view change as an opportunity for renewal (e.g., the birth of his granddaughter is "another nail in the coffin"). Suffering from hardening both of the arteries and of ideology makes Rabbit an average aging American male, in Updike's view, who tends to react instinctually rather than to act rationally with forethought. As a result, Rabbit's unrestrained sexuality in the sensual American climate leads to adultery and illegitimate children. In addition, feeling spiritually alienated in an increasingly godless, amoral culture, he fears death, hedonistically living for the moment. In his mid-fifties the utterly flawed Rabbit must face the consequences of his past, such as his baby Becky's bathtub death, to live out a mediocre life with implacable regret. There will be no golden years.

In the end Rabbit, desolate after having fled to Florida following a tryst with his daughter-in-law, Pru, comes to terms with his situation. With the smell of death all around, he does not have the will and the necessary reserve to override his present state of mental and physical decline. Even though Updike's superior mentality has breathed life into Rabbit up to this point, he is now "ready to succumb to the heaviness of being." Conversely, Janice, influenced by the movie *Working Girl*, achieves independence by embracing feminism. Because of Rabbit's infidelity with Pru, Janice's disinterest in his well-being shifts her attention elsewhere, motivating her to become a successful realtor. After running Springer Motors into the ground, Nelson attends rehab for cocaine addiction. He achieves a new life despite his mother's earlier denial and enabling and his father's refusal to continue family therapy. In the final analysis, Rabbit's lack of inner resources causes his inability to change and to embrace life, leaving him in a state of perpetual male angst (n.b., Updike's surname choice of Angstrom). Even an attempt at redemption (a basketball pickup game with street kids) fails. The *Rabbit* series is an epic American tragedy, and in *Rabbit at Rest* Updike keenly portrays not only an unsympathetic, aging American male but a disintegrating society at large. It is fitting that Rabbit unsentimentally accepts his fate and dies just after thinking one last thought: "Enough."

But life goes on in Brewer without Rabbit, as Updike explains in the novella, "Rabbit Remembered," a postscript to the series published in *Licks of Love* (2000). Now approaching the new millennium, Janice has married Rabbit's nemesis (Thelma's former husband), and Nelson is a divorced father and a drug-free social worker. Through them Updike somewhat redeems a culture seen in decline, thereby expressing hope the old and new generations can change for the better. Ultimately, by treating the subject of disease and death in *Rabbit at Rest* so artistically, Updike triumphs over its dire reality enough to make Rabbit exemplar of a deteriorating body. The book thusly teaches us a lesson in health-care issues and ethics. But it is too late for Rabbit, whose rapid decline is metaphorically America's story. However, in our medically flourishing times, Updike's wise reader who identifies with Rabbit's mistakes may achieve a cathartic revelation. That is, as in the realm of all great tragedy, he or she may be transformed by the novel's events enough to embrace contemporary medical education and to adopt a healthful lifestyle. Otherwise, if Rabbit represents the average man (or woman) who does not take personal responsibility for his health, the real American tragedy extends beyond the pages of Updike's book.

SYNOPSIS OF THE NOVEL

It is the end of December 1988. Harry "Rabbit" Angstrom is a white, middle-class, married male with a dysfunctional family, whose years of self-abuse surface in this last novel of Updike's famous *Rabbit* series. Now 55, he is a grandfather who has lived anxiously through the end of the Cold War and into the War on Drugs with both his family and country still in crisis. The social backdrop includes political references to the Ronald Reagan and George H. W. Bush administrations and multiple death references, including to AIDS, Roy Orbison, and Pan Am 103 exploding over Scotland. Thus, the novel's tone is elegiac, echoing the past decades of discontent and foreshadowing Rabbit's demise. Rabbit and his wife Janice meet their son, Nelson, and his wife, Pru, and their two children, Roy (age 4) and Judy (almost 9), at the Miami airport. Right away the family situation becomes stressed when Rabbit takes Judy to buy candy and then cannot find his car; later there are more quarrels over nixing a Disneyland trip and making sleeping arrangements. Additional problems arise because the drug-addicted Nelson has taken over the family car sales business inherited by Janice, but he lacks the competency to manage it. One conflict after another stresses Rabbit's plaque-narrowed arteries. Three days later Rabbit saves Judy from drowning after their sailboat capsizes; he has a mild heart attack and is taken to the hospital. While floating in a world of Demerol, Rabbit learns he has a typical aging American heart, "tired and stiff and full of crud." The whole family visits him. The doctor explains the diagnosis, then discusses interventions like angioplasty and bypass grafting surgery. He recommends a new dietary plan. Nelson's family returns home to Brewer, Pennsylvania.

In part 2 it is mid-April, and Rabbit and Janice return to springtime Brewer. While Janice looks for a job, Rabbit reflects on his dismal past, visiting his ill lover, Thelma, whose disease, systemic lupus erythematosus, has depleted her family's income and spirit. Rabbit learns from her that Nelson is a cocaine addict, causing Rabbit additional worry about AIDS. He visits Springer Motors, discovering Nelson has taken down his old basketball star photos, has hired a woman, and that the homosexual AIDS-inflicted bookkeeper refuses to show him the books. Janice takes Penn State extension real estate courses, while Rabbit frets about Nelson. They talk about Nelson's drug addiction and bleeding the company then receive threatening calls from his unpaid drug dealers. They are guilt-ridden for raising Nelson to be so troubled. Rabbit asks his friend Charlie Stavros for advice, and they discuss Brewer's drug problem at large. Late one evening after the drugged-up Nelson attacks Pru, she calls Janice and Rabbit for help. They are divisive in their approach to Nelson.

In mid-May Rabbit undergoes an angioplasty, fully described in the novel, to widen the narrowing arteries to his heart. He feels sandbagged when he learns that what was described to him as a simple Mickey Mouse procedure requires the surgeon, two attending nurses, and a bypass team standing by. His nurse may even be his illegitimate daughter. Later Rabbit resents Charlie Stavros for advising and consoling Janice. Janice fires the bookkeeper, Lyle, and Rabbit feels threatened by her taking charge of the business rather than managing their household. Dr. Breit tells Rabbit his angioplasty was not totally successful because there is still 80 percent blockage in his right coronary artery. Also, because he may have suffered a postoperative MI, Dr. Breit strongly recommends the more drastic coronary artery bypass graft. "[T]hey split you right open like a coconut and rip veins out of your legs," Rabbit tells his sister, Mim, during a depressing phone call.

He is distrustful of Dr. Breit, suspecting he has a surgical quota to achieve. Janice, too busy with classes, has not visited him in the hospital, but when she does, she relates how the car lot revenue has gone to Nelson's drug habit and Lyle's AIDS medicines. Rabbit's former lover, Thelma, and her husband, Ronnie, visit Rabbit. She is demoralized from dealing with her disease. Nelson goes to a nearby rehab facility, learning the Narcotics Anonymous first principle of "admitting you are powerless and dependent on a higher power." Rabbit, released from the hospital into Pru's care because Janice is busy taking real estate tests, makes love to her. Back running the car lot, Rabbit uncovers Nelson's malfeasance and reinstalls his own enlarged high school basketball photos on the wall. Rabbit, whose strange brand of religion has been replaced by cynicism, reluctantly attends family counseling. To Rabbit's chagrin, Nelson, who reminds him of Hitler and sounds like a minister, hugs him for the first time in their adult lives.

In part 3, appropriately called "MI," Rabbit marches as Uncle Sam in the Mount Judge Fourth of July parade. He attends Thelma's funeral, where her husband Ronnie argues with him. In early August the Toyota representative visits Rabbit on the lot and cancels the franchise. Janice warns Rabbit about his health habits, and Nelson returns from rehab, his life plan being to change "A day at a time with the help of a higher power." Janice and Nelson dash Rabbit's high expectations about running the business again. They want to get grant money to turn it into a drug treatment center. The Toyota loan is paid with a second mortgage on the property. When Janice talks of moving in with Nelson and Pru to save money, the latter tells Janice of her affair with Rabbit, who then takes off on a marathon drive to their Florida condo. Eating junk food along the way, he learns on the radio of Bart Giamatti's death at age 51. Living alone in the condo, Rabbit becomes depressed, making an appointment with Dr. Morris, who advises him on a health plan: eat right, walk, and "[g]et interested in something outside yourself, and your heart will stop talking to you." Nelson, Pru, and Janice are moving forward with their lives, while Rabbit reflects on the past but tries new food and exercise regimens. Healthy foods are unpalatable to him, but as a former athlete he has chosen to walk. While on one trek he plays a pickup basketball game with teenagers. Back at the condo, he tries the food again. The next day, playing a stressful one-on-one pickup game with a young black man, Rabbit suffers a massive heart attack. Janice flies to Florida to see and to forgive him; a remorseful Nelson begs him not to die. But Rabbit assures his son, "[I]t isn't so bad," and thinks laconically to himself: "Enough."

TOPICS FOR ORAL AND WRITTEN DISCUSSION

1. Describe how Rabbit is an antihero like Kesey's Mack and how his self-image and existential angst contribute to his unfortunate lifestyle and health problems. Add to your discussion Updike's poem "The Ex-Basketball Player."
2. Correlate Rabbit's lifestyle (diet, exercise, stress) with his increasing cardiac symptoms in a case study of how it contributed to his cardiac arrest. Use medical terms and apply the saying "It's time to pay the piper" to Rabbit's final outcome.
3. How did the specific decades through which Rabbit lived culturally acclimate him to bad personal habits? In particular, how does Tom Wolfe's description the "Me Decade" apply to Rabbit?
4. If *Rabbit at Rest* is an American tragedy, what part does Rabbit play in the novel? Apply the terms existentialism and free will to your discussion. Ethical query: If you were a medical professional and observed someone like Rabbit, not your patient, who exhibited heart disease symptoms, would you tell him to see a doctor?
5. Describe the effects of Nelson's cocaine habit, including to his family relationships with his wife, children, and his mother and father. Who enables him? Who helps him?
6. Define the traits Updike attributes to Rabbit, such as narcissistic, hedonistic, bigoted, misogynistic, xenophobic, and homophobic, then argue both sides, that either he is or he is not the product of his times and typifies an average aging American male with a propensity for heart disease.
7. Describe, medically, the effects of Rabbit's hedonism and indolence on his body (heart), then discuss 1) the first medical procedure he underwent, 2) the more aggressive medical procedure another doctor recommended, and 3) the doctor-patient relationship in each event. If Rabbit's bypass doctor has a quota to meet, as Rabbit suspects, would this be ethical?
8. Because Rabbit vicariously relates to various sports heroes, how do they, and specifically the Pete Rose-Bart Giamatti debacle, affect his well being?
9. What part does Rabbit's isolation in Florida play in his failure to recover from myocardial infarction (MI)?
10. Life goes on in Brewer, Pennsylvania, after Rabbit dies. Describe how by the specific processes of rehabilitation and feminism Nelson and Janice reclaim their lives.

BIBLIOGRAPHY

Alliance for Aging Research. http://www.agingresearch.org/.
American Heart Association. http://www.americanheart.com.

American Society for Bariatric Surgery. http://www.asbs.org. See also International Bariatric Surgery Registry and related sights for calculating obesity.

Decades History Timelines. http://www.decades.com.

Family Caregiver Alliance. Hypoxic-Anoxic Brain Injury Fact Sheet. http://www.caregiver.org/caregiver/jsp/content_node.jsp?nodeid=575.

Framingham Heart Study. National Heart, Lung, and Blood Institute. http://www.nhlbi.nih.gov/about/framingham/index.html. For risk assessment see http://www.framingham.com/heart/.

Gawande, Atul. "The Man Who Couldn't Stop Eating." In *Complications: A Surgeon's Notes on an Imperfect Science,* 162–83. New York: Holt, 2002.

IRS Table 1. http://www.retirelink.com/education/LifeExpectancy.html.

Knapp, Tom. "John Updike: Shared Recollections." *Rambles, a Cultural Arts Magazine.* http://www.rambles.net/updike_report.html (February 1996).

Nuland, Sherwin B. *How We Die: Reflections on Life's Final Chapter.* New York: Knopf, 1994.

Oates, Joyce Carol. "A Beautiful Brainless Guy." In *Books of the Century* (*The New York Times* Book Reviews), ed. Charles McGrath, et al., 449–51. New York: Three Rivers Press, 2000.

Selzer, Richard. "Liver," "Skin." In *Mortal Lessons: Notes on the Art of Surgery,* 62–77. New York: Simon & Schuster, 1987.

Updike, John. "The Ex-Basketball Player." *The Carpentered Hen and Other Tame Creatures.* New York: Knopf, 1982.

———. "From the Journal of a Leper." In *Problems,* 201–18. New York: Fawcett, 1981.

———. *Rabbit at Rest.* New York: Fawcett, 1990. Winner of the Pulitzer Prize.

———. "Rabbit Remembered." In *Licks of Love.* New York: Knopf, 2000.

SUGGESTED FURTHER READING

Harvard Lampoon. http://www.harvardlampoon.com.

Living to 100 Life Expectancy Calculator. http://www.livingto100.com/.

Montagu, Ashley. *TOUCHING: The Human Significance of the Skin.* New York: Harper and Row, 1986.

Selzer, Richard. "Skin." In *Mortal Lessons: Notes on the Art of Surgery,* 105–15. New York: Simon & Schuster, 1987.

Wolfe, Tom. "The 'Me' Decade and the Third Great Awakening." *New York Magazine,* 23 August 1976, 26–40.

MARGARET EDSON'S
WIT (1999)

Once I did the teaching, now I am taught.
—Dr. Vivian Bearing, *Wit*

HISTORICAL CONTEXT

Margaret Edson was born on July 4, 1961, in Washington, D.C. Her medical social worker mother and her newspaper columnist father encouraged her high school drama interests. After she received a bachelor's degree in Renaissance history, magna cum laude, from Smith College in 1983, she traveled for two years working at odd jobs. Then in 1985 she became an oncology and AIDS patient clerk and volunteer social worker at the National Cancer Institute in Bethesda, Maryland, where she witnessed protocols being developed to treat patients for ovarian cancer and HIV. She wrote a training manual titled "Living with AIDS: Perspectives for Caregivers." In 1991, from observing the medical teams and patients on the ward and from listening, she wrote *Wit* (also known as *W;t*), initially a regional theater and off-off Broadway production. Edson received a master's degree in English from Georgetown University in 1992, then she taught English as a second language and first grade in a Washington, D.C., public elementary school until 1998. Since then she has become an Atlanta kindergarten teacher, a career briefly interrupted in 1999 when she accepted the Pulitzer Prize for drama. As an extraordinary first-time playwright, at the age of 37 she became one of only 10 women recipients up to that time. Nonetheless, Edson remains committed to innovative teaching as her life's work and has no other published plays to her credit. She lives near Atlanta with her partner, Linda Merrill, a curator at the High Museum of Art, and their son, Timothy.

Wit has the rare quality of being simultaneously funny and heartbreaking as it deals with the subject of ovarian cancer, an often fatal disease if not caught in its early stages. The play also reviews clinical trial methods, including the effects of experimental drugs administered to terminal patients without offering any hope of cure. It dramatically depicts medical science in its hustle-and-bustle attempt to find better treatments and cures, subordinating the research subject's human needs. Therefore, the play scrutinizes the doctor-patient relationship, especially relating to respect shown for or withheld from the patient whose palliative care may therefore be lacking. Although there is no possibility of healing *Wit*'s protagonist, Dr. Vivian Bearing, of stage 4 cancer, avoiding medical mistakes is also at issue. Patients achieve autonomy, or the right to self-determination, in part when their medical professionals learn to listen to them, a skill that can be modeled in narrative literature as illustrated here. Lastly, as a practicum in clinical trial methods, *Wit*'s analysis describes how institutional review boards (IRBs) take their ethical philosophy from the Belmont Report and follow Federal Drug Administration (FDA) regulations in drug studies. They oversee methods for ensuring the study participant's informed consent and privacy as well as work to avoid doctor and drug company conflicts of interest. Managing the patient's pain and utilizing hope for increasing the quality of life are also hands-on doctor-patient issues. In the mid-twentieth century *One Flew Over the Cuckoo's Nest* sharply criticized mental health care, bringing reform; now into the twenty-first century *Wit* casts a light on end-of-life issues.

Cancer is a leading cause of death in Americans, second only to heart disease. While breast cancer kills the most women, many gynecological cancers are part of the overall cancer statistic. Ovarian cancer, the so-called whispering disease because of its insidious nature, is detected in one in 70 predominantly perimenopausal and postmenopausal American women and often metastasizes undetected. Risk factors include family history of ovarian and breast cancer, high dietary fat, delayed menopause, and no or late childbearing. The use of oral contraceptives appears to decrease risk. Ovarian cancer often presents itself with a cluster of three persistent and severe symptoms: a swollen abdomen, a bloated feeling, and urgent urination. Other symptoms associated with the disease include gas pains, anorexia, backache, and indigestion. Unfortunately most women seek medical advice when their ovarian cancer is in the advanced stage because the symptoms might be associated with other gynecological conditions. A routine pelvic exam or sonogram can detect an abdominal mass; however, because benign cysts are common, a cancer antigen blood test such as CA 125 and/or surgery may be needed to rule out malignant tumors. The ovaries of postmenopausal women are small so an enlarged ovarian mass is of significant concern. For comprehensive information on diagnosis and treatment see chapter 241, "Gynecological Neoplasm," in the *Merck Manual of Diagnosis and Therapy* and the Ovarian Cancer National Alliance.

Legislation proposed in 2003 as the Gynecologic Cancer Education and Awareness Act (HR3438), called "Johanna's Law" after Johanna Silver Gordon who died from ovarian cancer, outlines a national early detection and awareness program to give women and their health-care providers the latest information on the symptoms and risk factors of gynecologic cancers, with ovarian cancer being the deadliest. In 2004, 26,000 women will have been diagnosed with late-stage ovarian cancer and 16,000 will have died from it, the American Cancer Society estimates. In 80 percent of the cases the five-year survival rate is only 35 percent. At the U.S. National Cancer Institute clinical trials are under way on a breakthrough proteomics diagnostic test for detecting bloodstream proteins produced by early-stage cancer cells. This exciting news builds hope for early diagnosis followed by new treatments in development such as the antiangiogenesis drugs that shut off a tumor's blood supply, causing it to shrink.

With one million cancer diagnoses in the United States each year numerous clinical trials are under way to develop early diagnostic tests and treatments beyond surgery and chemotherapy. Researchers who enroll about two percent of adult cancer patients into drug studies get valuable data; desperate patients hope for a miracle. However, the reality of clinical trials conducted first in nonhumans and then in humans often is pure research promising no therapeutic value for the participants, which brings into focus the question of their rights. Primarily, at hospital admission patients are asked about any advance directives they have signed including living wills, health-care powers of attorney, and organ donation. A patient advocate is always available to field questions and general complaints. The attending doctor reviews the patient's medical history, performs a physical examination, and presents a plan for healing. Along the way, the patient may seek an ethics consultation, which is a reasoned conversation with a professional about the values and choices made in healthcare. When the patient enrolls in a drug study, as *Wit*'s Dr. Bearing does, in reality an institutional review board (IRB) acts as a disinterested party to oversee research protocol. IRBs take their philosophy on what ethical research is from the Belmont Report commissioned by the U.S. Department of Education, Health, and Welfare (now the Department of Health and Human Services). See the full details on the referenced Belmont Web site. In 1974 the National Research Act created the National Commission for the Protection of Human Subjects of Biomedical and Behavioral Research. The Nuremberg Code, derived from the World War II war crimes, was a prototype for the commission's guidelines. For the purposes of this discussion, some of the ethical principles and guidelines for the protection of human subjects include defining how participants are selected, how informed consent is obtained, how to assess the risk-benefit ratio, and how to avoid conflict of interest. The boundaries between practice and research are defined. The basic ethical principles it sets out are: 1) respect for persons (acknowledging autonomy and diminished capacity), 2) beneficence (securing well-being and the Hippocratic maxim, "First, to do no harm"), and 3) justice (observing fairness in who bears the burden or receives the benefits).

Besides monitoring these practices and obtaining legally effective informed consent from the subject or his or her legal representative, IRBs must carefully observe privacy regulations created by the Health Insurance Portability and Accountability Act of 1996 (HIPAA). Therefore, respect for the patient's autonomy and guarding against any possibility of deceit or undue influence in a potentially vulnerable participant is paramount. Furthermore, in drug trials an IRB must carefully apply various titles of FDA codes of regulation. Investigational new drugs (IND) go through a three-phase investigational process, as determined by the FDA. Phase 1 introduces a new drug into 20 to 80 healthy human volunteers to determine metabolic and pharmacological actions, the side effects with increasing doses, and early evidence of effectiveness. Phase 2, in conjunction with the data learned from the earlier clinical study, introduces the IND to several hundred patients with the targeted disease or condition to determine short-term side effects and risks. Phase 3 includes several hundred to several thousand people who receive the IND for the evaluation of its effectiveness and safety (risk-benefit ratio). From here, FDA approval is sought and physician labeling procured. Vivian Bearing is probably enrolled in a phase 3 frontline drug study in which it may be deemed proper to push the dosage. The distinction here must be made between suffering that the patient would undergo as a part of her disease and that which may evolve from research participation. Any toxicity in the full dosage given Bearing could be evaluated by laboratory values and the parameters determined that could kill the patient. That is, administering the full dose may not be necessarily painful. In particular, the duties of IRB watchdogs include giving the research participant the opportunity to ask questions. Pertinent information must be explained so that the participant fully understands the terms and risk-benefit ratios, all under FDA regulations.

When a patient becomes a study participant, like *Wit's* Dr. Vivian Bearing, facing illness—especially disease and dying—may take the courage of a lion tamer, to borrow from Virginia Woolf in *On Being Ill*. While such studies are vital to medical training and can affect the future care of patients, often they are not in the best interests of terminal patients. In addition, distraught family members may insist on keeping a patient alive through heroic measures, merely prolonging their loved one's suffering. Economics in a health-care system in crisis is another primary concern. More than 50 percent of Medicare dollars goes to health care during the last six months of life, but increased technology and managed care policies distance doctors from their patients and cause a disconnection. In lieu of legalized assisted-suicide in the United States, restoring the doctor-patient relationship may be one solution to enable private, apolitical end-of-life decisions. Ongoing interdisciplinary talks between clinicians and humanists address what it means to die in the twenty-first-century United States. They discuss how technology alters our conceptions of death, and they assess the implications for end-of-life caregiving, such as new ways to perceive patient pain, to acquire medical professional empathy, and to determine duration in the dying process.

At the crux of the health-care debate is how the doctor-patient relationship affects patient care. The ancient Hippocratic oath ("to be useful, but, first, to do no harm") addresses a doctor's fundamental responsibility. Another principle used since the time of the "most influential physician in history," Sir William Osler (1849–1919), is detached concern. This psychological distancing, the theory goes, allows a doctor to remain objective so that he or she is not overwhelmed emotionally by each patient's plight. Another description of this tension between clinical reasoning and human emotion is head versus heart, as illustrated in chapter 1. The wisdom of the ages notwithstanding, new studies show that when doctors engage with patients, learning to listen and to touch, it builds trust rather than fostering vulnerability. Indeed, the additional sensitivity and bonding benefit both the patient and the doctor alike. Doctor paternalism gives way to creating a health-care relationship in which the patient is more likely to understand and to comply in the interest of mutual participation. Dealing daily with disease, pain, and dying takes a toll on any doctor, of course. Some still choose detached concern to cope with human misery, while others find that emotionally connecting keeps their focus on the patient.

Another end-of-life issue Dr. Jerome Groopman discusses is the role of hope in treating terminal patients: "People say where there is life, there is hope. I believe the flip side of that is true: where there is hope, there is life." Hope is a vital emotion distinguishable from mere optimism. Hope, he believes, can change physical well-being, and patients "flourish when you believe that the future can be different from the present—that you have some level of control or choice" (Yale Medical School, 6 November 2003). So besides the latest medication, Groopman prescribes hope—"the very heart of healing" (*The Anatomy of Hope*, 212). Hope's various forms include the hope of recovery, the hope pain will stop, the hope that before you die you achieve a goal, and the hope that eternal life follows death. Hope is not a cure, but, when used in a subtle negotiation between a patient and doctor, it may contribute to quality of life. Even in the face of apparent futility, Norman Cousins says a doctor delivering the bad news should ask, "Is it possible to communicate negative information in a way that is received by the patient as a challenge rather than a death sentence?" In an open and honest healing partnership, a doctor who chooses the right words offers a lifeline to the patient (Cousins, xiii).

The idea of giving a terminal patient hope is a contemporary issue developed within the field of narrative ethics. Therefore, hope is not merely an ethereal "thing with feathers," in the words of Emily Dickinson, but rather its substantive quality defined in the literature and applied to patient care changes the way doctors respond to vulnerable patients. Learning caring values and sensitivity falls within the broader context of medical humanities, which includes literature and medicine, an interdiscipline based on anecdotal learning with the doctor and patient becoming cotellers in a story of healing. Accordingly, it is natural and normal to teach the art of medicine through stories that require emotional involvement and can offer both escape and therapy. Edson's literature-and-medicine play *Wit*, for example, incorporates topics such as hope, kindness, and touching, helping medical practitioners understand human behavior and relate it to their technical practices, making for better doctoring.

Former Nazi war prisoner Viktor Frankl broadens the concept of hope, writing, "Man's search for meaning is the primary motivation in his life . . ." (Frankl, 105). He coined the term *logotherapy* to signify its importance. In the death camps Frankl, a psychiatrist, witnessed the universality of how the mind-body-spirit interrelated in humans fighting hard to exist. The unimaginable horrors they experienced brought acute self-knowledge. For many death soon followed. Just as then, everyone is in a different place in grasping and in dealing with the death of friends, of loved ones, and even of national figures like John F. Kennedy and Martin Luther King, Jr. When it comes to our own deaths, it is a process as well, often best addressed through personal philosophy, religion, and poetry. Although better health care promises to extend the average human life span, biological sciences professor

Robert Arking says on the cellular level it does not change that "you will still age as humans have throughout history" (Arking, 508).

In working through loss, however, thanatologist Elisabeth Kübler-Ross in *On Death and Dying* says everyone experiences five stages of grief: denial, anger, bargaining, depression, and acceptance. Emotional acceptance may be facilitated by feeling one has lived a good life, it is time to make way for the new, and that death is the natural next step, as expressed in Ecclesiastes 3:1–2: "To every thing there is a season, and a time to every purpose under the heaven: A time to be born, and a time to die." Death can come suddenly in unexpected ways. Or its approach can linger. Some will fight to the end, and others will surrender in quiet anticipation with courage and dignity. When feeling secure in life, we ignore death. Nonetheless, on a lifelong journey toward self-discovery, our time of death may offer us the greatest personal understanding. Ultimately, however, as much as philosophy, religion, and poetry might help, there is no escaping that death is the price we pay to live. But, come—"Grow old with me! / The best is yet to be, / The last of life, for which the first was made" (Robert Browning, "Rabbi Ben Ezra").

LITERARY ANALYSIS

There is no mistaking who is in charge. Right from the beginning *Wit*'s protagonist, Dr. Vivian Bearing, a tough-minded Renaissance literature professor, addresses the audience directly: "Hi. How are you feeling today?" This metatheatrical device, breaking the fourth wall, makes the audience self-consciously aware of its role while preserving the illusion of unfolding action. Then Bearing abruptly says, "I think I die at the end." Such a declaration might reduce dramatic tension except her stoical wit fills the void, drawing the audience into the story in a way whimpering could not. This analysis focuses on how *Wit* is a play about Bearing's journey toward death and how through simple human kindness she finds meaning in life. Edson says her intent was to show a person gradually acquiring self-knowledge through the capacity for love, then ultimately receiving God's grace. In doing so, Edson walks the fine line between heartbreaking and humorous, knowing when something is funny you hear the truth a little louder. *Wit* is used to teach lessons on humanity in medical practices and procedures.

Bearing, a 50-year-old, postmenopausal, childless woman, fits into the profile of an ovarian cancer patient, especially because her life of the mind helped mask awareness of the disease's vague physical symptoms. Now in stage 4 with metastatic spread to distant organs, late detection means little possibility of significant recovery. The play begins *in medias res* with Bearing, a researcher herself, signed up for an eight-month research protocol involving chemotherapy and high-dose experimental drugs given fictional names. To shrink her grapefruit-size tumor healthy cells will die along with the cancer. By consenting to the study she contributes to knowledge but suffers harsh side effects, including hair loss, nausea and vomiting, compromised immunity, fatigue, and pain. Cancer in a no-nonsense university professor, now a research subject detached from the outside world, causes her to become vulnerable.

Wit, a teaching play benefiting both the actors and the audience alike, at first portrays Bearing unsympathetically. She is a disciplined professor who has sacrificed friendship for intellectual achievement. Once ill, she wages a personal battle for survival by drawing on the only resources she has built up: the metaphysical poetry of John Donne (1572–1631). Donne was a seventeenth-century Anglican priest who became the dean of St. Paul's Cathedral in London in 1621. Family deaths—including wife Anne More and several children—and his own extended illness caused him to write a series of spiritual meditations, *Devotions upon Emergent Occasions*. In these essays and in his earlier *Holy Sonnets* salvation anxiety questioning his faith was prevalent. Although he died after a lingering illness, hope of salvation swept into his later years. His dramatic sonnets are an intellectual exercise for Bearing featuring conceits, complex poetic devices including simile, metaphor, puns, hyperbole, and paradox. Edson integrates the genius of metaphysical poetry into the structure of her whole play by creating surprising comparisons and elaborate parallels between dissimilar things in disparate fields of knowledge. For example, the compulsively focused Professor Bearing researches her medical condition as she has with her literary scholarship on Donne's *Holy Sonnets*, compiling a bibliography, analyzing data, and so forth. Her running dialogue on metaphysical wit contrasts with the scientific jargon of ovarian cancer protocols, showing how Bearing tries to understand her illness through language. Hence, set into the framework of interrelated disciplines, literature and medicine, come lessons on kindness and detachment, hope and grace, and ultimately life and death.

In *Wit*, a character-driven quest narrative, Edson at first closely aligns Bearing's illness journey with Donne's, at times even referencing his early scholars. Along the way other characters reveal human values easily compared with and contrasted to Bearing's. For instance, cancer specialist Dr. Harvey Kelekian, who is an academic professor on the same sociocultural plain with Bearing, mirrors her emotional distancing from students. At their first meeting Bearing takes comfort in an intellectual exchange with Kelekian, but this meeting of the minds soon collapses with the stark reality of her dire situation. Told her prognosis, she signs an informed consent for the full dose of an investigational drug. Paradoxically, such a protocol that may offer a fair test to help distinguish useful from useless or harmful treatment, contributing to knowledge and benefiting others, may kill her. The ethical dilemma of delivering a nonbeneficial dose too high to tolerate (Hippocrates' "First, to do no harm") and keeping Bearing alive to reap medical data conflicts with Kelekian's obligation to inform her fully about the drug, including whether it is FDA approved and has possible side effects. Furthermore, he must periodically review his patient's pain level and quality of life. At first Bearing is as eager to help researchers as she has been to solve Donne's intractable mental puzzle. But along the way technicians treat her inhumanely, as a number rather than a person, causing her to become cynical. Bearing is terminally ill, in intractable pain from the cancer and its treatment, and alone.

Like Bearing's scholastic tunnel vision, the data-oriented Kelekian and his research fellow Dr. Jason Posner, in a relentless pursuit of knowledge, also forget their subject is a person like themselves. Jason mindlessly asks her, "How are you feeling today?," a rhetorical question indicating detached concern or his learned ability to compartmentalize the fear and anxiety that proximity to death brings. This formulaic hospital greeting doubles the conviction that the old way, defensively disconnecting from a patient to maintain objectivity, still exists. Bearing feels proud that Jason, once her undergraduate student, is a dedicated researcher also. But as a scientist he is more interested in his patient's cancer cells than he is in her emotions, humiliating her during a disrespectful pelvic exam. He callously observes and records Bearing's suffering without offering solace. Bearing masks her loneliness with *bravissima* repartee. For example, after taking her medical history Jason remarks, "Well that about does it for your life history," to which Vivian wittily replies: "Yes, that's all there is to my life history." The sarcasm is lost on the rushed doctor who does not choose his words carefully. In the beginning both Bearing and her like-minded young doctor are dispassionate, but with increased pain her arrogance gives way to fear. Only when Jason inadvertently calls a code blue on Bearing, making a medical mistake, does he feel any humility. For Edson, once a hospital worker herself, kindness and humility need to balance out the fervor of scientific endeavor.

In stark contrast to the detached, fact-oriented Jason, nurse Suzie, although portrayed as a dim bulb, epitomizes a compassionate caregiver. Professor Bearing is a master teacher of the highest intellectual order with an unsurpassed curiosity for words; however, having read about death her entire professional career, she does not have a fundamental understanding of compassion. It is modeled when Suzie, her unofficial patient advocate, meets her needs by listening and showing simple human kindness. Of course, there is no way to know when given the bad news how anyone, whether the most learned theologian or a cancer-stricken child, will face a date with mortality. But with hope of recovery lost—the cancer is not in remission and only palliative measures are undertaken—Bearing appears to subsume her fear and accept her fate with equanimity. In the comfort of Suzie's arms, she is getting "the medicine of friendship," as put by Jerome Groopman's patient in *The Anatomy of Hope* (Groopman, 135). Suzie calls the once erudite ranked professor the familiar "sweetheart" to assuage her fear, although it is both a rational and emotional response. Indicative of Kübler-Ross's stages of grief, Bearing's peaceful acceptance contrasts with Dylan Thomas's famous poem in which he invokes his dying father to put up a fight by raging against death. To make the actions more declarative, Edson antagonistically casts Jason's detachment with Suzie's kindness, seen in simple acts such as applying skin lotion and adjusting Bearing's baseball cap over her bald head to help maintain her dignity. When her patient's condition deteriorates, Suzie splits a Popsicle with her while having a talk about codes. Thus, an emotionally involved nurse gives her dying patient experiencing loss of control and privacy a choice and offers her compassion along the way. In an act of educated nonadherence to protocol Bearing signs a do-not-resuscitate order, contrary to Jason's and Kelekian's desire to keep her alive to collect more research data. But Bearing has deprived death of its power over her, just as Donne hoped meditating on mortality and salvation would do for him.

Edson's focus on how the incredibly patient, pragmatic nurse Suzie interacts with Bearing of course belies the fact that it is a way of life for any nurse to have at least five other jobs to do at once. But by portraying characters *in extremis* Edson shows how, combined, they become an ideal caregiver who simultaneously develops both rational and kind qualities. They need not be mutually exclusive. That is, the faculties of reason are not weakened by the growth of compassion. In fact, Neurology Professor Antonio Damasio believes emotions are cognitive guides that contribute to logical decision-making (*Descartes' Error*). Self-aware doctors are conscious of connecting to patients. And by doing so, doctors tap into both their head and heart to build trust. Jason and Suzie, shown as opposites, reveal how different levels of empathy affect patient care. In *Walden* Henry David Thoreau argued that meaningful learning, such as acquiring the quality of empathy, derives from an actual experience—from hands to head. The proliferation of medical humanities literature-and-medicine courses taught throughout the country at every level of medical education—from high school bioethics clubs to postgraduate medical training—demonstrates widespread belief that empathic sparks can also be ignited from the vicarious experience of identifying with models presented in literature. In essence, medical humanism develops the qualities of respect, integrity, and compassion to add to the technical, scientific know-how in medical training. It teaches important ethical values like maintaining patient confidentiality and being sensitive to age, gender, culture, and disability. Clinical competence and professional values, taught together, blend into the art of medicine, indicating the real tasks of medicine require skill in diagnosis and therapy as well as in empathy, reflected in kindness.

Like Suzie, the heroic nurse who gives Bearing what she needs the most—the kindness of a simple human touch, and listening—Professor E. M. Ashford, Bearing's former mentor and only outside visitor, contrasts with the portrayal of uncaring medical personnel. In a 28-year flashback Ashford converses with her young student Vivian Bearing about Donne's "Holy Sonnet Six" and its profoundly simple meaning. Citing the authentic Gardner edition of the text, "And death shall be no more, Death thou shalt die," Ashford affirms in that line "nothing but a breath—a comma—separates life from life everlasting." But at this time Bearing fails to understand how "simple human truth [and] uncompromising scholarly standards" inform each other. In a moment of dramatic irony the audience feels like shaking Bearing for focusing solely on ideas rather than on building personal relationships. Lifelong immersion in the *Holy Sonnets* sparked her use of wit, certainly; however, other than providing an intellectual challenge, it did not engage her in real life. Donne's attempt to relate matters of the soul and its salvation were lost on Bearing. Later at the hospital—in the most sentimental yet realistically played scene—Ashford crawls into bed with the dying Bearing. Nestled in her mentor's arms, Bearing has regressed from intellectual posturing into childlike trust as Ashford reads to her not Donne but an uncomplicated child's tale, *The Runaway Bunny.* Simply put, no matter where the bunny runs to or hides, its mother will find it. It is a "little allegory of the soul" to show God's love, Ashford comments. This scene, as a litmus test indicating emotional reader response, helps show how Bearing's growing capacity to receive love extends into her saving grace.

While eight months of cancer treatments seem interminable, Bearing's death is swift. In her "playes [sic] last scene," borrowed from Donne's poetic description of the brief moment at death when the soul leaves the body, she takes leave of the audience. Because Bearing has helped tell her own story up to this point, interjecting witticisms and tears, now others must take over. Jason enters Bearing's room and seeing no vital signs begins CPR. He brazenly calls a code team to resuscitate her, even though Suzie who knows she is no code pleads for him to stop. Intellect and reason have devised palliative care measures during Bearing's extended life, but now only their complement, compassion, dictates it is time to stop intervening. From scene 1 it is clear Bearing is terminal and will die. But feeling secure in life, she has ignored death until her illness becomes a short journey of self-discovery and the search for meaning in life. In her memorable death-bed scene, redemption comes to the flawed intellectual. As the soul departs the body, Bearing experiences grace through her ability to give and to receive love. The transcendent ending—not revealed here—nonetheless surprises.

Margaret Edson has written an extraordinary play, both intellectually challenging and emotionally immediate. Bearing is an unforgettable character whose intractable pain and dehumanizing end-of-life isolation are not unusual. In the beginning of the play as a John Donne scholar knowing the importance of contributing to knowledge, Bearing is vociferously in charge. She approaches her illness as she had the study of Donne: aggressively probing and intensely rational. By the end, virtually friendless and having spent her entire life in intellectual pursuit, she is quietly vulnerable. The frequent references to Donne help develop his "death be not proud" as a major theme, illustrating how Bearing's growing humility precedes her courageous death. They also show how poetry can be keener than prose in explaining complex human ambiguity, especially as the mind, body, and soul interrelate. Other themes focus on preserving humanity in the quest for scientific knowledge, on man's ultimate search for meaning in life—culminating in God's grace, and, of course, on the play's salient characteristic, wit, which evokes both verbal skill and an ability to understand.

Besides wordplay that delights, surprises, and lightens the mood, *Wit*'s metatheatrical elements and dramatic devices drive the play. As an important storytelling feature, flashbacks to Bearing's childhood, to her student days, and to the linear trajectory—research, teach, publish—of her busy professor's life, contrast with seeing what her friendless life is like during the last months and hours. They reflect the effect of her choices while preserving the illusion of her once productive life, which is now embroiled in a struggle. Bearing's directly addressing the audience is powerful, adding immediacy by intermingling reality with illusion. Her repeating "Hi. How are you feeling today?" is a leitmotif mocking the detached concern inbred into medical professionals who are not listening for a response anyway. Later her silence makes it necessary to shift to other storytellers. One scene flows into the next—there are no intermissions—with the hustle and bustle of diurnal medical schedules to be met, realistically portraying what a patient endures. A play of opposites—hope and kindness revealed by showing characters without them—*Wit*'s layered literature-and-medicine approach ultimately pits life against death.

Wit has been criticized for being sentimental and melodramatic, as well as for portraying stereotypical medical professionals. Unfortunately, it is not unrealistic to the degree a recent study cites "woefully inadequate" care for end-of-life patients, including lack of respect, failure of physicians to communicate, and insufficient pain medicine and emotional support (Teno et al., 291:88–93). At first Bearing appears one-dimensional as a prideful full professor, until cancer drains the life out of her. Even in these earlier times a witty sensibility peaks through. But it is fully ironic that a scholar who researches and writes over an entire career about illness and death seems not to have gained an iota of wisdom from her subject matter; rather, only Bearing's obsession with language and retention of a semblance of Donne's wit are easily communicated to the audience. Arguably, she learned from Donne's writings neither courage nor his faith and beliefs. Only a caring nurse can tap into Bearing's emotions to assuage her fears.

The hospital's busy environment, with beeping technology and rushed medical personnel, is incongruently filled with the silences, both metaphorical and literal, that disease and dying create. Critically ill patients need answers to end-of-life human rights questions, which candidly addressed can fill a dark room with light. In particular, the medical issues and ethics *Wit* evoke concern specific guidelines in research study protocol. For instance, Dr. Kelekian simply tells Bearing she must be tough, then without further counsel she signs the informed consent. He fails to mention the risk-benefit ratio for her aggressive treatment and does not declare any conflict of interest. Later on, insufficient discussion of palliative care measures results in increased pain, lessening the quality of her short life. Although each institution and state have their own ethics committee policies, an IRB observes the research process. At admission patients are asked about living wills including notarized health-care proxies, and, as necessary, a doctor decides with his or her patient or a designated proxy on do not resuscitate orders to be placed in the medical chart. Understandably, Edson took dramatic license and omitted or consolidated some of these steps. But end-of-life authorizations are especially important to medical ethicists who oversee protocol for experimenting on terminal patients who have brain function but would die without life support. As eerie as it sounds, while cancer makes Vivian Bearing ineligible as an organ donor following cardiac arrest, machines might be able to revive her vital processes enough so that her warm body could continue to benefit research. This type of research as well as that on the unquiet dead, the brain-dead kept alive on machines, is occurring more frequently, writes Nell Boyce in "Science Calls at the Deathbed." But the obvious problem with processing the nearly dead as research subjects is, if the doctor is wrong about no hope of recovery, the patient may be harmed. Nonetheless, interns have long used the recently dead in CPR training as real Resusci-Annies and to practice inserting arterial lines.

Hypothetically, Edson's readers might imagine a scenario in which Drs. Kelekian and Posner try to further use Vivian Bearing's body to contribute to scientific knowledge, except Suzie, her last friend on earth, will not let them. The compassionate nurse would insist Bearing retain her dignity. However much *Wit* talks about death, though, it focuses more on Bearing's struggle to preserve her humanity in an end-of-life research experiment. During the course of her illness she reassesses her life and her work with a profundity and humor that transform both her and the audience. Other riveting characters provide narrative conflict that creates debate on important contemporary medical issues, and within rising life-to-death plot action many ethical questions are probed. Thereby *Wit* maintains its momentum from the beginning even through Bearing's death. Wordplay provides relief, offsetting the comitragedy's paradox that Bearing had to experience dying before kindness brought meaning to her life. A moment of tranquility precedes the chilling, epiphanous resolution.

SYNOPSIS OF THE PLAY

Professor Vivian Bearing, literary researcher, is now herself the subject of cancer research. Two dissimilar fields of study form the foundation of a moving play looking at the boundaries of the intellect and the expanses of the heart. Primarily set in a University Hospital Comprehensive Cancer Center room, there are no action breaks between scenes and no intermission in the 90-minute play. Therefore, lighting changes signify important transitions. Dr. Bearing enters an empty stage pushing an IV pole, giving immediacy to her dire situation. She wears two overlapping hospital gowns for modesty and a hospital ID bracelet, and covers her baldness with a baseball cap. Out of a cast of nine, Bearing carries the play, intermittently breaking the fourth wall by directly addressing the audience. Setting the tone for the play, in her professorial voice she asks the audience, "Hi. How are you feeling today?" Then in a witty academic response slightly mocking, she analyzes the question's ironic significance, indicating its rhetorical rather than sincere quality because no one is listening any way.

In a flashback scene Chief of Oncology Dr. Kelekian dispassionately announces to Dr. Bearing in medical jargon that she has stage 4 metastatic ovarian cancer with tumors spreading quickly. She will receive eight months of aggressive but experimental chemotherapy, taking the full dose to significantly contribute to knowledge. She must be very tough, he says, and she signs an informed consent. Given this drastic news, Bearing retreats into her intellect, making a mental note to create a bibliography for studying her disease. Both doctors, as academics, commiserate on the state of their students' scholarship. Bearing learns the treatment for her insidious cancer will have pernicious side effects, but she views her plight as a challenge, taking comfort in applying her lifelong discipline of exploring mortality in Donne's *Holy Sonnets*.

Twenty-eight years earlier Bearing's mentor E. M. Ashford berates her for emotionally analyzing Donne's "Holy Sonnet Six" rather than critically reading it with a correctly punctuated line: "And death shall be no more, Death thou shalt die." In this uncompromised version a mere comma, a breath, separates life from everlasting life. A future academic, Bearing eagerly returns to the library, although Professor Ashford suggests she join friends. Back in the present, Bearing deals with the impersonal hospital regimen, save for her compassionate nurse, Suzie. The emotionally detached young doctor, Jason, once Bearing's student, oversees the study protocol. Bearing answers his battery of questions, wit intact, describing her progressive symptoms.

Then Jason in a dehumanizing manner performs a pelvic examination, excitedly confirming her ovarian mass. Tests and treatments ensue as do Bearing's nausea and vomiting. Her only visitors are medical students on rounds.

In another flashback Dr. Bearing is five, reading Beatrix Potter's *The Tale of the Flopsy Bunnies* to her father, who explains the word "soporific" (sleepy) to her. Hence, her love of words began early and extended into the wonders of metaphysical poetry, as it does now less evocatively to medical terms. She has endured her outpatient chemotherapy but now rushes to the hospital shaking, feverish, and weak. Suzie suggests Bearing's dose be lowered; Jason insists on the full dose, which paradoxically imperils her health but is done in the interest of knowledge. The scene shifts, spotlighting Dr. Bearing's metaphysical lecture on the doctrine teaching that God forgives overweening intellect. But Suzie preempts it, taking her unwilling patient for more tests. Growing weaker, Bearing, evoking Donne's sensibilities, visualizes this to be her "playes last scene." However, Jason enters. He explains his enthusiasm for studying cancer, but acknowledges he lacks the bedside manner only "troglodyte" clinicians are trained for. Bearing tries to tap into Jason's emotions but is put off. Even though she is now in a "pathetic state as a simpering victim," Bearing realizes they both have exalted research at the expense of humanity. Thinking her confused, Jason denies the touch of human kindness she needs.

Next Bearing's inhumanity appears in her teaching methods. In a profound classroom moment later easily applied to Bearing's illness, a student sees Donne as a man who is "scared, so he hides behind all this complicated stuff, hides behind this *wit*." Bearing finds her student's view that simple is better a "perspicacious remark" but puts down his "heroic [mental] effort." An uncompromising teacher, Bearing flatly denies a student's paper extension due to her grandmother's death. This lack of compassion later becomes a regret. Back during the hospital's graveyard shift the agitated Bearing appears to be sundowning and creates a little emergency so Suzie will come see her. Bearing is scared, having lost control in her life; she is in need of comfort. Suzie shares an orange Popsicle with her, and they talk about Bearing's advancing cancer and code status. Despite the cancer researchers' desire for more knowledge, Bearing wants no heroic measures to restart her heart, which is noted in her chart. She is afraid, and only aggressive pain management—palliative care—helps now. Jason enters the room while in the background Bearing lapses into a drug-induced sleep. He tells Suzie his theory that all the while Donne conjured his "brilliantly convoluted" sonnets—not unlike trying to quantify the increasing levels of complexity in medical research puzzles—it ironically never released his salvation anxiety. Jason hastily adds, the sentimental "meaning-of-life garbage" is not for him.

In the penultimate scene Professor Emerita Ashford visits the semiconscious Bearing, crawls into her hospital bed, holds her, and reads *The Runaway Bunny,* a book for her five-year-old grandson. Ashford gently kisses the sleeping Bearing and says upon departing, "It's time to go. And flights of angels sing thee to thy rest." Then Jason stridently enters, notes his patient's lack of vital signs, and without checking her chart calls a code blue. Frantically he pounds her chest and performs mouth-to-mouth resuscitation. Suzie enters and announces his mistake: Bearing is no code. But a frenzied code team swoops in, at first deaf to Suzie's pleas to stop. At last the violent activity ceases, and the audience focuses on the bed as Suzie lifts the blanket from her patient. The surprise ending—with Bearing embraced by God's light—will not be revealed here. House lights fade to black.

TOPICS FOR ORAL AND WRITTEN DISCUSSION

1. What different health-care lessons do Rabbit Angstrom and Dr. Vivian Bearing teach? Apply the sayings *mememto mori* and *carpe diem* specifically to each.

2. Describe the medical professional-patient relationships that Vivian Bearing has with Dr. Kelekian and with Suzie. Who helps? Who adds insult to injury?

3. Correlate Jason's and Bearing's personality characteristics to show first their similarities and then their growing differences. What events cause each to turn pride into humility?

4. Describe how *Wit* defines the role of communication in treating patients, specifying how listening, empathy, hope, humor, and silence relate to medical mistakes and/or patient quality.

5. Distinguish detached concern from compassionate care in research protocols.

6. Discuss Donne's meditation on humility and death, a major theme in *Wit,* and relate it to Bearing's saving grace.

7. Describe ovarian cancer and the tests and legislation hoping to eliminate this silent killer.

8. The subjects of disease and death are done artfully in *Rabbit at Rest* and *Wit,* but the latter work is uplifting. Describe how literary devices such as wit, dramatic irony, and audience metatheatrical self-consciousness keep the reader entertained so the dire subject remains palatable.

9. In clinical trials is using experimental drugs that may not benefit the study participant and may even eliminate the last peaceful moments necessarily sacrificing patient autonomy to advance research? Review IRB rules, regulations, and philosophies as set out in the Belmont Report and FDA regulations. Argue both sides.
10. What specific issues does *Wit* illuminate to help bring reform in end-of-life care, as *One Flew Over The Cuckoo's Nest* criticized mental institutions to bring sweeping changes?

BIBLIOGRAPHY

Arking, Robert. "Aging: A Biological Perspective." *American Scientist* 91, no. 6 (November–December 2003): 508–15.

Belmont Report. http://ohrp.osophs.dhhs.gov/humansubjects/guidance/belmont.htm.

Boyce, Nell. "Science Calls at the Deathbed." *U.S. News & World Report,* 12 January 2004, 50–1.

Cousins, Norman. Introduction to *Medicine as a Human Experience* by David E. Reiser and David H. Rosen. Rockville, Md.: Aspen, 1985.

Damasio, Antonio R. *Descartes' Error: Emotion, Reason, and the Human Brain.* New York: Avon, 1994.

Dickinson, Emily. Hope is the thing with feathers / That perches in the soul, / And sings the tune without the words, / And never stops at all.

Donne, John. *Devotions upon Emergent Occasions and Death's Duel.* New York: Vintage Spiritual Classics, 1999. A series of meditations on illness and recovery. Introduction by Andrew Motion; biography by Izaak Walton (1640).

Ecclesiastes 3:1–2. The Holy Bible. Authorized (King James) Version.

Edson, Margaret. *W;t.* New York: Faber, 1999.

Federal Drug Administration. http://www.fda.gov.

Frankl, Viktor. *Man's Search for Meaning.* Boston: Beacon, 1992.

General Requirements for Informed Consent. Title 45 Code of Federal Regulations, Part 46.116. http://www.hhs.gov./ohrp/humansubjects/guidance/45cfr46.htm.

Groopman, Jerome. *The Anatomy of Hope.* New York: Random, 2004.

———. "Telling the Truth While Sustaining Hope." Yale Medical School Program for the Humanities Lecture Series, 6 November 2003.

Gynecology and Obstetrics. The Merck Manual of Diagnosis and Therapy. http://www.merck.com.

Kübler-Ross, Elisabeth. *On Death and Dying.* New York: Macmillan, 1969.

Ovarian Cancer National Alliance. http://www.ovariancancer.org.

Teno, Joan M., Brian R. Clarridge, Virginia Casey, Lisa C. Welch, Terrie Wetle, Renee Shield, and Vincent Mor, eds. "Family Perspectives on End-of-Life Care at the Last Place of Care." *JAMA* 291 (2004): 88–93.

Thomas, Dylan. "Do Not Go Gentle into That Good Night." The Academy of American Poets. http://www.poets.org/poems/poems.cfm?45442B7C000C07040C7A. The poet's audio recording.

Thoreau, Henry David. *Walden and Other Writings.* New York: Modern Library, 2000.

Woolf, Virginia. *On Being Ill.* Ashfield, Mass.: Paris Press, 2002.

SUGGESTED FURTHER READING

Albom, Mitch. *Tuesdays with Morrie.* New York: Doubleday, 1997. A teacher's dying lesson.

Broyard, Anatole. "Doctor, Talk to Me." In *On Doctoring,* eds. Richard Reynolds, et al., 175–81. New York: Simon & Schuster, 1995. Pathography.

Butler, Sander, and Barbara Rosenblum. *Cancer in Two Voices.* Gardena, Calif.: Spinsters Ink, 1996.

Nuland, Sherwin B. "Hope and the Cancer Patient." In *How We Die,* 222–41. New York: Knopf, 1994.

Olsen, Tillie. *Tell Me a Riddle.* New York: Dell, 1977. A woman's cancer affects her family.

Paget, Marianne A. *A Complex Sorrow: Reflections on Cancer and an Abbreviated Life,* ed. Marjorie L. DeVault. Philadelphia: Temple University Press, 1993. A sociologist writes about cancer misdiagnosis.

Tolstoy, Leo. *The Death of Ivan Illych.* New York: Bantam, 1988. Emotions of a dying man.

Williams, William Carlos. "A Face of Stone." In *The Collected Stories of William Carlos Williams,* 167–76. New York: New Directions, 1996. A paternalistic doctor lashes out.

Afterword

> I find nothing so singular in life, as that everything appears to lose
> its substance, the instant one grapples with it. So it will be with
> what you think so terrible.
> —Nathaniel Hawthorne, *The House of Seven Gables*

Dramatic medical advances ushered in with the twenty-first century include AIDS inhibitors, early multiple sclerosis treatment, and Alzheimer's vaccine. They promise to ameliorate but not to cure specific diseases. Nonetheless, these technological achievements give perspective on how far we have come. For instance, in 1900 pneumonia, tuberculosis, and heart disease were among the leading causes of death. Now vaccinations and antibiotics developed over the years offer a great measure of control, although cancer, followed by heart disease and stroke, remains the number one challenge. In 2000, with the decoded human genome, often called the discovery of the century, nanotechnological applications of recombinant DNA get down to the molecular level, promising therapeutic results even before symptoms manifest. Nonetheless, throughout the ages the lesson remains the same: prevention and early diagnosis are paramount. Unfortunately, technologies available to all on the Internet through government open-access rules bring fears that rogue scientists present potential dangers, and while infectious diseases like smallpox and polio are nearly eradicated, an unvaccinated population is at risk for bioterrorism.

Science is moving so fast, in fact, that things merely theoretical when

I began *Bioethics and Medical Issues in Literature* are now a reality, such as cloning human beings. Science continues to change life as we know it, with discoveries embraced by the parents whose "engineered child" is free from genetic disease and by recipients of cloned, rejection-free organs. There is no stopping science, but we can regulate the environment and educate scientists facing increasingly difficult ethical choices. They will need guidance into a future we cannot even envision. Along with great strides in knowledge come tremendous responsibilities, and each new discovery offers challenges in bioethics, legislation, and commerce. This book grapples with bioethics and medical issues by actively engaging teachers and students in literature. We have now figured out that science integrated with literature helps us understand what it means to be human. In fact, Harvard University's new interdisciplinary curriculum, which influences others, educates all students in science as well as in the humanities, a pedagogically sound principle because the brain loves diversity. Students work in an environment with current technology, which fosters creative ideas and sparks new research. Today's progressive scientists understand humans in their environment just as knowledgeable bioethicists draw from biology and human values. The fruit of widespread education reform is an enlightened citizenry that shapes the future by analyzing social issues with dual facility.

This book's literary tour from the birth of modern medicine into third-millennium science and humanities builds an understanding of the world we live in. Along the way I have posed provocative questions to create insights and to develop critical views drawn from diverse disciplines. I have plunged undaunted into *Bioethics and Medical Issues in Literature,* and by this last page my ideal reader will feel comfortably situated in many issues never thought about before but that will be faced in our brave new world. Knowledge properly harnessed is power. Having deciphered the human genome and with the advent of stem cell technologies, exciting and perhaps alarming therapies are forthcoming. But, as evidenced in bringing back into use the nineteenth-century leech and twentieth-century electroshock therapy, we should never underestimate the value of the past and cannot know what the future holds. With the ushering in of a hopeful yet fear-filled biotechnical revolution, "A terrible beauty is born" (William Butler Yeats).

FINIS

Glossary of Terms:
Literary, Medical, and Scientific

The following terms apply specifically to the readings in each chapter and to Western medicine; therefore, the definitions are limited in nature.

abortion. The termination of a pregnancy. The U.S. Supreme Court ruled in *Roe v. Wade* (1973) that restrictive state regulation of abortion was unconstitutional.

absurdism. Philosophy espousing that human life is irrational, morally indifferent, and rendered meaningless by death.

advance directives. Signed authorizations including medical powers of attorney in living wills designating another person, or proxy, to make health-care decisions in your stead.

affective family. The family entity evolving from freely expressed emotions.

agriterrorism. Using agricultural weapons against livestock or grain fields.

AIDS. Acquired immunodeficiency syndrome. A human immune-system disease caused by HIV infection transmitted through blood and bodily secretions, rendering its victim susceptible to life-threatening pneumonia and Kaposi's sarcoma. *See also* **HIV.**

allegory. A narrative with a primary and secondary meaning. Related to fable and parable, it is understood on two levels. After reading an allegory, ask yourself, What is the story *also* about?

alpha male. The top dog; exemplified by "Bull Goose Loony" in *One Flew Over the Cuckoo's Nest*.

alterego. The second self or other side of the personality.

alternative medicine. A mind-body-spirit approach to self-healing.

amalgamate. Integrate, fuse, merge.

amoral. Existing outside of a standard moral code of right and wrong.

angina. Sharp, spasmodic pain attacks, indicative of heart disease. *See also* **arteriosclerosis.**

angioplasty. An artery-clearing procedure (also known as cardiac balloon catheterization) to unblock clogged arteries that reduce blood flow to the heart muscle, followed by clot-busting drugs.

anthrax. An acute infectious disease caused by spore-forming bacterium *Bacillus anthracis,* infecting warm-blooded hoofed animals like cattle and sheep but transmittable to humans. Characterized by external ulcerating nodules or lung lesions. *See also* **bioterrorism.**

a priori. Latin, meaning "from the former." Derived from previous analysis; that is, deductive.

archetype. Primordial, structural elements of the human psyche (Jung).

ars moriendi. Latin, meaning the "art of dying."

ars vivendi. Latin, meaning the "art of living well."

arteriosclerosis. Arteries progressively blocked or narrowed by cholesterol plaque, causing a chronic oxygen and nutrient shortage to the heart, generating a "protest," or angina pain.

asylum. A mental institution or a sanctuary and inviolable place of refuge.

attention deficit hyperactivity disorder (ADHD). A condition characterized by behavioral and learning disorders.

autonomy. Each person's individual right to respect and self-determination.

baby boomers. Americans born between 1946 (after World War II) and 1964 (when the birthrate peaked).

back shots. Painful spinal taps used to procure neurological evidence for study.

bad blood. The vernacular, or common term, for syphilis-infected blood.

bariatrics. From the Greek *baros,* meaning "weight" and *-iatrics,* meaning "medical treatment." A branch of medicine relating to obesity and its treatments, including surgery.

Beat Generation. An American post–World War II literary and social movement promoted by 1950s writers Allen Ginsberg, William Burroughs, Jack Cassady, and Jack Kerouac, who attacked capitalism, the military, racism, consumerism, and the destruction of the environment. At the end of the 1960s hippies replaced beatniks as an alternative American culture.

bildungsroman. A novel about the main character's moral and psychological growth.

bioethics. For biomedical ethics. Concerns ethical issues situated in scientific and health-care disciplines. Van Rensselaer Potter coined the term in 1970 to describe "a new discipline that combines biological knowledge with a knowledge of human value systems" (Jonsen, *The Birth of Bioethics*).

biotechnology. The use of biological processes to produce a product or process for human use and benefit. As a branch of molecular biology it might include using microorganisms to perform specific industrial processes such as making beer and cheese as well as producing genetically altered bacteria to solve a horticulture problem or altering genes for recombinant DNA in an attempt to cure human diseases or in human reproduction processes. Often the stuff of science fiction, it merges science and engineering. [See Schacter's *Issues and Dilemmas of Biotechnology*, p. 1].

bioterrorism. Terrorist acts using biological weapons like anthrax or small-pox.

black satire. Genre ridiculing human vices with a turn toward the grotesque.

blank verse. Common, unrhymed verse (usually in iambic pentameter [five feet per line, stressing the second beat of each foot]) seen in Shakespeare's plays. Do not confuse blank verse with free verse *(vers libre)* that commonly has no fixed meter and number of feet.

blood pressure. A pressure cuff placed around a patient's arm measures the "push" of the circulation system (i.e., the top, systolic, number measures the pressure of the heart pumping blood out; the bottom, diastolic, number measures the pressure in between pumps). A reading over 120 systolic means the heart is working too hard, stressing arteries, leading to heart disease, stroke.

botulism. An inhaled or eaten bacterial toxin causing a muscle-paralyzing disease.

brain death. As defined by the Uniform Determination of Death Act, brain death is "irreversible loss of all functions of the entire brain, including the brain stem." However, these activities of the brain may continue: 1) evoked potentials of auditory and visual pathways; 2) brain wave activity; and 3) neurohormonal regulation producing the arginine vasopressin hormone keeping fluid-electrolytes balance.

bubonic plague. From Greek *boubon,* meaning "groin." A disease caused by the bacterium *Yersinia pestis* that is spread to humans by fleas from infected rodents and that causes swelling of the lymph glands. Early symptoms include headache, nausea, vomiting, and aching joints, followed by fever and chills. In advanced cases the skin turns black, hence the alternate name Black Death. *See also* **plague.**

Calvinism. The theological system of John Calvin and his followers, marked by emphasizing the sovereignty of God, the depravity of mankind, and the doctrine of predestination.

carapace. The shell of a turtle or crab, for instance.

cardiac arrest. Sudden stoppage of the heart resulting in heart damage and death unless immediate resuscitation is achieved.

cardiac death. The irreversible loss of circulatory and respiratory functions, as defined by the Uniform Determination of Death Act. The traditional cardiopulmonary criterion of death is when blood stops circulating, and non-heart-beating protocols determine exact time an organ can be harvested for transplantation to reduce degradation.

carpe diem. Latin, meaning "seize the day." Enjoyment of the moment without concern for the future.

catch-22. Derived from Joseph Heller's novel *Catch-22;* a contradictory situation, paradox, or absurdity in which the only solution is denied by a circumstance inherent in the problem and is therefore impossible to achieve.

catharsis. An artistic purging of emotions (pity and fear, for example), bringing about renewal.

chagrin. To be vexed or unsettled by, disappointed.

cholera. An acute diarrheal illness caused by intestinal bacterial infection.

cholesterol. A type of liver-produced fat found in the blood and used by the body to make hormones and build cell walls. Elevated cholesterol levels may increase the risk of heart disease. Cholesterol became a common household term in the 1970s.

chronic. Having a long duration or always troubling.

cingulotomy. Psychosurgery in which the trigeminal cranial nerve and intracranial lesions are targeted, often with a noninvasive Gamma Knife in an outpatient procedure to relieve intractable depression, obsessive-compulsive disorder (OCD), chronic pain, and other disorders.

civil rights and liberties. Every U.S. citizen is entitled to protection against infringement by the government, and other specific rights include freedom of speech, press, religion, and assembly, as well as property rights and equal treatment under the law. Refer to the U.S. Constitution's first 10 amendments (Bill of Rights) and the Civil Rights Acts of 1957, 1960, 1964, and 1968.

cloning. Creating a genetic duplicate through somatic cell nuclear transfer (SCNT).

code blue. A signal for calling a hospital resuscitation team.

colonialism. The state of being colonial; a colony subject to another government's policies that may involve cultural oppression and the domination of one country over another.

coma. A state of unarousable unconsciousness requiring a medical evaluation.

Combine, The. A combination, especially business or political interests; also, in agriculture, a grain-threshing machine. In *Cuckoo's Nest* the Chief believes the omnipotent Combine is a huge organization running the world, both inside and outside of the institution. A metaphor for repressive America.

comitragedy. A dramatic mixture wherein comic elements offset the tragic.

compassion. From Latin *com* and *pati,* meaning "to bear with" the consciousness of another's distress, together with a desire to alleviate it. Syn. Pity. *See also* **patient.**

conceit. A fanciful and complex figurative literary device often incorporating simile, metaphor, oxymoron, hyperbole, and puns.

concomitant. Accompanying in an incidental way.

confidentiality. In the medical practitioner-patient relationship there is an express and implied oath standing since Hippocrates' time that no professional confidence shall be broken.

counterculture. Alternative or against the prevalent culture; also known as bohemian, beat, hip.

CPR. Cardiopulmonary resuscitation. An emergency procedure involving external cardiac massage and artificial respiration, attempting to restore blood circulation and prevent brain damage. Also know as "the kiss of life." Consult the American Heart Association for specific details.

criminal insanity. As derived from the M'Naghten rule, the statutory definition states: "Criminal responsibility is excused where the actor, because of mental illness, does not understand the nature of his actions or does not understand that those actions are wrong." That is, he is criminally insane because he does not know the difference between right and wrong.

cultural relativism. A philosophical concept that claims moral rules are customs specific to particular cultures and that consequently no moral rules are universal. Advocates for international human rights, by their very nature, reject the primacy of cultural relativism.

cyberterrorism. Terrorist acts (such as computer hacking and spreading viruses and worms) infiltrating computer systems in the nation's infrastructure (financial institutions, government databases, water delivery systems, etc.).

cyborg. Cybernetic or bionic organism with automatic brain and nervous system.

cynicism. Showing a character or attitude of pessimism, misanthropy, gloom, and distrust. It incorporates a growing emotional distance and sense of futility.

Dante's *Inferno.* Part I, Hell, of the *Divine Comedy.* Virgil conducts Dante (1265–1321) into Hell where damned souls suffer eternal punishments appropriate to their sins. In the anteroom reside those who did nothing in life, neither good nor evil. Then follow nine levels of Hell, descending conically into the Earth.

death. A legal term describing the cessation of brain function. Death usually occurs within two to four minutes of oxygen deprivation to the brain. Initially, the pupils of the eyes become fixed and dilated. Finally an electroencephalograph determines lack of brain activity.

depression. A common depressive mood disorder ranging from mild to severe. When clinical, it is characterized by persistent sadness interfering with daily activities. Other symptoms include headaches, crying, loss of interest, feelings of worthlessness, sleeplessness, low energy, irritability, weight loss or gain, and, in extreme cases, difficulty in concentrating and a preoccupation with dying.

detached concern. In a doctor-patient therapeutic relationship, as taught by Sir William Osler, a defense mechanism medical professionals use to dissociate emotionally from a patient.

discipline. A field of study; imposing order.

disease. A harmful medical condition inhibiting normal human functioning.

DNA. Deoxyribonucleic acid. The nucleic acids that are the molecular basis of heredity reconstructed as a double helix. *See also* **recombinant DNA.**

doctor-patient relationship. Emphasizes the human bond or partnership between doctor and patient essential to the art of medicine.

domesticating death. Medicalizing or hiding death with intervening technology.

do not resuscitate (DNR) order. A hospital code ordering no patient resuscitation.

doula program. A program to assign a companion to a friendless dying person; based on a Greek word for a woman who assists mothers in childbirth.

dramatic irony. A tension built into the play, usually occurring when the audience understands the unfolding situation and its meaning and the characters do not.

dystopia. Anti-utopia.

Ebola virus. A Filoviridae named after a river in Zaire, identified in 1976, affecting humans and nonhuman primates with severe outbreaks and hemorrhagic fever; fatality rates of 90 percent.

electroshock therapy (EST). Also called electroconvulsive therapy (ECT). Administering electroshocks to an anesthetized patient to relieve depression or mania.

elegiac. Mournful, sad, expressing sorrow.

elixir. A medical concoction capable of prolonging life.

emigrate. To leave one's country to live elsewhere.

empathy. Observing and vicariously understanding another's feelings but keeping a safe distance between yourself and the other; experiencing the feelings of another as yours.

empirical thought. New scientific discoveries are often based on empirical thought springing from Aristotle's ideas: 1) examine what everyone says about the issue; 2) make several observations; and 3) derive general or probable principles on the matter from both 1 and 2.

endemic. Prevalent in a particular area or environment.

Enlightenment, the. Also called the Age of Reason. An eighteenth-century philosophical movement in which rational thought prevailed and individual happiness was paramount.

epidemic. A contagious disease outbreak affecting a large number of individuals within a population.

epistolary novel. The plot unfolds through a series of letters; note who is speaking to whom.

ethics. From Greek *ethos*, meaning "character." The discipline focusing on what is good and bad and what is one's moral duty and obligation. Ethics helps iron out conflicting values and principles to help make sound decisions, or at least ones with which a person can live.

eugenics. The scientific improving of hereditary qualities of a race or breed; term coined by Francis Galton.

euthanasia. Greek, meaning "easy or good death"; also known as mercy killing or doctor-assisted suicide. The practice of assisting in the death of terminal patients. The countries that have legalized it consider it a profoundly compassionate response to help end a life in suffering.

existentialism. A twentieth-century philosophy emphasizing that individual experience in an unfathomable but sometimes hostile or indifferent universe, while inexplicable, offers freedom of choice without knowing what is right or wrong or good or bad, and we are responsible for the consequences of our actions.

fatalism. A doctrine advancing the idea that future events are fixed and that we are powerless to change them.

female genital mutilation (FGM). An ancient ritual practiced mostly in some African, Middle Eastern, and Far Eastern countries that consists of two surgeries: excision and infibulation. Excision removes the outer genitals; infibulation sews up the vagina leaving a small opening for urination and menstruation.

First World (Third World). Having electricity, sewers, and governmental policies that contribute to citizens' health and welfare (not having the same). Or, highly industrialized Western nations, generally.

fortunate fall. Latin, *felix culpa*. A theme in early American literature, out of evil comes some good, in which a person's painful experiences become instructive and beneficial. Put otherwise, a man's tortured heart may lead to spirituality and understanding of the humanity around him.

fourth wall. A theatrical term describing the invisible wall between the audience and the on-stage actors. When an actor speaks directly to the audience, as does the narrator stage manager in Thornton Wilder's *Our Town*, he breaks the fourth wall.

Frankenfood. A food that has been genetically engineered.

Frankenscience. A scientific creation that has the potential to destroy its creator. Examples include bioterrorism, cyberterrorism, and agriterrorism. The term has its origins in Shelley's *Frankenstein*.

free verse. Verse that has no metrical pattern but depends on internal rhyme, images, etc.

free will. Freedom, without prior coercion or even divine intervention, to choose or decide the course of one's life, whether another person agrees or not. For example, "I do this of my own free will."

Galenic. Of or relating to the work of Galen (A.D. 130–200), Greek physician who tried to synthesize what was known of medicine and to develop a theoretical framework for explaining the body and its diseases. His anatomical and physiological discoveries included heart-muscle action, kidney secretion, respiration, and nervous-system function. William Harvey's seventeenth-century discovery of blood circulation was a major step away from Galenic medicine.

galvanism. Relating to the 1790s work of Italian physician Luigi Galvani who jolted frog muscles with an electrostatic spark, demonstrating twitching nerve impulses. In *Frankenstein* galvanism implied the release, through electricity, of mysterious life forces.

geriatrics. Medical specialty dealing with the diseases and problems specific to old people.

globalization. The integration of nations that makes applying social, medical, and economic principles worldwide in scope.

gluttony. Overindulgence, especially eating and drinking too much; one of the Seven Deadly Sins, along with pride, envy, anger, sloth, greed, and lust, codified after Jesus' death.

golden years. Usually the retirement years when people should be free to explore life, ideally free of health and money problems.

gothic. Gloomy castles, threatening ghostly figures, and vulnerable heroes are all gothic elements, which Hawthorne and Poe used to reveal or to explain the supernatural.

grace. In Christian theology, the unearned beneficence of God; that is, to become sanctified by a saving grace. God's grace becomes manifest in the salvation of sinners.

habeas corpus. Latin, meaning "you should have the body." A habeas corpus writ is issued to bring a person before the judge for a ruling as a protection against illegal imprisonment.

hallucination. Sensory perceptions that occur without any objective stimulus; a mental disturbance common in schizophrenics.

hallucinogenic drugs. Drugs that induce delusions, pushing the limits of physical and psychological endurance. LSD, for instance.

head versus heart. Exalting the mind at the expense of the heart.

hedonism. The doctrine that pleasure (happiness) is the chief good in life.

heroism. The qualities of a hero, especially fulfilling a higher purpose or attaining a noble end.

hippies. A 1960s counterculture group that took psychoactive drugs, wore psychedelic clothing, and as nonconformists reacted against wartime by engaging in peace demonstrations.

Hippocratic oath. The oath taken by doctors, who pledge "to be useful; but, first, to do no harm."

HIV. Human immunodeficiency virus. Any retroviruses that infect and destroy immune-system T cells, becoming diagnostic of AIDS.

holistic. Relating to the whole system rather than to the analysis or treatment of parts. For example, modern medicine attempts to treat the mind, body, and spirit.

homeopathy. From Greek *homos*, meaning "similar," and *pathos*, meaning "suffering." The principle "like can cure like" is the basis of homeopathy and dates back to the Greek physician Hippocrates in the fifth century B.C., who believed patients could help themselves.

hope. Expecting good. Hope, faith, and charity are three Christian virtues. The opposite of hope is despair.

hubris. Exaggerated pride or self-confidence.

humor. A quality appealing to the sense of the absurd or ridiculous; also can be a patient's coping mechanism.

hypospadias. Abnormal urethral construction of the penis.

ideology. The aims, assertions, and theories constituting a sociopolitical view.

immigrate. To come into another country as a nonnative.

implacable. Not capable of being changed, appeased.

impostor syndrome. When a doctor feels he or she can never know enough.

indolent. Habitually lazy; averse to activity.

infection. The state produced by an infective agent in a suitable host.

informed consent. A research participant must be adequately informed of and fully understand the risks and/or benefits of medical procedures and be relatively free from external influences before legal and ethical consent can be freely given.

in medias res. Latin, meaning "in the middle of things."

insanity. A legal term, meaning having a deranged or unsound mind and lacking the mental capacity, that removes the person from civil or criminal responsibility; includes the mental disorder schizophrenia (excludes mental retardation).

institutional review boards (IRBs). Multidisciplinary research institution committees charged with reviewing human experimentation standards of practice and ethics.

intern. A medical school graduate who begins his or her first year of residency to gain supervised practical experience (houseman in the United Kingdom).

intersexuals. Also called hermaphrodites. People born with intermediate or ambiguous genitals, neither completely male nor female. Conditions that cause intersexuality include Klinefelter's Syndrome (XXY chromosomes), congenital adrenal hyperplasia, androgen insensitivity syndrome, and a host of other syndromes. Intersexual characteristics are sometimes not determined until puberty.

in vitro fertilization. Combining sperm and ova in a glass dish to reap embryos.

irony. Using words to express the opposite of the literal meaning.

irresistible impulse. Legal principle stating that even if a person knowingly performs a wrongful act he or she can be absolved of responsibility if driven by an irresistible impulse to perform the act or if having a diminished capacity to resist performing the act. The legal principle employed in the movie *Anatomy of a Murder.*

Jim Crow era. From the 1870s to the 1950s discriminatory practices toward blacks (often local custom not law) proliferated, in spite of the 1863 Emancipation Proclamation and the 14th Amendment to the U.S. Constitution. They included discrimination in education, sports, hotels, restaurants, and so forth. For instance, blacks had to sit at the back of the bus, and drinking fountains were labeled "White only" and "Colored only," with only water in the white fountain cooled. In most areas of the South, the practice did not end until the 1960s. The term derived from Jim Crow, a stereotypical black song-and-dance man.

laconically. Using concise, minimal words to make a point.

leitmotif. A recurrent theme in a work that represents an emotion or character.

litmus test. An acid-base indicator test that turns red in acid solutions and blue in alkaline solutions.

lobotomy (psychosurgery). Surgically severing the nerve fibers connecting the brain's frontal lobes to the thalamus, a drastic technique thought to relieve specific mental disorders.

logotherapy. Viktor Frankl's term for understanding that the search for meaning is man's primary motivating force.

LSD. Lysergic acid diethylamide. An organic compound that induces psychotic symptoms similar to those of schizophrenia. In 1938 Swiss chemist Dr. Albert Hofmann first synthesized it from ergot fungus on the rye plant as a headache remedy, but he was not aware of its hallucinogenic properties until several years later. In the 1950s American experiments began on humans for treating alcoholism, schizophrenia, drug addiction, and behavior modification. Tests proved ineffective, and the FDA has never approved LSD for therapeutic use.

Luddite. One of a group of early nineteenth-century workmen who destroyed laborsaving machinery as a protest; broadly, one who is opposed to technological change. The movement is probably named for the eighteenth-century Leicestershire workman Ned Ludd who destroyed a knitting frame. Today, the Unabomber, who targeted computer industry executives and researchers, is considered a neo-Luddite.

Me Decade. Author Tom Wolfe coined this term to represent the period from 1971 to 1980, a self-centered time incorporating hedonism, hipness, and tragedy.

medical humanism. A view or teachings that add professional values such as respect, empathy, and integrity to the technical and scientific know-how of medicine (clinical competence), combining into the art of medicine.

medical humanities. An interdisciplinary blend of medicine and humanistic ideals to reveal the beauty in healing. In the field of literature and medicine, for instance, literature and scientific knowledge reveal a healing art, giving insight into the human condition.

medical power of attorney. Authorizations directing another to make specific medical decisions in your stead.

meditation. An attempt to focus thoughts for reflection and guidance.

melancholia. A mental disorder with symptoms of depression, physical complaints, and possibly delusions.

melodrama. A highly theatrical, sensationalized drama filled with intense action, extravagant sentiment, and agonizing situations; overdramatic.

memento mori. Latin, meaning "remember that you must die."

mental illness. Various disorders of the mind often caused by inherited genetic and learned environmental factors as well as external emotional stresses. Major categories include psychoses like schizophrenia and manic depression, neuroses like obsessive-compulsive disorder and hysteria, and personality disorders like drug dependence and alcoholism. Twenty-first-century psychiatry looks at causes in a patient's brain biology and genetics, as well as childhood influences and daily stresses.

mental retardation. Intelligence defects, a condition that affects 2 percent to 3 percent of the U.S. population. Genetic advances help us understand abnormalities in the brain. Related terms include feebleminded, moron, imbecile.

Merry Pranksters. Philosophical existentialists, acting spontaneously against authority. Namely, Ken Kesey and his psychedelic-era compatriots such as Jack Kerouac.

Metamorphoses. A series of Latin verse tales written by Ovid around A.D. 8 dealing with mythological, legendary, and historical figures. *See also* **Prometheus.**

metaphor. A figure of speech describing one thing in terms of another.

metaphysical poetry. A seventeenth-century poetry defined in the work of John Donne that intellectually persuades, engages in discussion, and seeks psychological analysis through images, analogies, elaborate parallels between dissimilar things, and a dramatic event.

metatheater. A play self-consciously declaring itself theater, especially with an actor speaking to the audience and breaking the fourth wall but maintaining dramatic illusion. Also "in-yer-face" theater or theater about theater.

miasma. A vaporous air quality believed to cause disease (e.g., a miasma of tobacco smoke).

moral. Relating to principles of right and wrong behavior; ethical, virtuous.

morale. The mental and emotional level of psychological well-being.

morbidity. Affliction with disease.

morbid obesity. Having a body mass index (BMI) of 40, or 100 pounds overweight.

mot juste, le. French, meaning "just the right word."

mutilation. Cutting off or destroying a person's or animal's limb or other essential body part.

nanotechnology. The branch of engineering that creates incredibly small machines and materials dealing with things smaller than 100 nanometers (a metric unit of length equivalent to one billionth of a meter). This new science and technology will allow us to snap together the fundamental building blocks of nature within the laws of physics. The far-reaching hope is that nanomedicine, by manipulating molecules, will eliminate all common twentieth-century diseases, pain, and suffering, as well as augment mental capabilities. Using devices the size of a few nanometers, often involves the movement of a small number of electrons.

narcissistic. Love (sexual desire) for one's own body; egocentric.

narrative ethics. The use of narrative, stories in particular, to help medical professionals make ethical choices by illustrating clear examples of right or wrong decisions. In fictional stories and case histories the viewpoint is considered. Also known as literary ethics, narrative knowledge.

neurasthenia. An emotional disorder with psychosomatic symptoms involving fatigue and feelings of inadequacy.

neutraceutical. A food or dietary supplement ingredient (such as ginseng in tea, isoflavone-laced soy products, and high quality herbal extracts) that provides health benefits.

nontherapeutic research trial. A research trial performed to benefit future patients, not those of the instant study.

Nuremberg Code. A code derived from the World War II Nuremberg Trials setting permissible standards for approved medical research.

obsessive-compulsive disorder (OCD). Besieged by a neurotic state of recurring obsessions and compulsions such as repetitive hand-washing or counting.

Odysseus syndrome. Derived from an episode in Homer's *Odyssey* in which Odysseus asks his men to tie him to the mast so he does not become crazed by the Sirens and have his power of reason affected. When applied by a bioethicist, it states that medical professionals should rely on a patient's decision when it is made in his right mind.

original sin. The state of sin that according to Christian theology characterizes all human beings as a result of Adam's fall.

Orpheus. In Greek mythology, a poet and musician who almost rescues his wife Eurydice from Hades by charming Pluto and Persephone with his lyre. In Gluck's opera, separated lovers journey underground to be united.

pain. A subjective experience effecting an unpleasant emotion relating to real or imagined touch. Medicine keeps revising and improving ways patients can relate and describe their pain.

palliative care. Improving the quality of life in patients, addressing physical, psychosocial, and spiritual needs; to soothe.

pandemic. The outbreak of disease affecting a wide geographical area and a high percent of the population.

Pandora's box. Derived from ancient Greek mythology, a box filled with implacable curses, but near the bottom there is hope.

pantheism. A doctrine equating God with the forces and laws of the universe; toleration of the worshipping of all gods of different creeds, cults, or peoples.

Paradise Lost. John Milton's 1667 epic poem of the story of Adam and Eve, Lucifer and Satan, good versus evil.

Paracelsian. Relating to the teachings of Paracelsus (1493–1541) who believed the activities of the human body are chemical; health depends on the proper chemical composition of the organs and fluids; the object of chemistry is to keep this essential balance.

passion. Emotions (as distinguished from reason) driving feelings and interests, promoting enthusiasm and even anger.

pathogen. A specific causative agent of disease, such as a bacterium or virus.

pathography. Life writing on one's own illness.

pathology. The study of the nature of disease, especially what deviates from normal.

patient. Latin "to suffer." A person who is under medical care.

patient advocate. Usually a hospital employee who responds to patient needs and complaints.

patriarchal medicine. The doctor is the all-knowing father; the patient is an inexperienced child.

pejorative. Having negative connotations; disparaging.

penicillin. A nontoxic acid produced by molds and found to be a useful antibiotic against syphilis and other bacteria. Accidentally discovered by British bacteriologist Alexander Fleming in 1929.

personifying, personification. Attributing personal or human qualities to a thing or abstraction.

placebo. Latin, meaning "I shall please." An innocuous substance prescribed for mental relief to soothe; used in controlled experiments to test the efficacy of another protocol. Also known as a sugar pill.

plague. An extremely contagious bacterial disease caused by the bacillus *Pasteurella pestis.*

plug drug. A new type of drug not related to genetic sequencing, but promising to halt flu viruses that invade the body.

polemics. Aggressively refuting the opinions and principles of another; a controversial argument.

poliovirus. An enterovirus occurring in several antigenically distinct forms causing human poliomyelitis.

post-traumatic stress disorder (PTSD). A term arising out of World War II when psychologists diagnosed returning soldiers with problems such as loss of concentration, sleep disturbances, nightmares, flashbacks, intrusive thoughts, and emotional stress.

predestination. The doctrine that all-knowing God infallibly guides those destined for salvation.

preimplantation genetic diagnosis. The technique for examining and pre-selecting embryos to identify sex, inherited diseases, and even cell donor capability. The selected in vitro fertilization embryos are then implanted in a womb. Also called embryo-sorting technique.

prescient. Anticipating or having foreknowledge of events.

presumed consent. A term facilitating the harvesting of organs from the deceased unless individuals or families object. *See also* **informed consent.**

preternatural. Existing outside of nature; exceeding the natural; atypical.

progenitor. Originator; direct-line ancestor.

Prometheus. Greek, meaning "forethought." In Greek mythology Prometheus, a champion of men against the gods, stole fire from heaven and gave it to humans. As punishment, he was nailed to a mountain, where an eagle tore out his liver by day and it grew back by night. According to some stories, Prometheus was the creator of man, molding him from mud. *See also* ***Metamorphoses.***

Prometheus syndrome. Relates to the Greek legend of Prometheus who created man and gave him fire. This concept relates to man's invention of technology, altering nature, including man, without thinking ahead about the consequences.

protocol. A detailed plan for scientific experiments, treatments, and procedures.

psoriasis. A chronic skin disease characterized by red patches with white scales.

psychopathic personality. An emotional and behavioral disorder involving realistic perceptions but often characterized by antisocial and immoral behavior, with immediate personal gratification in criminal acts, sexual perversion, or drug addiction.

psychosocial. Involving both psychological and social aspects, for instance as in mental health analysis or marriage adjustment.

psychosomatic. Physical symptoms caused by emotional disorders.

psychotic. Losing contact with reality; mental derangement.

Public Health Service (PHS). An agency of the U.S. government established in 1798, now within the Department of Health and Human Services, that promotes and safeguards national health and coordinates services internationally.

puerperal fever. Childbed fever or puerperal sepsis. An infection of the placental site leading to fever, which in serious cases may infect the uterine wall and then pass into the bloodstream leading to death. Dr. Oliver Wendell Holmes first identified it in *The Contagiousness of Puerperal Fever* (1843). Dr. Semmelweis theorized on prevention.

Puritanism. A doctrine preaching strictness and austerity especially in matters of religion and conduct. Puritans were a sixteenth- and seventeenth-century Protestant group in England and New England.

quotidian. Occurring every day; commonplace.

rationalism. Emphasizing man's ability to think for himself; it valued reason and experience over sense perception to gain knowledge.

recombinant DNA. In vitro genetically engineered DNA spliced together from various organisms.

regenerative medicine. A new field of medicine researching how to restore diseased organs with new healthy cells.

research subject (research participant). A person from whom research data is obtained (a social science term describing a person who may influence study design and give full and informal consent to being studied).

road literature. A literary genre in which the protagonist on a trip faces challenges along the way. Examples include Homer's *Odyssey,* Jack Kerouac's *On the Road,* Tom Wolfe's *Electric Kool-Aid Acid Test,* Mark Twain's *Huckleberry Finn,* and the movie *Thelma and Louise.*

romantic love. A mode of sentimental feeling traced to eighteenth-century novels such as Goldsmith's *The Vicar of Wakefield* (1766) and to the natural world described by the poets Keats, Coleridge, and Wordsworth. A key element is sexual passion, with the premise that your mate's personality is ideal, without normal faults, and only one person in the world can be your soul mate. Feminist Mary Wollstonecraft regarded romantic love as an invention of male novelists adopted to cover sexual lust (Lawrence Stone, 282, 284).

sandbag. To conceal or misrepresent one's intent; to take advantage of.

sardonic. Scornful, mocking.

satire. A literary device holding up human vices and follies to ridicule or scorn.

schizophrenia. A psychosis characterized by loss of reality and deterioration in everyday functioning. Two million Americans with schizophrenic psychosis have lost touch with reality, experiencing hallucinations and delusions and often expressing hostility. Probable causation is a complex interaction between heredity and environment.

science fiction. A literary genre questioning man's relationship to technology and science. Science fiction writers imagine change, horrify, and pique our interest to prepare us for the future.

scourge. The cause of great affliction; sometimes used interchangeably with "plague."

secular humanism. A humanistic philosophy antagonistic to traditional religion.

self-actualization. The process occurring in the construction of identity; self-knowledge.

self-esteem. Confidence and belief in oneself.

sensual. A carnal gratification of the senses.

sentimental. Resulting from feeling rather than thinking; emotional rather than rational.

sex assignment surgery. For instance, genetically male babies born with ambiguous genitals surgically transformed into girls by reforming the testes and the secondary sexual characteristics and given female hormones at puberty. In the 1950s American psychologist John Money believed babies, a blank slate, can environmentally change gender identities (nature versus nurture). In the 1970s, genetic testing called his view into question.

shaman. Wound healer. A person, usually a priest, who uses magical powers and belief in gods, demons, and spirits to cure the sick.

silver bullet cure. Also called "magic bullet." A miraculous solution to a complicated problem.

smallpox. A highly contagious disease with no cure caused by the variola virus. Within two weeks of exposure symptoms include high fever, fatigue, headache, and backache. Two to three days later a skin rash develops enlarging into pustules (pox) and scabs. During the second week death occurs in 30 percent of the infected. It is spread by infected saliva, by face-to-face contact, or through contaminated fabric. Its warfare use dates to 1750s British soldiers who deliberately spread smallpox among American Indians on contaminated blankets. Vaccination wiped out smallpox in developed countries in the mid-twentieth century. Routine vaccinations ended in the United States in 1972 because the risk of side effects outweighed the risk of the disease. The last known public case was in Somalia in 1977. Worldwide vaccinations stopped in 1980, making it ironic that medical victory over the disease leaves populations vulnerable to bioterrorist attack.

Social Darwinism. Classifying a cultural system on Charles Darwin's nineteenth-century principles of survival of the fittest and natural selection; individuals or countries fail due to inherent weakness. Social policy should allow the weak and unfit to fail and die.

social sciences. Social studies. They comprise the scientific study of the relationships humans have within the world, including how a sense of responsibility and civic competence develops.

solipsism. Each of us is the center of the universe.

soporific. Sleepy; causing sleep.

soul. The seat of faith where man and God connect and into which His grace comes.

soul pain. Emotional in nature, such as described in DeVries' *Blood of the Lambs.*

sterilization. To deprive of reproducing children; includes vasectomy or salpingotomy.

sundowning. Unsettled behavior evident in patients in the early evening, including agitation or restlessness.

symbolism. An object standing for something else (e.g., the flag symbolizes patriotism).

syphilis. A chronic, contagious usually venereal and often congenital disease caused by a spirochete. Left untreated, it produces chancres, rashes, and systemic lesions in a clinical course with three stages over many years (primary, secondary, and tertiary syphilis).

systemic lupus erythematosus. An autoimmune disease with no known cure or cause that runs in families. The body harms its own healthy cells and tissues, leading to inflammation and tissue damage, including to the joints, skin, kidneys, and heart. Treatable symptoms include extreme fatigue, arthritis, fever, reddish raised skin rashes, and kidney problems.

taboo. The cultural mandate not to discuss a topic or to practice an act (e.g., incest).

tabula rasa. Latin, meaning "blank tablet." A young mind capable of absorbing new knowledge.

technology. From Greek *teche*, meaning "art, skill." The practical application of knowledge in a particular area.

telemedicine. Rural medicine administered through broadband interest systems to provide health care to sparsely populated areas where medical professionals are scarce.

terminal illness. A diagnosis of no hope of recovery.

terminal wean. Patients with brain function who would die without life support.

tetralogy. Four in a series; a quartet.

thanatology. The study of death and dying.

totalitarian. Authoritarian; an autocratic leader having strict, centralized control.

toxic. Poisonous. Toxic plants include mistletoe, hyacinth, daffodil, and narcissus.

tragedy. A literary genre describing a situation engendering pity and fear so that it can bring catharsis or a purging of these emotions.

tragic flaw. A character flaw (or error) leading to downfall (e.g., Dr. Rappaccini's hubris).

tragic hero. One whose misfortune is brought on by misjudgment, through error or flawed character, and whose life goes from happiness to anguish.

tuberculosis. A communicable disease of the lungs caused largely by the tubercle bacillus and characterized by allergic and toxin symptoms, including chest pain and a bad cough that progresses into coughing up blood.

unpardonable sin. Failing to ask for forgiveness; not repenting.

unquiet dead. The brain dead kept alive on machines for organ harvesting or research.

vaccine. A preparation administered to produce immunity to a particular disease; made of killed microorganisms, living attenuated organisms, or living fully virulent organisms.

vivisection. Cutting into or operating on a living animal.

West Nile virus. A virus identified in Uganda in 1937; invaded New York City in 1999. Transmitted from birds to mosquitoes to humans, often causing the elderly or immune-challenged to contract brain encephalitis and/or polio-like virus and die. Not spread from person-to-person.

wit. A mental ability or verbal skill evoking laughter or understanding.

women's studies. A multidisciplinary academic program emphasizing the contributions of women in society, history, politics, the humanities, arts, and sciences.

worried well, the. People overanxious about their health (first used in the late 1980s).

xenotransplantation. From *xeno* (guest); cross-species transplantation.

yellow fever. A warm-region, sudden onset, acute infectious disease with prostration, fever, albuminuria, jaundice, and hemorrhage; caused by a virus transmitted by the yellow-fever mosquito.

A

Recommended Movies

CHAPTER 1

Frankenstein

Elephant Man, The (1980). Directed by David Lynch. Anthony Hopkins, John Hurt, Anne Bancroft, John Gielgud. A doctor in turn-of-the-century London shows a deformed man compassion.

Frankenstein (1931). Directed by James Whale. Colin Clive, Mae Clarke, Boris Karloff, Lionel Belmore. A scientist's creature has a criminal brain. Restored censored footage in 1987. Three sequels are Whale's *The Bride of Frankenstein* (1935) with Boris Karloff, Colin Clove, Ulna O'Connor, Elsa Lanchester; Rowland Lee's *Son of Frankenstein* (1939) with Basil Rathbone, Boris Karloff, Bela Lugosi; Erle Kenton's *Ghost of Frankenstein* (1942) with Cedric Hardwicke, Lon Chaney, Jr., Lionel Atwill, Ralph Belamy, Bela Lugosi.

Godsend (2004). Directed by Nick Hamm. Greg Kinnear, Robert De Niro, Rebecca Romijn-Stamos. A cautionary tale about the dangers of cloning.

Island of Lost Souls, The (1933). Directed by Erle Kenton. Charles Laughton, Bela Lugosi. Based on H. G. Wells's 1896 novel *The Island of Dr. Moreau* about a scientist who melds animals and humans.

Jekyll & Hyde (1990). Directed by David Wickes. Michael Caine, Cheryl Ladd, Lionel Jeffries. Robert Louis Stevenson's story of man tinkering with science and his own humanity.

Mary Shelley's Frankenstein (1994). Directed by Kenneth Branagh. Robert De Niro, Tom Hulce, Helena Bonham Carter, Aidan Quinn, Ian Holm,

John Cleese. A faithful rendition of the novel allowing us to understand Frankenstein and his creature.

Young Frankenstein (1974). Directed by Mel Brooks. Gene Wilder, Peter Boyle, Marty Feldman, Teri Garr, Madeline Kahn, Cloris Leachman. A parody of *Frankenstein* movies.

"Rappaccini's Daughter"

The Crucible (1996). Directed by Nicholas Hytner. Daniel Day-Lewis, Winona Ryder, Joan Allen. Based on Arthur Miller's classic 1953 play. The 1692 Salem witchcraft trials bring freedom of conscience into question. Parallels 1950s McCarthyism in America.

Rappaccini's Daughter (1980). Directed by Dezsö Magyar. Kristoffer Tabori, Kathleen Beller, Michael Egan, Leonardo Cimino. In Padua, Italy, Giovanni loves a beautiful girl who tends her father's poisonous garden. Available in most public libraries.

Truman Show, The (1998). Directed by Peter Weir. Jim Carrey, Laura Linney, Ed Harris. Truman lives in seaside village where his life is televised 24-hours. Satire on commercialized lives.

Twice Told Tales (1963). Directed by Sidney Salkow. Vincent Price, Sebastian Cabot, Brett Halsey, Beverly Garland. A Nathaniel Hawthorne horror tales trilogy, featuring "Dr. Heidegger's Experiment," "Rappaccini's Daughter," and "The House of the Seven Gables."

CHAPTER 2

Brave New World

Animal Farm (1955). Directed by John Halas. Joy Batchelor. Animated British version of Orwell's satire.

Boys from Brazil, The (1978). Directed by Franklin J. Schaffner. Gregory Peck, Laurence Olivier, James Mason, Lilli Palmer, Anne Meara. Dr. Josef Mengele breeds a new race of Hitlers. Olivier plays an aging Jewish Nazi-hunter. Based on the Ira Levin novel.

Jurassic Park (1993). Directed by Steven Spielberg. Sam Neill, Laura Dern, Jeff Goldblum. Michael Crichton cowrote the screenplay from his novel.

2001: A Space Odyssey (1968). Directed by Stanley Kubrick. Keir Dullea. An expedition to the moon. Oscar-winning special effects. Screenplay by Arthur C. Clarke.

Coma

Awakenings (1990). Directed by Penny Marshall. Robert De Niro, Robin Williams. From Oliver Sacks novel about the affective bond between doctor and patient.

Coma (1978). Directed by Michael Crichton. Genevieve Bujold, Michael Douglas, Rip Torn. Based on Robin Cook's novel.

Girl in White (1952). Directed by John Sturges. June Allyson, Arthur Kennedy, James Arness. Biography of Emily Dunning Barringer, who graduated near the top of her class from Cornell Medical School but was initially refused an internship because of her gender.

Hospital, The (1971). Directed by Arthur Hiller. George C. Scott administers a municipal hospital coping with a nursing shortage, incompetence, greed, and other personal sources of stress.

Return to Me (2000). Directed by Bonnie Hunt. Minnie Driver, David Duchovny, Carroll O'Connor. Engaging drama/romantic comedy about heart transplantation.

CHAPTER 3

The Plague

And the Band Played On (1993). Directed by Roger Spottiswoode. Matthew Modine, Alan Alda, Richard Gere, Lily Tomlin, Steve Martin, Anjelica Huston, Swoosie Kurtz, Ian McKellan, Phil Collins. A dramatization of the early years of the AIDS epidemic.

Hero (1992). Directed by Stephen Frears. Dustin Hoffman, Geena Davis, Andy Garcia. A dramatic comedy.

The Last Angry Man (1959). Directed by Daniel Mann. Paul Muni, Billy Dee Williams, Cicely Tyson, and Godfrey Cambridge. Old-time doctor ruins his health caring for a Brooklyn neighborhood.

Of Human Bondage (1934). Directed by John Cromwell. Leslie Howard, Bette Davis. Deformity, tuberculosis, and prostitution, including a scene where two doctors "light up."

Outbreak (1995). Directed by Wolfgang Petersen. Dustin Hoffman, Rene Russo, Morgan Freeman, Kevin Spacey, Cuba Gooding, Jr., Donald Sutherland. An African virus invades the United States.

Picture Bride (1994). Directed by Kayo Hatta. Youki Kudoh, Akira Takayama, Toshiro Mifune. Young Japanese woman leaves an unhappy past for Hawaii in the early 1900s.

Symphony of Six Million (1934). Directed by Gregory La Cava. Ricardo Cortez, Irene Dunne. A young doctor from the immigrant community loses sight of his commitment to the poor.

Miss Evers' Boys

The Black Stork (1917). Directed by Leopold Wharton, Theodore Wharton. Jane Fearnley, Allan Murnane, Harry J. Haiselden, Hamilton Revelle. A film about a doctor who "lets" deformed infants die (a famous case).

Judgment at Nuremberg (1961). Directed by Stanley Kramer. Spencer Tracy, Burt Lancaster, Richard Widmark, Marlene Dietrich, Judy Garland, Maximilian Schell, Montgomery Clift, William Shatner. Portrays the German war trials.

Miss Evers' Boys (1997). Directed by Joseph Sargent. Alfre Woodard, Laurence Fishburne. Syphilis patients are uninformed subjects of research.

CHAPTER 4

One Flew Over the Cuckoo's Nest

Asylum: A History of the Mental Institution in America. Mondale and Patton. Documentary on St. Elizabeth Hospital in Washington, D.C.

A Beautiful Mind (2001). Directed by Ron Howard. Russell Crowe, Ed Harris, Jennifer Connelly. John Forbes Nash, Jr., a brilliant mathematician with schizophrenia, has conspiratorial hallucinations and is treated with insulin-shock therapy and Thorazine.

Fear Strikes Out (1957). Directed by Robert Mulligan. Anthony Perkins, Karl Malden. Catatonic baseball player received electroconvulsive therapy.

I Never Promised You a Rose Garden (1977). Directed by Anthony Page. Bibi Anderson, Kathleen Quinlan. An institutionalized 16-year-old girl struggles with reality.

Of Mice and Men (1939). Directed by Lewis Milestone. Lon Chaney, Jr., Burgess Meredith, Charles Bickford, Bob Steele. Chaney plays the feeble-brained Lennie whose expectations for a peaceful life are failed. From John Steinbeck's morality tale. Several remakes.

One Flew Over the Cuckoo's Nest (1975). Directed by Milos Forman. Jack Nicholson, Louise Fletcher, Danny DeVito, Christopher Lloyd. A misfit inspires reform. Based on Kesey's novel.

Ordinary People (1980). Directed by Robert Redford. Mary Tyler Moore, Donald Sutherland, Timothy Hutton. An understanding therapist absolves a patient of guilt.

Patch Adams (1998). Directed by Tom Shadyac. Robin Williams, Peter Coyote, Michael Jeter. A doctor desperately wants to help patients but rejects the sober protocol of the medical environment.

Shock Corridor (1963). Directed by Samuel Fuller. Peter Breck. A reporter receives electroconvulsive therapy.

Snake Pit, The (1948). Directed by Anatole Litvak. Olivia de Havilland, Mark Stevens, Celeste Holm. Set in a mental institution, the story reveals mental breakdowns and the slow recovery process.

Spellbound (1945). Directed by Alfred Hitchcock. Gregory Peck, Ingrid Bergman. A thriller emphasizing dream analysis.

Three Faces of Eve, The (1957). Directed by Nunnally Johnson. Joanne Woodward, Lee J. Cobb. About multiple personality disorder.

What's Eating Gilbert Grape (1993). Directed by Lasse Halström. Johnny Depp, Leonardo DiCaprio. A young man in a dead-end town cares for his retarded brother and obese mother.

Yellow Wallpaper, The (1996). Directed by Tony Romain. Rachael Lillis, Michael Slayton. A nineteenth-century woman slowly goes mad. Based on the Charlotte Perkins Gilman novel.

Possessing the Secret of Joy

Color Purple, The (1985). Directed by Steven Spielberg. Whoopi Goldberg, Oprah Winfrey, Margaret Avery, Danny Glover. Drama based on the Alice Walker novel.

Girl Interrupted (1999). Directed by James Mangold. Winona Ryder, Angelina Jolie, Whoopi Goldberg, Vanessa Redgrave. Adaptation of Susanna Kaysen's autobiographical book. A girl enters a mental institution in the 1960s feeling normal compared to others.

Life and Times of Sara Baartman, The (1998). Directed by Zola Maseko. Documentary on a young Khoi woman called "The Hottentot Venus" who was taken to Europe in the early 1800s and exhibited in a freak show. She was examined for proof of inferiority of her race.

CHAPTER 5

Rabbit at Rest

Little Foxes, The (1941). Directed by William Wyler. Bette Davis, Herbert Marshall, Teresa Wright, Richard Carlson. Based on the Lillian Hellman play about a man dying from ischemic heart disease in 1900.

Rabbit, Run (1970). Directed by Jack Smight. James Caan, Anjanette Comer, Jack Albertson. Based on the Updike novel.

Wit

Death and Dying (2000). Bill Moyers's six-part PBS series.

Doctor, The (1991). Directed by Randa Haines. William Hurt, Christine Lahti. Based on Dr. Ed Rosenbaum's pathography, *A Taste of My Own Medicine.*

Doctor's Dilemma, The (1906). Play by George Bernard Shaw. Medical ethics, and should a doctor decide who dies and who lives?

Our Town (1937). Play by Thornton Wilder. Pulitzer Prize-winning drama. "Do human beings ever realize life while they live it? The Saints and poets, they do maybe."

Shadow Box, The (1975). Pulitzer Prize-winning and Tony Award-winning play by Michael Cristofer. Three California hospice patients deal with family, friends, and death.

Whose Life Is It, Anyway? (1978). Play by Brian Clark. Paralyzed sculptor in a battle of wills pleads with doctors who are sworn to preserve life. Right to die movement.

Wit (2001). Directed by Mike Nichols. Emma Thompson. Based on the Edson play. A must-see play for its emotional payoff.

RECOMMENDED MOVIE REFERENCES

The Internet Movie Database. http://www.imdb.com.

Maltin, Leonard. *Leonard Maltin's 2004 Movie and Video Guide*. New York: Signet, 2003.

Dans, Peter E. *Doctors in the Movies: Boil the Water and Just Say Aah*. Bloomington, Il.: Medi-Ed Press, 2000. Compilation of physician film reviews.

B

Recommended Internet Sites

CHAPTER 1

Frankenstein

Foresight Institute (preparing for nanotechnology): nanorobots FAQ. http://foresight.org/Nanomedicine/NanoMedFAQ.html#FAQ19.

Frankenstein. http://www.mostweb.cc/Classics/Shelley/frankenstein/. An electronic version of the story.

Frankenstein Castle: Ultimate Frankenstein Film Site. http://members.aon.at/frankenstein/.

Literary Gothic. http://www.litgothic.com.

National Nanotechnology Initiative. http://www.nano.gov.

Resources for the Study of Mary Shelley's *Frankenstein*. http://www.georgetown.edu/irvinemj/english016/franken.html.

Ultimate Science Fiction Web Guide. http://www.magicdragon.com/UltimateSF/SF-Index.html.

Visible Human Project. National Library of Medicine. http://www.nlm.nih.gov/research/visible/visible_human.html.

"Rappaccini's Daughter"

Nathaniel Hawthorne Society. http://asweb.artsci.uc.edu/english/HawthorneSociety/nh.html.

William Harvey Medical Research Foundation. http://www.williamharvey.org/wm_harvey.htm.

CHAPTER 2

Brave New World

Aldous Huxley. http://somaweb.org.
Human Genome Project. http://www.ornl.gov/hgmis/.

Coma

Center for Ethics and Human Rights. http://www.nursingworld.org/ethics/
index.htm.
Integrity in Science. http://www.integrityinscience.org. A nonprofit watch
group.
Medline Plus. http://www.nlm.nih.gov/medlineplus/organdonation.html.
Transplant Network. The Timeline for Transplantations. http://www.the
transplantnetwork.com.
United Network for Organ Sharing (UNOS). http://www.unos.org.
University of Houston Law Center. http://www.law.uh.edu. Analyzes recent
developments in health-care law.

CHAPTER 3

The Plague

Healthfinder. http://www.healthfinder.gov.
HealthWeb. http://www.healthweb.org.
HIV InSite. http://hivinsite.ucsf.edu/InSite.
HIV Testing. National Centers for Disease Control site at www.cdc.gov/hiv/
testing.htm and *The New England Journal of Medicine* site, www.nejm
.org, both discussing the proposal for routine HIV tests to help control
the epidemic.
Pandemic Facing AIDS. http://www.pandemicfacingaids.com. Proactive AIDS
awareness organization.
World Health Organization. http://www.who.int.

Miss Evers' Boys

African American Newspapers: http://www.aasm.com/pubs.html.
Altrius Biomedical Network. http://www.e-medical-ethics.com/.
CANDLES Holocaust Museum. http://www.candles-museum.com.
Directives for Human Experimentation: Nuremberg Code. http://www.nih
training.com/ohsrsite/guidelines/nuremberg.html. http://ohsr.od.nih.gov/
nuremberg.php3.
History of Jim Crow. http://www.jimcrowhistory.org. Educator's site includ-
ing historical resources.
Javanoir. http://www.javanoir.net/guide/index.html. Guide to African Amer-
ican Resources on the Internet.

Rise and Fall of Jim Crow. http://www.pbs.org/wnet/jimcrow/. PBS special on the Jim Crow era.

Timeline: The Tuskegee Syphilis Study. http://www.cdc.gov/nchstp/od/tuskegee/time.htm.

Tuskegee University National Center for Bioethics in Research and Health Care. http://www.tuskegee.edu/Global/category.asp?C = 35026. CDC Tuskegee Syphilis Study Page. http://www.cdc.gov/nchstp/od/tuskegee/index.html.

CHAPTER 4

One Flew Over the Cuckoo's Nest

American Academy of Child and Adolescent Psychiatry: http://www.aacap.org.

Child and Adolescent Bipolar Foundation. http://www.bpkids.org.

Depression and Related Affective Disorders Association. http://www.drada.org.

Mythology of Suicide. http://darkwing.uoregon.edu/~counsel/newpage5.htm.

National Alliance for the Mentally Ill. http://www.nami-org.helpline.

National Depressive and Manic Depressive Association. http://www.ndmda.org.

Official Ken Kesey Site. http://www.key-z.com/.

Possessing the Secret of Joy

Anniina's Alice Walker Page. http://www.luminarium.org/contemporary/alicew/.

Bioethical Themes in Popular Literature. http://www.georgetown.edu/research/nrcbl/hsbioethics/fbooks.html.

Female Genital Mutilation. Amnesty International. http://www.amnesty.org/ailib/intcam/femgen/fgm1.htm.

Kennedy Institute of Ethics High School Bioethics Curriculum Project. http://www.georgetown.edu/research/nrcbl/hsbioethics/.

National Coalition Against Domestic Violence. http://www.ncadv.org.

National Women's Health Information Center. http://www.4women.gov.

Roe v. Wade. http://www.roevwade.org.

CHAPTER 5

Rabbit at Rest

American Heart Association. http://www.americanheart.org.

Centurian. http://userpages.prexar.com/joyerkes/. A John Updike Web site.

"Learn CPR." http://depts.washington.edu/learncpr.

Wit

American Cancer Society. http://www.cancer.org.

Gilda's Club. http://www.gildasclub.org. Support group.

Groopman, Jerome. http://www.jeromegroopman.com. Books, articles, and biography.

Hospice Information. http://www.hospiceinformation.info.

Journal of Medical Ethics. http://jme.bmjjournals.com/misc/links.shtml.

President's Council on Bioethics. http://www.bioethics.gov/.

Pulitzer Prizes. http://www.pulitzer.org. See "History of the Prizes."

Stripling, Mahala Yates. http://www.medicalhumanities.net. An introduction to medical humanities and suggestion for teaching.

GENERAL INTEREST WEB SITES

American Journal of Bioethics. http://bioethics.net/. An interdisciplinary journal.

American Medical Association. http://www.ama-assn.org/ama/pub/category/1929.html. Chronology of the AMA.

American Society for Bioethics and Humanities. http://www.asbh.org/.

Harvard Center for Cancer Prevention. Disease Risk. http://www.your diseaserisk.harvard.edu.

Hastings Center. http://www.thehastingscenter.org. Leading bioethics into the future.

Literature, Arts, and Medicine Database. http://endeavor.med.nyu.edu/lit-med/lit-med-db/topview.html.

National Library of Medicine. Frankenstein: Penetrating the Secrets of Nature. http://www.nlm.nih.gov/hmd/frankenstein/frank_birth.html.

Perspectives in Biology and Medicine: http://muse.jhu.edu/journals/pbm/.

United States Department of Health and Human Services. http://www.hhs.gov.

C

Recommended Books and Articles

CHAPTER 1

Frankenstein and "Rappaccini's Daughter"

Bacon-Cohen, Simon. *The Truth about the Male & Female Brain: The Essential Difference.* New York: Perseus, 2003.

Beauchamp, Tom L., and James F. Childress. *Principles of Biomedical Ethics.* New York: Oxford University Press, 2004.

Duffin, Jacalyn. *History of Medicine: A Scandalously Short Introduction.* Toronto: University of Toronto Press, 1999.

Maddox, Brenda. *Rosalind Franklin: The Dark Lady of DNA.* New York: Harper, 2002.

McElheny, Victor K. *Watson and DNA: Making a Scientific Revolution.* Cambridge, Mass.: Perseus Press, 2003.

Miller, Arthur. *The Crucible.* New York: Penguin Plays, 1953.

Miller, Judith, et al. *Germs: Biological Weapons and America's Secret War.* New York: Simon & Schuster, 2001.

Narby, Jeremy, and Francis Huxley, eds. *Shamans through Time: 500 Years on the Path to Knowledge.* New York: Penguin, 2001.

Nuland, Sherwin B. *The Doctor's Plague: Germs, Childbed Fever, and the Strange Story of Ignac Semmelweis.* New York: Norton, 2004.

Ridley, Matt. *Genome.* New York: Harper, 2000.

Sulston, John, and Georgina Ferry. *The Common Thread: A Story of Science, Politics, Ethics, and the Human Genome.* Washington, D.C.: Joseph Henry Press, 2003.

Ullman, Ellen. *The Bug*. New York: Doubleday, 2003. Reinvents the *Frankenstein* story as computer.

Wade, Nicholas. *Life Script: How the Human Genome Discoveries Will Transform Medicine and Enhance Your Health*. New York: Simon & Schuster, 2001.

Watson, James D. *The Secret of Life*. New York: Knopf, 2003.

CHAPTER 2

Brave New World and *Coma*

Alschuler, Albert W. *Law without Values: The Life, Work, and Legacy of Justice Holmes*. Chicago: The University of Chicago Press, 2002. Justice Holmes upheld laws leading to the sterilization of 18,000 imbeciles.

Black, Edwin. *Eugenics and America's Campaign to Create a Master Race*. New York: Four Walls, 2003.

Eiseley, Loren. *All the Strange Hours*. Lincoln, Neb.: University of Nebraska Press, 1975. Autobiography. Sacrificing research animals with which researchers have developed a close relationship.

Grant, Madison. *The Passing of the Great Race*. New York: Arno Press, 1970.

Henig, Robin Marantz. *Pandora's Baby: How the First Test-Tube Babies Sparked the Reproductive Revolution*. New York: Houghton, 2004.

LeGuin, Ursula K. "The Ones Who Walk away from Omelas." In *The Wind's Twelve Quarters*. London: Orion Publishing Group, 1990. A dystopian parable about a town's happy citizens—but their happiness depends on the suffering of a child.

Power, Samantha. *A Problem from Hell: America and the Age of Genocide*. New York: Perennial, 2003. Won a Pulitzer Prize for documenting genocide in the twentieth century.

Ridley, Matt. *Nature VIA Nurture: Genes, Experience, and What Makes Us Human*. New York: Harper, 2003.

Slater, Lauren. *Opening Skinner's Box: Great Psychological Experiments of the Twentieth Century*. New York: Norton, 2004.

CHAPTER 3

The Plague and *Miss Evers' Boys*

Annas, George J., and Michael A. Grodin, eds. *The Nazi Doctors and the Nuremberg Code: Human Rights in Human Experimentation*. New York: Oxford University Press, 2004.

Barry, John M. *The Great Influenza: The Epic Story of the Deadliest Plague in History*. New York: Viking, 2004.

Brooks, Geraldine. *Year of Wonders: A Novel of the Plague*. New York: Penguin, 2001. A seventeenth-century village besieged by plague uses herbal medicine, common sense, and a barber surgeon to relieve suffering.

Chase, Marilyn. *The Black Death in Victorian San Francisco*. New York: Random, 2003.

Dowbiggin, Ian. *A Merciful End*. Oxford: Oxford University Press, 2003.

Drexler, Madeline. *Secret Agents: The Menace of Emerging Infections*. Washington, D.C.: J. Henry Press, 2002.

Friedman, Lester D., ed. *Cultural Sutures: Medicine and Media*. Durham, N.C.: Duke University Press, 2004.

Gray, Fred D. *The Tuskegee Syphilis Study: The Real Story and Beyond*. Montgomery, Ala.: Black Belt Press, 1998.

Lax, Eric. *The Mold in Dr. Florey's Coat*. New York: Henry Holt, 2004. Extends the penicillin story.

Mermann, Alan. *Some Chose to Stay: Faith and Ethics in a Time of Plague*. New Haven, Conn.: Humanities Press, 1998. Essays.

Proctor, Robert N. *The Nazi War on Cancer*. Princeton, N.J.: Princeton University Press, 2000.

Verghese, Abraham. *My Own Country: A Doctor's Story of a Town and Its People in the Age of AIDS*. New York: Simon & Schuster, 1994. Memoir of an AIDS doctor in Tennessee.

CHAPTER 4

One Flew Over the Cuckoo's Nest and *Possessing the Secret of Joy*

Coulehan, Jack. *Medicine Stone*. Portland, Ore.: Night Shade Books, 1991. Alternative medicine, Native American medicine, prayer as medicine, mind and soul.

Diagnostic and Statistical Manual of Mental Disorders (DMS). Washington, D.C.: American Psychiatric Association, 1994. Standard reference classifying mental disorders.

Koplewicz, Harold S. *More than Moody: Recognizing and Treating Adolescent Depression*. New York: Putnam, 2002. Describes signs of four main types of teen depression.

Leamer, Lawrence. *The Kennedy Women: The Saga of an American Family*. New York: Villard, 1994. Describes the lobotomy of Joe Kennedy's retarded daughter, Rosemary, sister to President John F. Kennedy. She inspired her younger sister Eunice to found the Special Olympics for mentally disabled athletes. Rosemary died in 2005 after lifelong institutionalization.

Schlaler, Jeffrey A., ed. *Szasz under Fire: The Psychiatric Abolitionist Faces His Critics*. Chicago: Open Court Publishers, 2004.

CHAPTER 5

Rabbit at Rest and *Wit*

Gottlieb, Sidney, ed. *Approaches to Teaching the Metaphysical Poets.* New York: MLA, 1990.

Jonsen, Albert, Mark Siegler, and William Winslade. *Clinical Ethics.* New York: McGraw-Hill, Inc., 1992.

Kleinman, Arthur. *The Illness Narratives: Suffering, Healing, and the Human Condition.* New York: Basic Books, 1988.

Lowey, E. H. *Textbook of Health Care Ethics.* New York: Plenum, 1996.

McCue, J. "The Naturalness of Dying." *JAMA* 273, no.13 (5 April 1995).

McKee, D., and J. Chapple. "Spirituality and Medical Practice." *The Journal of Family Practice* 35, no. 2 (1992). See Web site: http://seeingthe difference.berkeley.edu.

GENERAL RECOMMENDATIONS

Coles, Robert. *The Call of Stories.* Boston: Houghton, 1989.

Dittrich, Lisa R., and Anne L. Farmakidis, eds. "The Humanities and Medicine: Reports of 41 U.S., Canadian, and International Programs." *Academic Medicine* 78, no. 10 (October 2003).

Halpern, Jodi. *From Detached Concern to Empathy: Humanizing Medical Practice.* New York: Oxford University Press, 2001. Argues doctors gain from allowing patients to move them emotionally.

Hastings Center Report. Journal, six issues a year. Garrison, N.Y.: The Hastings Center. World's leading bioethics journal anticipating provocative questions.

Hawkins, Anne Hunsaker, and Marilyn Chandler McEntyre, eds. *Teaching Literature and Medicine.* New York: MLA, 2000. Includes additional resources.

D

Recommended Methods for Teaching

CHAPTER 1

Frankenstein

1. Compare and contrast two movies, *Mary Shelley's Frankenstein* (1994), the more faithful Branagh version, and James Whale's *Frankenstein* (1931), which relates to pop culture.
2. Just for fun: Bobby "Boris" Pickett and the Crypt Kickers recorded the hit sensation "The Monster Mash" in 1962. The dance, something like the "mashed potato," goes like this: holding your arms in a ghoulish position, grind one foot on the floor in mashing footwork as if putting a cigarette butt out; pull that foot backward; then step onto the opposite foot and do the same thing. At the same time, walk in place and swivel your foot. See Novelty Dances, http://www.eijkhout.net/rad/dance_specific/novelty6.html.
3. Discuss how attitudes toward death differ from one generation to another. For example, when Percy Bysshe Shelley drowned in a sailing accident off the coast of Italy, Mary Shelley was only 24. Because relics were acceptable keepsakes in lieu of photographs, she asked for his heart from the cremated remains. She kept it "[w]rapped in silk between the pages of his *Adonais* until her death" (Seymour, 306). At Percy's death, Mary had to fend for herself.
4. A feminist view of *Frankenstein* sees an aggressive male scientist who rapes nature (the passive female). In fact, Frankenstein's Professor Waldman taught him scientists "penetrate into the recesses of nature, and show how she works in her hiding places." Taken a step further, some think tech-

nology's ability to fulfill our desperate need for resources is raping the environment and destroying the delicate ecological balance in nature. Discuss Francis Bacon's misogynist rape metaphor, "In Defense of Francis Bacon," http://www.uno.edu/~phil/bacon.htm.

5. The corset, essential in the nineteenth-century wardrobe, is blamed for ill health. Did surgeons remove women's ribs to narrow waists; did corsets oppress women; why has there been a revival of its use; and what Victorian views of sexuality caused doctors to examine women fully dressed? See: Valerie Steel's *The Corset: A Cultural History* (New Haven, Conn.: Yale University Press, 2001).

6. Discuss nineteenth-century swaddling, which is blamed for killing babies when done in the extreme. It is used again, as explained in Dr. Harvey Karp's *The Happiest Baby on the Block* (New York: Bantam, 2002).

7. Study how Coleridge's "Rime of the Ancient Mariner," http://www.sangfroid.com/rime/, influenced Shelley (Coleridge's hero was stalked by "a frightful fiend," and there is reference to the icebound sea).

8. Read Michael Crichton's *Prey* (New York: Harper Collins, 2002) and discuss it in terms of Frankenscience and nanoparticles escaping to plague humankind.

"Rappaccini's Daughter"

1. First read the short story, then show the movie after the first class discussion.

2. Read Conan Doyle's story "The Adventure of the Copper Beeches," then discuss the scientific mind.

3. Read John Donne's "The Flea," then discuss the place of women in society.

4. Read, compare, and contrast "Rappaccini" with two other Hawthorne stories, "The Birthmark" and "Dr. Heidigger's Experiment," then discuss scientific obsession, the romantic notion of distrusting science, and being wary of boundless dreams of physical perfection.

5. Late-twentieth-century forensic science put a strange twist on the Salem witch trial more than 300 years ago. Linnda Caporael, a behavioral psychologist at New York State's Rensselaer Polytechnic Institute, writes in "Ergotism: The Satan Loosed in Salem?" that hallucinogen LSD, derived from the common grain fungus ergot, caused the bizarre behavior reported in Salem. Ergot naturally occurs in rye grain under the right weather conditions. When made into bread, it caused a toxicity in the people who ate it, resulting in bizarre behavior. Similar outbreaks identified in medieval peasants were called St. Vitus' dance and St. Anthony's fire. What other recent scientific theories explain this phenomenon?

6. Consider "Rappaccini's Daughter" as an allegory relating to Genesis 2–3; compare those Bible chapters to Hawthorne's Garden of Eden with "the tree of the knowledge of good and evil."

7. Compare Dr. Rappaccini's and Baglioni's archrivalry with James Watson's and Francis Click's scientific rivalry over the discovery of DNA. See McElheny, Voctor K. *Watson and DNA: Making a Scientific Revolution.* Cambridge, Mass.: Perseus Books, 2003.
8. Research and define "romantic love." How do hormones affect it, and can you die from a broken heart? Research: *Broken heart syndrome* and *stress cardiomyopathy.*

CHAPTER 2

Brave New World

1. How often and in what context does the term *brave new world* appear in today's headlines? How often do you see DNA related to forensic science in criminal cases?
2. Review human population genetics, including the work of Halden, Wright, and Fisher.

Coma

1. Review and discuss the dramatic stories at "The Gift of Life Donor Program's" Web site: http://wwworgantransplants.org.
2. Explain the current U.S. medical criteria for determining death, including rules for brain death, the dead donor rule, and cardiac death.
3. Set out *Coma*'s hospital hierarchy and determine how it affects patient care (upper world—chiefs and above; mid-world—chief resident; lower world—residents, students).
4. Read William Carlos Williams's "Old Doc Rivers" and put him on trial for his actions, determining causes of action and assigning prosecutors and defendants.
5. Organ Transplants Timeline (student resources). http://www.timeline science.org/Resource/Students/tplant/orgtplant.htm. Review this interesting historical source.

CHAPTER 3

The Plague

1. In England in 1500 children sang a rhyme and played a game called "Ring around the Rosies." In Canada in the 1940s, children still held hands in a circle and chanted:

    Ring around the rosies
    A pocketful of posies
    Ashes, ashes
    We all fall down.

The rhyme originated from the flulike symptoms, skin discoloration, and mortality caused by bubonic plague. Discuss how the meaning was that life could be both unimaginably beautiful and horrible.

2. Study and report on the romanticization of tuberculosis in the nineteenth century, especially focusing on famous cases such as the poet John Keats.

3. Report on the science of immunology. What is a vaccine and how does this agent in the war on disease work in the immune system? Define the terms antibodies, pathogens, antigens, macrophages and dendrites, T cells, cytokines, white blood cells, and lymph nodes. What are the pros and cons of administering vaccines? See the National Vaccine Information Center, http://www.909shot.com.

4. Study Dark Winter, a 2001 exercise simulating a covert smallpox attack in the United States. How have the senior-level policy makers met the challenge of containing the outbreaks of this highly contagious disease? The scenario is available at the University of Pittsburgh Medical Center, Center for Biosecurity, http://www.upmc-biosecurity.org/pages/events/dark_winter/dark_winter.html.

5. Discuss the 1997 U.S. Supreme Court decision on assisted suicide and its Fourteenth Amendment view that there is no constitutional right to die. Review ongoing federal legislation, specifically the Assisted Suicide Funding Restriction Act prohibiting federal money to support physician-assisted suicide. House and Senate bills were introduced in 1999 to revoke a doctor's license for prescribing federally controlled drugs used in an assisted suicide. If these laws pass, Oregon doctors would be subject to federal sanction.

6. Compare Dr. Jack Kevorkian, who advocated complete patient autonomy with an in-your-face defiance of the suicide law, to Dr. Haiselden's 1915 actions as described in *The Black Stork*.

7. Reflect on the Pope Pius XII controversy following World War II, when he, as a moral leader, was accused of falling culpably silent in the face of known Nazi crimes against the Jews.

8. A small Texas boy, Audie Murphy, was the most decorated soldier of World War II. He epitomized American heroism and in 1945 received the Medal of Honor. Learn about Murphy's heroic activities and the Medal of Honor to discuss courage and heroism. Place Murphy on Aristotle's Golden Mean of courage, in which an excess of courage is rashness; the mean is courage; and a deficiency is cowardice. See Aristotle, *Ethics* (London: Penguin Classics, 1976).

Miss Evers' Boys

1. How did Alexander Fleming's "accidental" discovery, penicillin, take so long for widespread use?

2. Explain the need to monitor ethical standards, such as those 1) leading to

the disastrous 1950–60s use of thalidomide in pregnant women; 2) leading to the 2001 tragic death at Johns Hopkins of a healthy 24-year-old woman who inhaled hexamethonium; and 3) leading to the placebo-controlled African AZT trial for preventing maternal-to-fetal transmission of HIV. How are colleges monitored in treating student volunteers to keep the public trust from eroding?

3. Some surviving Tuskegee Syphilis Study (TSS) investigators argue the study was ethical. Analyze their arguments and compare them to the study's majority condemnation.

4. Describe Negro Health Week, established in 1915 by Tuskegee Institute founder Booker T. Washington, and discuss how by 1932 it provided a positive national context for public health work in black communities and contributed to the TSS.

5. There are many examples of research abuse like the TSS, including: 1) Nazi concentration camps; 2) Willowbrook State School hepatitis experiments on mentally retarded children; 3) elderly patients injected with cancer cells without consent at the Jewish Chronic Disease Hospital; and 4) the 1950–60s human radiation experiments in the United States at the Nevada Test Site. What Nuremberg Code principles were broken that an institutional review board would stop today?

6. Harvard University philosopher John Rawls devised the Rawls Test to highlight questions of right and wrong. For him an ideal society includes the principle relationship that asks, would the best-off people accept the arrangements if they believed that they might at any moment find themselves in the place of the worst off? How in good faith would you answer this role reversal question about 1) slavery, 2) Nazi concentration camp inmates, and 3) the TSS?

CHAPTER 4

One Flew Over the Cuckoo's Nest

1. Discuss how *Cuckoo's Nest,* written in stream of consciousness for immediacy, is absurdist like *The Plague,* reflecting counterculture attitudes and the lifestyle of the 1940s and 1950s Beat Generation, seen also in Kerouac's *On the Road* and Wolfe's *Acid.*

2. Relate *Cuckoo's Nest* characters to Melville's in *Moby Dick* and *Billy Budd.*

3. Political figures: What did Senator Eagleton say about his mental illness that caused him to leave politics, and how did Kitty Dukakis find relief?

4. Drugs, often a godsend in treating mental disorders, also have disastrous side effects. Learn about the Haldol lawsuits and the plaintiffs' claims of being turned into vegetables.

5. Teenagers often forced against their will into mental institutions do not have the rights of an adult. Discuss this hot topic, relating the more progressive measures some states take.

6. Trace the effects of 1) the ability to diagnose mental illness and 2) the establishment of civil rights laws on filling and then emptying mental institutions. Why has there been a return to the mentally ill roaming the streets? Read Dr. John Friedberg's *Shock Treatment Is Not Good for Your Brain* and Dr. Max Fink's *Electroshock: Restoring the Mind* to discuss psychiatric battery and involuntary admissions. What is a psychiatric protection order?

7. Psychiatrists monitoring depression also manage communicable diseases. Ratched fumigates the men, for instance. Through shared needles Hepatitis C infects 20 percent with severe mental illness such as depression and schizophrenia, with the standard treatment being alpha interferon, an injection, with ribavirin, a pill, a combination difficult to tolerate. Discuss interrelated aspects.

8. Nobel Prize-winning economist John Nash, a Princeton professor, suffered with the debilitating mental illness schizophrenia. Read and discuss Sylvia Nasar's *A Beautiful Mind* and compare and contrast it to the movie *A Beautiful Mind* that has been called a sentimental fairy tale about mental illness. Is Dr. Nash, who is described as having a willpower that controls his symptoms, a typical schizophrenic? Research project: What are the three categories of schizophrenics and what newer medications are effective with fewer side effects?

9. Read Chekhov's "Ward Number Six" and demonstrate how "the norm of reciprocity" (open and free communication—cooperation between doctor and patient; and truth-telling) does not apply in psychiatry, especially in a totalitarian state such as *Cuckoo's Nest*. Comment on why it is particularly disturbing that some inmates choose voluntarily to be committed.

10. Opponents of the widespread use of Ritalin for ADHD say it kills the creative spark. Thomas Edison, Albert Einstein, Salvador Dali, and Winston Churchill may have had this disorder defined by impulsiveness, daydreaming, and disorder. Discuss.

Note: Cuckoo's Nest is rich in SAT–type words: chronic, pinochle, replica, grievance, prototype, acoustic, matriarchy, maudlin, folio, vulnerable, punitive, hallucinate, and lobotomy.

Possessing the Secret of Joy

Note to teachers: This novel contains mature sexual themes, explicit language, and graphic descriptions, all of which serve to enhance the subject matter, culturally perpetuated female genital mutilation. While *Possessing* is often taught in 11th and 12th grade, some teachers who do not have school board approval choose to get parental permissions for students under 18. Alternatively, students who are very uncomfortable with reading the text may be assigned the less graphic *The Color Purple*, also ultimately adding to the conversation.

1. Compare the ubiquitous 1950s tonsillectomy to male circumcision. Is either medically necessary? Cite research.
2. Compare the culturally entrenched habit of smoking to female genital mutilation. The World Health Organization estimates 47 percent of men smoke compared to 12 percent of women, and because tobacco companies market to women and girls in developing countries the Centers for Disease Control and Prevention recommend programs be developed specific to gender warning of the serious health consequences of tobacco use.
3. Compare and contrast the Prime Directive and cultural relativism. According to *Star Trek*, a television show and a movie, the Prime Directive states it is forbidden for Starfleet to interfere with the normal development of any culture or society, which is more important than the protection of spaceships or members of Starfleet. Losses are tolerated as long as they are necessary to observe this directive. Cultural relativism is a philosophical concept claiming moral rules are customs specific to particular cultures; consequently no moral rules are universal. International human rights advocates reject the primacy of cultural relativism, by its very nature, in dealing with the abolition of slavery, the fundamentalist treatment of women, abuse of children in workshops, and so forth.
4. Walker's new interests include protecting indigenous cultures in their natural environment. How do you do this when you interfere with their traditions?
5. Research birth control methods, including RU-286, and review how they have changed the course of history, comparing their availability in the United States and in Third World countries.
6. For related issues *Possessing* touches upon, please read and discuss the following:

   - Alice Walker, "Abortion" (poetry).
   - Richard Selzer, "Abortion" (essay).
   - Ernest Hemingway, "Hills Like White Elephants" (short story).
   - Charlotte Perkins Gilman, *The Crux* (*The Charlotte Perkins Gilman Reader*). A woman, who has been denied medical knowledge about transmission, prevention, and so forth almost marries a man with venereal disease. Issues: taboos; doctor-patient confidentiality; and misogyny.
   - Perri Klass, "Invasions" in *A Not Entirely Benign Procedure*.
   - Unknown author, "Indian Poem," *Lancet* 13 (March 1993): 669–72. A mother must decide how to divide her limited resources between her three children: a strong son with no immediate need, a weak son soon to die, and a girl "who is a girl anyway."

7. Read Mirella Ricciardi's lush descriptions in *African Saga* for a colonist's viewpoint of cultural history, which underscores a tribe's ability to subsist on what it has, and that colonists often exploit natives with no attempt to introduce social and political measures. Note the effects of political change and the seductive safari imagery. Excerpts:

   - "The tribes I visited differed greatly from each other, but they all shared one similarity, which I discovered later was very important to the survival of the human race. They had adapted to their environment and did not crave for things beyond their immediate needs. They seemed primitive by our standards, but their simple code of life was built on the basic laws of survival: eating, sleeping and reproducing. They solved their problems in their own ways, and law and order were kept by the elders of the class. Women never questioned their positions as perpetuators of the tribe and the children grew up naturally, according to the teachings of the elders for generations back" (164).
   - "[W]hites in Africa were like an army of occupation, to be tolerated but never accepted" (298).
   - "The modern world where all men are to be equal is closing in around us and there is nowhere left to run" (300).

8. For works covering misdiagnosis (misperception of patient experience), psychosomatic disorders, hysteria, and neurasthenia, read Charlotte Perkins Gilman's "The Yellow Wallpaper" and Kate Chopin's *The Awakening*. Isolate the issues in the works, touching upon the protagonists' relationships to their husbands and the relationships' effects on their well-being. How does this relate to the Andrea Yates case in Houston?

9. Define feminism. Contemplate Pope John Paul II's definition of feminism: "In transforming culture so that it supports life, women occupy a place . . . which is unique and decisive. It depends on them to promote a 'new feminism' which rejects the temptation of imitating models of 'male domination'."

CHAPTER 5

Rabbit at Rest

1. Read Updike's "From the Journal of a Leper," in *Problems and Other Stories* (New York: Knopf, 1976). Issues covered in the 10-page short story include body image and psychosocial medicine. A pottery artist suffers from psoriasis. He is humiliated and seeks modern medical help, but his retailer admires his beautiful pottery, and his girlfriend loves him. Write an essay on the ironic psychosocial effects of his modern medical treatment. Apply these sayings to your discussion: beauty is only skin deep; beauty is in the eye of the beholder. For a follow-up, read Dr. Ashley

Montagu's *TOUCHING: The Human Significance of the Skin* and Richard Selzer's "Skin" in *Mortal Lessons*.

2. Write a short literary analysis of Updike's poem "The Ex-Basketball Player," noting tone (the speaker's attitude toward the subject), citing imagery (the language that makes the reader see, hear, smell, taste, and feel while stimulating the imagination to understanding), and interpreting theme (essence of the knowledge gained). Compare and contrast to A. E. Housman's "To an Athlete Dying Young," Robert Frost's "A Road Not Taken," and Bruce Springsteen's "Glory Days."

3. Read Sherwin Nuland's *How We Die* (20–42, include diagram) on how the heart works.

4. Compare the health-care systems of the United States, Canada, Great Britain, and Germany.

5. Thelma's illness costs the Harrisons a fortune. Discuss how she emotionally deals with the ordeal: religious sect membership, holistic care, and alternative treatments.

6. On obesity, proponents of the Calorie Restriction (C.R.) regimen believe it will increase superlongevity and the quality of life. Argue the pros and cons. Scientific data are limited to animal studies and remote populations. For wisdom from the past, review Ben Franklin's ideas on moderation at The Quotable Franklin, www.ushistory.org/franklin/quotable, and Aristotle's concept of the *Golden Mean* at http://homepage.mac.com/mseffie/handouts/mean.html.

Wit

1. For a fun exercise in metaphysical conceit, read and discuss Donne's "The Flea."

2. Discuss the end-of-life/right-to-life case of Terri Schiavo (Florida, 2004). Are comatose people disabled? Discuss basic science, human rights, and medical authorizations.

3. For an exercise in mind-body revelation, substitute "hope" for "love" in the following poem:

> Love cannot fill the thickened lung with breath,
> Nor clean the blood, nor set the fractured bone;
> Yet many a man is making friends with death
> Even as I speak, for lack of love alone.
> —Edna St. Vincent Millay

4. Poetry readings, which must be done out loud, teach lessons:

> Maya Angelou, "The Last Decision."
> Margaret Atwood, "The Woman Who Could Not Live with Her Faulty Heart."

Raymond Carver, "My Death."

Emily Dickinson, "I Heard a Fly Buzz," "Because I Could Not Stop for Death."

James Dickey, "Cancer Match."

Robert Frost, "Home Burial."

Sharon Olds, "The Father."

Linda Pastan, "The Five Stages of Grief."

John Stone, "Death."

Alice Walker, "Medicine."

William Carlos Williams, "The Last Words of my English Grandmother."

The above poems appear in *In Doctor*, Ed. Reynolds and Stone.

William Wordsworth, "We Are Seven." www.bartleby.com.

Index

About the Author

MAHALA YATES STRIPLING is an independent scholar who lectures widely at such places as Yale Medical School and the University of Texas Medical Branch, and who publishes extensively in medical humanities journals. Her work has appeared in *The Journal of Medical Humanities*, *Medical Humanities Review*, *Studies in Psychoanalytic Theory*, and other publications.